89-3565

Inflation in the
Twentieth Century

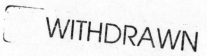

# Inflation in the Twentieth Century

## Evidence from Europe and North America

George Horsman

*Lecturer in Economics*
*University of Glasgow*

HARVESTER · WHEATSHEAF

ST. MARTIN'S PRESS · NEW YORK

First published 1988 by
Harvester · Wheatsheaf
66 Wood Lane End, Hemel Hempstead
Hertfordshire HP2 4RG
A division of
Simon & Schuster International Group

and in the USA by
St. Martin's Press, Inc.
175 Fifth Avenue, New York, NY 10010

© 1988 George Horsman

Printed and bound in Great Britain by
Billing & Sons Ltd., Worcester

---

British Library Cataloguing in Publication Data

Horsman, George
Inflation in the twentieth century : evidence
from Europe and North America.
1. Western world. Finance. Inflation, 1900–
1987
I. Title
332.4′1
ISBN 0-7450-0074-6

---

Library of Congress Cataloging-in-Publication Data

Horsman, George,
Inflation in the twentieth century : evidence from Europe and
North America / George Horsman.
    p.  cm.
"Wheatsheaf books."
Bibliography: p.
Includes index.
ISBN 0-312-01988-2 : $39.95 (est.)
1. Inflation (Finance)—Europe—History—20th century.
2. Inflation (Finance)—United States—History—20th century.
I. Title. II. Title: Inflation in the 20th century.
HG924.H64 1988                                    88-15057
332.4′ 1′094—dc19                                 CIP

1  2  3  4  5    92  91  90  89  88

To Mary, Elspeth, Eleanor and Susan Horsman

Quelqu'un pourrait dire de moi que j'ai seulement fait ici un amas de fleurs étrangères, n'y ayant fourni du mien que le filet à les lier. (Montaigne, Essais, III.xii)

It is no part at all of my intention to substitute institutional for Keynesian or monetarist explanation . . . My proposition is much simpler: demand inflation and deflation in market economies is a complex and highly irregular historical phenomenon. Anyone proposing a unitary explanation should have his head examined. Each moment of inflation and deflation is unique. There is no substitute for economic history. (Peter Wiles, *Economic Institutions Compared*, 1977, p.368)

# Contents

# List of Figures and Tables

FIGURES

TABLES

# Introduction

Anyone proposing to add yet another book about inflation to the many which already exist is called upon to justify his action. Can there be any aspect of the subject which has not yet been sufficiently propounded? Rash though the claim may be, this book is written in the belief that in one respect at least the answer is: yes. In the course of the present century Western man's experience of inflation, its causes, course, mechanisms and effects, has been vastly extended by a long series of inflationary episodes representing a wide range of different causal processes and countered by a wide variety of proposed remedies. Yet so far no one person has presented in a compact and unified form the stories of a wide and reasonably representative range of these inflations and asked how far they are consistent with the main widely-held theories about the nature of inflation. The object of this book is to attempt in some measure to fill this gap.

Such an attempt has necessitated selection of the most important and interesting episodes in recent history, narration in broad outline of the course of events in each episode, and discussion of the main questions involved. The writing of an economic – historical survey of this kind has called for a closely focused approach. First, brevity has had to be a predominant aim and in consequence it has been impossible to present in full detail all relevant facts, figures and arguments. Anyone wishing to pursue these is referred to the Bibliography. Second, this is not a textbook of economic theory and will not satisfy those readers who demand theory for its own sake. Indeed, no idea has been discussed here which is 'pure theory' in the sense that it was not advanced as a mechanism, explanation or proposed remedy for some particular inflation which actually occurred. Nor have I devoted much time to theories which have seemed to me to be only tenuously linked with observed events. In this sense the book is an exercise in what Professor Kindleberger has christened 'historical economics', an approach based on the conviction that economic judgement is best trained by studying the past and on the desire to move the subject away from model-building based on assumptions little if at all related to the real world. Third, the huge variation in the volume of literature on the different inflations, as well as their widely varying degrees of interest, has inevitably and desirably produced accounts which vary widely in length. Finally, though I have tried to treat each inflationary episode in a reasonably standardised way, usually proceeding from narrative to discussion of opinion and thence to points of particular interest, in the end the subject matter has largely determined the form of presentation. To have narrated events without even mentioning different views on such topics as causality would have been tiresomely evasive, and to have withheld all discussion of opinion until a later stage would have involved much intolerable repetition. Moreover, the interest of an inflation often arises from its peculiarities, which a highly standardised treatment would have tended to suppress. Although, therefore, for ease of reference I have tried to gather together related sections of each chapter into the groups mentioned above, I make no apology for a certain lack of water-tightness in this categorisation and warn readers that quick reference cannot be an adequate substitute for thorough reading.

Wide though the range of the book is, I am well aware that it is none the less restricted to this century and to Europe and North America, so that it can make no claim to be truly comprehensive. It remains possible that inflations which I have not studied (unlike several in Latin America and Europe which I did study at some length but had to omit for lack of space) may necessitate changes in some of the conclusions I have suggested. Yet despite these reservations I remain convinced that some general truths emerge from the investigation and that in an age when the literature of economics and economic history is exploding in volume, the need for broad surveys has never been greater. Indeed, but for the size of the task it would be surprising that economists have not made more attempts to assess the truth of proposed economic laws and other general hypotheses by examining a range of differing cases rather than by single country studies or by incorporating them in the usual aprioristic and assumptionist models.

In one respect my approach to the inflations studied reflects a compromise. Recent decades have seen an explosion of regression analysis as applied to macroeconomic data and in this respect data relating to inflation have been no exception. Within the profession of economics the limitations of this method are now increasingly recognised; and although not everyone would agree with the view which Sir Donald MacDougall (1974) discusses that 'running regressions between time series is only likely to deceive', or with Professor Kaldor's (1972) view that ' "econometrics" leads nowhere', there would probably be widespread assent to Leontief's statement (1971, p. 3) that 'In no other field of empirical enquiry has so massive and sophisticated a statistical machinery been used with such indifferent results.' The reasons for this state of affairs are various. In part they arise from the intercorrelation of different possible causes, which is widespread in economic data and often statistically irremediable. In part they reflect the fact that an econometric model by its nature excludes all immeasurable variables, which may well in practice constitute overwhelmingly the main influences at work. Even the remaining variables may, indeed, be very imperfectly measured (Morgenstern, 1963). Again, there may be no sound reason for believing the assumptions underlying the statistical methods used. Furthermore, even where regular conjunctions of a supposed cause and its hypothesised effect are found, there is often scope for different interpretations of the fact. The recent growing awareness of considerations such as these must prompt a degree of caution in approaching econometric studies. Even so, there have been cases where such studies have seemed to me to yield evidence which should be included, either because of its near-unanimity, or because it has lent support to a view which has seemed to me sensible on other grounds, or simply *faute de mieux*; and in those cases I have departed from a generally historical-analytical approach by quoting econometric findings.

One aspect of my approach to which I attach some importance arises from my belief that causality in economics has often been insufficiently differentiated and that as a result over-simple, even monocausal explanations, though usually implausible, have flourished. There is always a standing temptation to speak of 'the' cause of an economic phenomenon. Amazingly, indeed, this tendency has been most marked not in the distant past but in the most recent period covered, the 1970s. In practice, however, causes may be major or minor, proximate or ultimate, active or accommodating, necessary or sufficient. In the following pages I have tried, without falling into pedantry, to draw these distinctions where they seemed useful. For a similar reason − in order to introduce the reader most comprehensively to the full complexity of the causes of inflation right from the start − I have departed, in the early chapters, from a strictly chronological treatment.

The book is addressed to students of economic history and economics. I also hope that much the greater part will be accessible to the general reader who has some background in basic economics. With such people in mind, I have tried to eliminate as many technical expressions as possible. For explanations of those which seemed unavoidable but which could not be explained in the text the reader is referred to the Glossary and list of Acronyms at the back. These include many entries to which the reader is not specifically referred in the text, though, unsurprisingly, they stop short of including econometric terms. The result of my attempt to bring a broad theme to a wide readership may not always satisfy specialists in the different areas; but it remains my hope that the perspective afforded by the broad canvas I have chosen will yield a glimpse into the historic problems and arguments about inflation which will more than compensate for any corresponding failings.

Readers should note that I have used the term 'billion' to denote one thousand million throughout; 'trillion' correspondingly means one million million. The four quarters of calendar years are indicated after a colon. Thus, '1964:2' refers to the second quarter of that year.

I am indebted to Roger Clarke, Anne Crowther, Rick Trainor, David Vines and Terry Wanless for commenting most helpfully on early drafts of various chapters. The responsibility for any remaining errors of fact, logic or judgement remains, however, my own.

# 1 A Preliminary Framework of Hypotheses

Inflation, one of the great economic evils to afflict mankind, is also one of the most mysterious. Its onset has often been unpredicted; time and again its arrival has provoked perplexity and heated debate as to its causes; and its effects, including some which have scarcely been noticed by contemporaries, have often been enormous. In the following chapters we investigate some of the most important and interesting inflations of modern times. In this chapter, however, we confine ourselves to setting out briefly some of the main hypotheses which have been advanced about the causes, course and effects of inflation. The purpose is to lend unity to the accounts of particular inflations which follow – to pose the questions to be answered and outline the main theories to be assessed.

An approach of this kind presents obvious dangers. To begin by presenting theories is to run the risk that the reader's mind will be diverted into a chain of speculative logic which may serve as a substitute for examination of the facts. Again, economic hypotheses have a disarming habit of sounding like statements of fact, slipping from supposition to assertion; and in a world where party loyalties run deep, putting theory first involves the risk that readers may, by the time they have finished reading the theories, already have chosen their favourite without recourse to the facts. Even so, without hypotheses we have no means of knowing which facts are relevant, so that some basic hypotheses are necessary as a framework of thought. All that we can do, to avoid the dangers mentioned above, is to emphasis that this chapter gives no answers whatever but consists purely of hypothesis. It is presented, moreover, at an elementary level and intended only for those readers who have little background knowledge of economics. Other readers should turn to Chapter 2.

Perhaps the broadest and most fundamental hypothesis implicit in the chapters which follow is that inflation, defined as a persistent tendency for the general price level to rise, may be regarded as a spiral, with inflationary pressure arising at many possible points in that spiral. The market for goods and services may be one such point, with excess demand inducing suppliers to raise prices persistently. Excess demand in its turn may, in a widespread view, arise when the amount of money in circulation grows faster than the supply of goods, services or assets; and this may happen either when the government creates money to bridge a continuing budget deficit, or when the banking system creates excess money by expanding its lending to the private sector. An inflow of money due to a balance of payments surplus, if not withdrawn from circulation via, for example, the sale of government bonds, may also increase the stock of money in circulation. A further hypothesis claims that excess demand may result when the stock of money, even though fixed in quantity, begins to circulate ever more quickly (perhaps because its holders, expecting inflation, try to hold less of it) and so gives rise to a higher level of expenditure. More elaborate, though largely untested, theories try to explain how expectations are formed. Some posit, for example, that people base their expectations of future inflation on current rates of of change in the money supply.

According to a second group of hypotheses, an inflationary spiral may also be initiated or worsened by a rising trend in costs. The causes of this may in turn be various. Costs may rise persistently because of workers' pressure for higher pay, born either of a desire to raise wages or in an attempt to prevent their erosion by inflation. A particular case of the latter occurrence, known as 'fiscal drag', is said to be observed when money wages, rising in line with inflation, carry workers into progressively higher tax brackets and so increase the tax burden on a constant real income. Erosion from rising tax rates may also stimulate higher wage claims and settlements. Or competition between different wage groups may impel money wages upwards.

If wages push up prices while money demand remains constant, output and employment are likely to fall. Alternatively, if the government intervenes to boost demand for goods and services, or if a given money stock begins to circulate more rapidly, then the demand for labour may be little affected by wage increases, but the chance that wage inflation will persist, undamped by market forces, is to that extent increased. A further possibility is that persistently rising profit margins may necessitate rising prices, which again may be ratified by government policy in pursuit of full employment.

A factor likely to be of increasing importance in a world where international trade and payments have been soaring for four decades is the exchange rate. A devaluation of three per cent in many industrial countries' rates can bring about a rise of one per cent in their retail price level. Downward influences upon the exchange rate, at least in the short run, can include sharp increases in the prices of necessary imports, or falls in the prices of exports; such changes can arise from changing market forces, including those stemming from excess demand at home, or as a result of action on the part of cartels or monopolies at home or abroad. Capital outflows can also exert a major influence, taking such forms as direct investment abroad, military or development aid, reparations or flows of portfolio capital, whether long-term or short-term. Such flows may result from the rapid growth of domestic income or money stock, or from political impositions or other arrangements with foreign countries.

More complex links are also possible. A fall in the exchange rate may make imports dearer in domestic currency and so, it is suggested, drive up the prices of goods which incorporate imported materials, or allow domestic producers of import substitutes to raise *their* prices. If public expenditure rises with the resulting rise in the prices of goods and services generally – as when wages, a major component of public expenditure, are indexed either formally or by trade union action – a falling exchange rate may worsen the state deficit, pushing up expenditure faster than tax revenue rises. This may be so especially when inflation is fast and there is a time lag between the assessment of taxes and their payment, during which time the real value of tax revenues diminishes.

An equal variety of hypotheses exists as to the course of inflation. Inflation is said to redistribute income: between the public and private sectors (e.g. by cutting the real value of government debt, or via fiscal drag); between those with flexible and those with fixed incomes; between debtors and creditors; between bondholders and shareholders; and between those with access to foreign exchange and others. The overall effect of such redistribution may be to increase or reduce the private sector's real wealth and this in turn may affect the volume of private consumption and investment. The latter may also be influenced by changes in real rates of interest, the behaviour of which during inflation is itself the subject of several hypotheses. So are the questions: does inflation tend to accelerate? Is there a regular pattern in the relative rates of external and internal depreciation of a currency? If so how is it explained?

The many and various mechanisms advanced as causing inflation correspond with a wide variety of possible remedies. In the pages that follow we discuss proposals for the restraint of wages and profits, the support of the exchange rate, the control of demand and the money supply, and the curbing of public expenditure and the public sector deficit. Such policies may operate through government intervention in the market process, through voluntary restraint or through compulsion; and there are several ways of adopting each approach. In particular, we review cases of indexation intended to protect incomes, wealth or money balances from erosion by inflation and thereby either to lessen the hardships and distortions caused or, according to some proponents, actually to curb inflation. For consideration, too, are the possible means of altering inflationary expectations and so influencing the velocity with which money circulates in the economy.

As for stabilisation, a mass of hypotheses exists as to the ideal pace of attempting to achieve it, the role of changed expectations, the merits and defects of orthodox prescriptions stemming from the 1920s, and the case for centrally planned controls over wages and prices. From the latter arises consideration of the relative properties and dangers of open and suppressed inflation. The virtues of introducing a stable currency to circulate in parallel with the old eroded one are debated, as are the merits of making the central bank independent of government, or of instructing it to follow some firm monetary rule, such as one which prescribes steady monetary growth. The need for foreign loans during stabilisation is also scrutinised.

Most fundamentally, we note the recent revival of the view that inflation stems ultimately from inter-group conflict. The frequent appearance and role of such phenomena as the 'scissors' effect and transfer problem are central features of the ensuing debate. Through the latter we are led to consider the relationship of inflation to power, democracy, absolutism and equally balanced economic struggle, so that our enquiry ends by taking us well outside the confines conventionally ascribed to economics. From such political and social views of the causes of inflation spring, too, broader policy prescriptions for its cure. By the time we enter this field our seach for the general laws or tendencies underlying modern inflations has ranged very wide indeed.

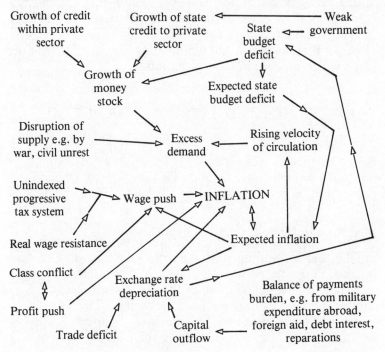

*Figure 1.1: Hypothesised Causal Mechanisms in the Course of Inflation*

# 2 The Great German Inflation

The inflation which reached its climax in Germany in November 1923 was, until the Hungarian hyperinflation of 1945–6, the greatest ever to have been recorded in the West. It began almost immediately upon the outbreak of World War I and was to continue, with only one break, for a total of over nine years, raising retail prices more than one trillionfold. Though not chronologically the first of the interwar inflations, it gave rise to such intense interest and so voluminous a literature that we here discuss it first, as a means of illuminating the complexity of the issues which modern inflations can raise.

## THE WAR AND IMMEDIATE POSTWAR PERIOD

Right from the beginning, the German government's intention was to finance its war expenditure entirely by borrowing. Not until 1916 was any rise in taxation even considered, taxes on war profits and on turnover then being belatedly introduced along with certain new indirect taxes. Even so, tax revenue over the period 1914–8 still fell, according to Stolper's estimate, some six billion marks short of covering total non-war expenditures, notably those resulting from currency depreciation and debt interest. Funds were also raised by the highly successful issue of war loans to the public, while the commercial credit banks showed great eagerness in purchasing Treasury bills. Nonetheless, the sums raised by war loans financed, according to Stolper (1967, p. 58), not more than 60 per cent of war expenditures.

The rest of the necessary funds were newly created via loans from the banking system. A variety of measures facilitated this policy. On 31 July 1914 the Reichsbank suspended convertibility into gold both for its own notes and for the notes of the five private banks of issue; and in August the Bank was authorised to discount short-term Treasury bills and count them, together with commercial bills, as cover for its notes. Further legislation provided for the organisation of Loan Banks which could extend credit on lenient terms both to the federal states and municipalities and to the newly created war corporations. The Loan Banks' funds, consisting of newly created notes, were to be counted with gold in the Reichsbank's 'ready money coverage', with which the note circulation was to be kept in a fixed ratio.

The effects of these measures, weakening as they did earlier safeguards against excessive note issue, were seen in a sixfold rise between 1914 and 1918 in the circulation of 'government money' (coins, banknotes, Loan Bank notes and the daily maturing Reichsbank liabilities); bank deposits also increased, nearly fourfold. The 'floating debt' of outstanding Treasury bills and bonds rose between June 1914 and December 1918 by a factor of 184. With demand at a high level as evidenced by low rates of unemployment, wholesale prices more than doubled and by the end of the war the stage was set, unless wartime trends were rapidly curbed, for a soaring demand inflation fuelled by monetary growth.

The immediate postwar months, however, saw the emergence of a second proximate source of inflation. During the war external trade had been severely limited and the dollar–mark exchange rate controlled by the Reichsbank. The reopening of freer trade and payments at once produced an external depreciation which threatened to destroy price stability by raising the price of imports and of import-using or -competing goods. From then on the exchange rate led the way in the inflation, rising even by May 1919 to over three times its prewar par value and carrying import prices with it, while the volume of the note circulation, the size of the floating debt and even the domestic price level lagged far behind. This ordering of the rates of increase of the various magnitudes was, except during a hiatus between February 1920 and May 1921, to persist until the final stages of hyperinflation in the summer and autumn of 1923.

The background to this renewal of inflation and to the change in its main symptoms was sombre. Although, apart from a small area of East Prussia, Germany's territory had not been devastated, manpower losses had been severe and prolonged undernourishment had reduced the productivity of the population. In addition Germany lost in the peace settlement all her colonies and was obliged to pay huge deliveries in kind to the Allies, including her entire navy and a very large part of her merchant fleet and railway rolling stock. The effects of the cession, under the Treat of Versailles, of territory amounting to 13.1 per cent of the prewar total and containing about 10 per cent of the population are also likely to have been adverse, especially as the territories lost included Alsace-Lorraine and part of Upper Silesia and accounted for three quarters of Germany's iron ore production and a quarter of its coal. The cession even of highly productive territory need not itself, as Graham (1930, pp. 18-25) points out, necessarily have occasioned a worsened balance of payments or a weaker exchange rate. High productivity and external surplus by no means always go together, and in Graham's view any weakening in external payments resulted from loss of the return on capital assets other than land. A majority view, however, dissents, with Stolper attributing the trade deficit of the time to the curtailment of raw material exports and to increased imports of food and minerals – both results of the cession of territory itself – and Kindleberger likewise (1984, pp. 313–4) expecting cession to have weakened the Reich's external trade balance.

Whatever the effects of territorial loss, there can be no doubt that a third burden, reparations, imposed an extermely serious charge upon Germany's international payments. Beginning as a demand for compensation, the Allies' claims grew quickly to include all the costs of their occupation troops as well as the value of capitalised pension payments to Allied combatants. When the Peace Treaty at last became known it stated no definite ceiling for reparations but only that Germany was to transfer to the Allies, as an instalment on her debt, bonds worth 100 billion gold marks, of which 20 billion were to be paid by 1 May 1921. Part of the payments was to consist of annual deliveries of coal, chemicals and other goods for the duration of the following decade, the value of early deliveries being credited against the 20 billion marks. Payments in kind in fact began in August 1919.

The large but undefined scale of the reparations led to a long period of Allied–German wrangling. From the period preceding hyperinflation two salient events may be picked out for special note. The first was the publication of the Paris Resolutions of January 1921 which presented Germany with a schedule of payments over a forty-two year period, envisaging them as rising from an initial 2 billion gold marks a year to a level of 6 billion for the last 31 years of the repayment period. Germany's rejection of these claims led to temporary French and Belgian occupation of several German towns. The second, a still more important reformulation of Allied reparations demands, was presented in the London Ultimatum of May 1921. The Ultimatum required Germany, under threat of further sanctions, to deliver bonds to a total value generally stated at 132 billion gold marks (though Sally Marks (1969) calculates the true total as closer to 126.3 billion) and in addition to make annual payments of 2 billion gold marks plus 26 per cent of the value of German exports. The commencement of payment, in short-term Treasury bills and gold marks, involved the sale of paper marks on the foreign exchange market and coincided with a renewed plunge in the exchange rate after over a year of stability. The effect of reparation payments was thus, at least proximately, to end Germany's last chance of stabilising its currency in reasonably normal conditions.


## THE 1920–1 HIATUS; THE COLLAPSE INTO HYPER-INFLATION

While the conflict over reparations raged, successive German governments made a variety of attempts to solve or alleviate their problems. In December 1919 a turnover tax and capital levy were introduced, the latter aiming to confiscate up to 65 per cent of the largest holdings of personal wealth. Unfortunately, such a tax inevitably took a considerable time to put into operation, involving as it did huge tasks of valuation and the need for a long payment period, and in the meantime the value of the tax, which was calculated in norminal terms, had fallen so much as to make the revenue not worth collecting. In 1922 it was accordingly suspended, to be replaced by a property tax.

Radical fiscal reforms were also introduced in 1920 by Finance Minister Matthias Erzberger, who much increased the federal government's control over the public finances of Germany's constituent states, upon which the federal government had up to that time been heavily dependent. With the extended powers which this reorganisation gave him Erzberger attempted to balance the budget, introducing new taxes on corporations and on the yield of capital. Again, however, the stricter policies failed of their purpose. Municipal governments continued to spend liberally, largely in order to curb unemployment, and the floating debt and note circulation continued to rise.

The period following Erzberger's reforms has often been cited as one in which, given sufficient strength and determination in the face of opposition from business interests and nationalists, the government could have introduced fiscal restraints strong enough to achieve the joint objectives of paying the necessary reparations and preventing further inflation. Whether Germany could possibly have paid enough in reparations to satisfy the Allies may depend crucially on the extent to which the official total of 132 billion gold marks announced in May 1921 was seriously intended – a point of contention between Sally Marks (1969, 1972) and David Felix (1971). But certainly there was also fierce political resistance to the imposition of higher taxes, which arose partly from the fear that fiscal orthodoxy, producing higher unemployment, could bring in its train socialist revolution of the kind already experienced in 1918 (James, 1986, p. 42), and partly from governments' reluctance to impose hardship upon the domestic populace for the benefit of the Allies. Scope for deflationary policies was thus severely limited by political and psychological considerations.

However limited the measures taken, the months between February 1920 and May 1921 certainly constituted a hiatus in the postwar inflation markedly diffeent from all other substantial periods. The chief difference lies in the fact that at all other times (except possibly the last few confused months before stabilisation) the mark's plunging exchange rate led the inflation, with the growth of currency and the floating debt lagging, whereas during the 1920–1 hiatus the reverse was true: the currency and the floating debt continued to rise but the exchange rate on balance held firm, with the overall result that the domestic price level remained for fifteen months broadly constant. This relative stability, as recently researched by Gerald D. Feldman (1982), proves to have been due mainly to the Reichsbank's intervention in the foreign exchange market to support the mark by selling foreign securities and by reintroducing forward exchange transactions and exchange purchase guarantees, a policy which evoked an inflow of capital from abroad. The policy was, however, aided by three further factors: the onset of world recession, which lowered the prices of imported food and raw materials (Feldman, p. 184); the failure of the Kapp *putsch* of March 1920, with its boost to confidence; and Allied agreement the same month to close the 'Hole in the West', a loophole in Germany's import and export controls in its occupied border areas. Policy and good fortune thus combined to stabilise at once the exchange rate and the price level.

It was, as we have seen, a blow to the exchange rate, in the form of the London Ultimatum, which ended the period of stability. As a result, in May 1921 the dollar soared, followed closely by the price level and at a greater distance by the note circulation and floating debt. Not only the capital levy but also the subsequent enactment of a compulsory interest-free loan from the public to the government, repayable in terms of non-depreciating 'gold marks', had failed to take much practical effect, with the result that there was nothing to check the renewed upsurge. From the summer of 1921, moreover, the approach of catastrophe was foreshadowed by several dramatic and in some cases sinister events.

In August 1921 nationalist assassins killed Erzberger. In October, to the accompaniment of a further slide in the exchange rate, Upper Silesia was partitioned in accordance with the Peace Treaty. A short respite, in the form of a falling dollar rate, followed the announcement of a partial moratorium on reparations payments. Then in June 1922 after further large payments had been made, Walter Rathenau, the Foreign

Minister and an advocate of conciliation with the Allies, was assassinated. The currency's downward course recommenced with renewed vigour, hastened the same month by the refusal of a loan on the part of a committee of international bankers set up by the Reparations Commission. The flight from the mark not only drove down the exchange rate and impeded the achievement of budgetary balance. It also created a credit shortage which threatened to bring on the long-feared recession. The result was that the Reichsbank, which had previously stopped discounting Treasury bills in deference to the wishes of the Cannes Conference of January 1922, now felt obliged for the first time to discount commercial bills on a large scale, thus swelling the money supply.

Worse was to follow. In January 1923 France and Belgium occupied parts of the Ruhr in retaliation for Germany's allegedly inadequate payment of reparations. The citizens of the Ruhr responded with passive resistance, which included a general strike, and at a stroke a vital part of Germany's economy fell idle. The German government undertook the support of those who thus lost their livelihoods, by handing out social security payments with newly printed notes. For a time during the period March–April the Reichsbank steadied the exchange rate by selling gold and foreign exchange and again the price level briefly stabilised. But the new development was not to last. From then on all the economic indicators soared. The dollar rate, whose movements had initially preceded price movements by a substantial period, now became the yardstick of value, with internal prices adjusting to it almost instantaneously. In many rural areas paper marks ceased to be acceptable. Many employers paid wages in kind; and as people devised ways of spending cash at maximum speed the velocity of its circulation rose, reaching, according to Bresciani-Turroni (1937, p.168),[1] ten times its prewar level by one method of calculation (involving retail prices), and nearly forty times by another (using wholesale). The consequence was that despite capacity working by the printing presses the real value of the currency stock fell dramatically, giving rise to what was described, without intentional irony, as a 'shortage' of money.

During the last year of the inflation, wage indexation and the more frequent payment of wages spread rapidly. Though

*Table 2.1: Indicators of German inflation, 1918–23 (1918 = 1)*

|  | Banknote circulation | Internal prices | Dollar exchange rate |
|---|---|---|---|
| Oct 1918 | 1.0 | 1.0 | 1.0 |
| Oct 1919 | 1.625 | 2.105 | 4.07 |
| Feb 1920 | 2.039 | 5.063 | 15.032 |
| Oct 1920 | 2.897 | 5.412 | 10.342 |
| May 1921 | 3.061 | 5.268 | 9.44 |
| Oct 1921 | 3.734 | 9.3 | 22.76 |
| Jul 1922 | 7.61 | 38.699 | 74.784 |
| Oct 1922 | 18.112 | 206.266 | 482.357 |
| Jun 1923 | 651.119 | 7040.896 | 16677.58 |
|  | (31 July 1923 = 100) | | |
| 31 Jul 1923 | 1.0 | 1.0 | 1.0 |
| 14 Aug 1923 | 2.67* | 3.913 | 2.454* |
| 15 Sep 1923 | 73.02 | 206.832† | 82.06 |
| 23 Oct 1923 | 12026.0 | 85000.0 | 50763.0 |
| 30 Oct 1923 | 57399.0‡ | 109938.0 | 66031.0 |
| 30 Nov 1923 | 131778.0 | 853664.6 | 381679.4 |

* 15 August 1923
† 18 September 1923
‡ 31 October 1923

*Source:* Bernholz (1982, p.29), derived from Bresciani-Turroni (1931).

sometimes reported to have reinforced the inflation, these practices did something to protect employees' living standards; it could not, however, be said that they were adopted soon enough or operated efficiently enough to avert grave hardship for many classes of society or major shifts in the distribution of real income. Among accounts of those classes whose real incomes suffered, government functionaries of the middle and upper ranks figure large; while the savings, denominated in paper marks, of large sections of society, notably the middle classes, were virtually wiped out. Share prices, on the other hand, moved variably, some broadly keeping pace with the postwar inflation, others falling far behind.

Along with the distortion of income distribution went distortion of the structure of economic activity. Since it was highly profitable to borrow money repayable in paper marks in order to buy real assets, the negotiation of loans for purposes of the most dubious economic merit became common, undeterred by wholly inadequate rises in interest rates – an apparent violation of Fisher's 'Law' that interest rates rise to the full extent of expected inflation. Speculation in chattels described as 'real values' (*Sachwerte*) likewise became profitable and the structure of industry was altered, without any lasting economic justification, by conglomerate mergers and takeovers of the kind most typically associated with the name of the millionaire magnate, Hugo Stinnes. In addition, the number of commercial banks increased in response to booming demand for credit, while throughout the economy large numbers of workers were employed in dealing with the vast amount of paperwork which the problems of pricing, purchase, sale and indexation necessitated.

The effects on output were also evident. The level of demand may be gauged from the figures for the percentage of trade union members who were unemployed. For the years 1920–3 these moved in fairly close inverse relationship with the rate of inflation in something resembling an early forerunner of the Phillips Curve relationship (see Glossary). Falling from an immediate postwar peak of over 6 per cent, unemployment reached the low level of 1.9 per cent in the first quarter of 1920 and then rose during the hiatus of 1921–2 to levels of 3.0–4.5 per cent. Thereafter, with the resumption of inflation, it fell progressively to 0.6 per cent in the second quarter of 1922. During the last stages of hyperinflation, however, it grew once more, first to a peak of 5.6 per cent during the disruption caused by the Ruhr invasion of January 1923 and then, after a slight relapse, to 9.9 per cent in the third quarter. This came before stabilisation and resulted largely from the chaos caused by inflation. Partly, however, it arose from the spread, right at the end, of methods of 'valorisation', which by tying prices to the dollar or some other stable standard of value, had the effect of stabilising real prices in some parts of the economy and so bringing about the collapse of purely factitious employment in just the same way as the stabilisation itself was later to do – a kind of pre-stabilisation stabilisation.

Nor was the linking of prices to the dollar exchange rate the only means used for creating stable values. Another solution was to add a surcharge to prices for currency depreciation. Yet another was to use one of the many unorthodox monies, legal or illegal, which had come into circulation. These were reported (Bresciani Turroni, 1937, p.343) to number about 2000, many of them claiming to have stable value. The latter included: foreign currencies; real objects of various kinds; paper notes issued, principally by provincial and municipal authorities and chambers of commerce, against the 'cover' of equivalent sums desposited in the Gold Loan securities which the government created in August 1923; similar paper issued against 'Dollar Treasury Bonds'; and 'emergency monies' issued with the government's encouragement, most notably by the railway administration but also by many private traders. Such monies, while not driving the depreciating paper mark completely out of use, went far to replace it as a store of value, as subsequently became clear when, after the stabilisation, large gold and foreign currencies were released for general use from domestic currency hoards. The hoarding was, indeed, one reason why there was not enough 'good' money, in relation to demand, for it to drive bad money out of use completely – an interesting variant on Gresham's supposed 'Law'. On inspection, however, the Law proves to be more complex than has often been thought; we return to it in Chapter 13.

Throughout the inflation the balance of trade was heavily adverse. In the course of the war the value of merchandise imports had, according to the Reich's Statistical Bureau, exceeded that of exports by 15 billion gold marks, and in the four years 1919–22 this deficit fell only as far as 11 billion, a total no longer offset, as it had been before the war, by income from German investment abroads, since these had largely disappeared. The available trade statistics do not enable us to trace with accuracy the course of changes in the visible trade deficit for the latter period but Bresciani-Turroni takes the view (p.87) that by the calendar year 1922 something approaching balance had probably been established, partly owing to the growth of exports, partly because of a high level of foreign tourist expenditure in Germany. Highly incomplete figures for the first ten months of 1923 suggest a possible continuance of roughly balanced visible trade during that period. While, therefore, the fall in the mark exchange rate in the early postwar years must have been helped along by a weak overseas trading position, there are no signs that the latter contributed much to the sharply accelerated plunge in the last two years of the hyperinflation.

## STABILISATION AND RECESSION

Stabilisation was finally achieved by means of measures affecting both internal and external balance. In September 1923, broadly in accordance with a proposal of the Finance Minister, Dr Hans Luther, radically new policies were introduced. The government suspended loans for passive resistance in the Ruhr, furnished itself with special powers for the period of emergency and declared itself willing to resume reparations payments. On 15 October a decree establishing a new and additional bank of issue, the *Deutsche Rentenbank*, was published. The new bank was to be permitted to issue a maximum of 2.4 billion Rentenmarks, the new unit of account, to circulate alongside the notes of the Reichsbank. Not more than half of this sum could be lent to the government. The Reichsbank was also temporarily to retain its function as a bank of issue, though it was forbidden to discount the Reich's or its constituent states' Treasury bills. Roughly simultaneous steps were taken to establish a Committee under the chairmanship of Charles G. Dawes, an American banker, which in April 1924 put forward proposals for solving the reparations problem. In the meantime reparations payments were suspended. On 15 November the Rentenmark was introduced and five days later the official rate of conversion − 1 trillion paper marks for one Rentenmark − was established. With the announcement of strict limits to the credit which the Rentenbank could extend to government, the latter's obligation to balance the budget thus became clear to all; and on 16 November the Reichsbank stopped discounting Treasury bills, thus complying with that obligation.

The package of measures met with instant and virtually total success. As from mid-November prices stopped rising and began slightly to fall back. The dollar exchange rate in Berlin stabilised and was held stable by Reichsbank intervention in the market. When, in December, the government requested an increase in the credit that could be extended to the Treasury, the

Rentenbank refused; and when, early in April 1924, prices once more showed signs of rising in response to a unintended continuance of monetary growth, the Bank responded by imposing a severe freeze on credit generally, restoring the threatened stability at once. On the face of things, a strictly orthodox policy of shock treatment had all but killed inflation at a stroke. In detail, however, the story was more complex; we return to it below.

With stabilisation there vanished from use the huge number of substitute currencies which had come into circulation. The value of these was high, though the more trustworthy of them had tended to be withdrawn into hoards. Bresciani (p.344) asserts that in the autumn of 1923 'the total value of the emergency monies became considerably higher than the total of the legal tender money', with 1.5–2 billion marks' worth of foreign exchange and currency rumoured as being in circulation; while Schacht (1927, p.106) puts the total value of emergency money at the end of the year at an estimated 400–500 quintillion marks, the gold equivalent of the entire Reichsbank note circulation. From November, however, government offices ceased to accept emergency monies, while the issuers were instructed to redeem in official currency any such monies held by the Reichsbank. For these reasons, and because the emergence of a stable currency rendered substitutes – with all their difficulties of recognition and valuation – redundant, the emergency monies quickly declined. To some (unknown but partial) extent, therefore, the decline in use of them must have offset the continuing rise which, despite intentions to the contrary, was still taking place in the volume of official currency in circulation.

As the new currency and Bank became more firmly established and the budget balanced, foreign exchange restrictions were gradually relaxed until in 1926 the dollar rate was permitted to vary in response to market forces and the convertibility of Reichsbank notes in gold was restored. The Dawes arrangements were a substantial aid to recovery, making reparations payable to a League of Nations Commissioner inside Germany who was empowered to delay payment across the exchanges until this could be done without jeopardising the economy's stability. With the end of inflation, time-lags in tax assessments and payments ceased to reduce the real value of the revenue and in 1924/5 the budget went into substantial surplus, with the result that the government felt able to reduce somewhat both its tax rates and the extreme rigour of its expenditure pruning.

The balance of merchandise trade seems, however, to have worsened. Between 1 July 1924 and 31 December 1925 the deficit is estimated to have amounted to some 4.8 billion marks, a sum which had to be offset by foreign borrowing in accordance with the Dawes Plan. The deficit continued through almost every year of the 1920s, with foreign loans exceeding the sum of reparations payments plus interest payable on loans. Germany was, in short, borrowing more than the total sum needed to pay reparations and so was failing to reduce her net indebtedness. The risks inherent in this trend were to become all too evident when, at the height of the Wall Street boom a few years later, the inflow of capital was abruptly reversed.

The short-term effect of stabilisation upon the level of activity and employment seems to have been stimulatory. The number of workers on short time halved between November 1923 and March 1924 and the number totally unemployed, though it rose in November and December, had fallen sharply by March. Early in April, however, the Reichsbank, alarmed by rumours of a new *Rentenmarkinflation*, took severe measures to restrict the growth of credit and from that time onward production slackened and unemployment grew. Even then the 'stabilisation crisis' took time to reach its peak. The increase in foreign loans which followed adoption of the Dawes Plan brought about some temporary recovery and it was not until the summer of 1925 that unemployment began to rise dramatically, from 195,000 in June to over one million in December and an estimated three millions in March 1926. The cash flow crisis of that time and the belated adjustment of production to a pattern of demand more sustainable in non-inflationary times were certainly accompanied by major recession. Since, however, productivity rose fast in 1925 and fell little in 1926, the impact of the recession upon employment was much more marked than upon industrial production (Graham, 1930, p. 287; Holtfrerich, 1983, p. 409).

## OPINION ON CAUSAL LINKS

Opinion on the main causal links in the inflation has oscillated so much over the decades as to render summary more than usually difficult. W. J. Angell (1926) could assert that 'The reality of the type of analysis which runs *from* the balance of payments and the exchanges *to* general prices and the increased issue of paper seems to be definitely established.' More recently monetarist writers have claimed general agreement for the view that monetary growth was the prime, or even the sole, cause of the inflation. The truth has always lain between the two extremes. Rather few writers, until the monetarist boom of the 1970s, have held either monocausal view. Bresciani-Turroni, often cited as an early 'monetarist', can be quoted for the monetary theory (1937, p. 401): 'I insist . . . on the financial and monetary policy of Germany as the fundamental cause of the fall of the internal as well as of the external value of the mark . . .'; but equally he can be quoted for the balance of payments theory, when, discussing a number of periods in the years 1921–3, he writes (p. 80): 'The characteristics of those last phases was the very close connection between the exchange rate and domestic prices . . . A rise in the exchange rate spread almost immediately to all prices; not only to those of imported articles but also to purely domestic goods.' Bresciani (p. 54) is also willing to admit that the flight from the mark, which prompted exchange depreciation at such times, arose from psychological influences connected with reparations, such as the signing of the Treat of Versailles.

Similarly, Frank D. Graham's less 'monetarist' view lies between the two monocausal explanations. On the one hand, he writes (1930, p. 147): 'Exchange rates may in turn affect prices, regardless of the volume of note issues, through changing the rate of monetary turnover. It can scarcely be said therefore that the causal sequence runs any more strongly in one direction than in the other. Prices and exchange rates are in part determined independently of one another, in part react upon one another, and in part are self-determined.' On the other hand (p. 115): ' . . . while prices therefore do not respond in nice symmetry with the volume of circulating medium, there can be no doubt that the ultimate causal sequence runs from volume of money to prices.' The classic writers on the episode thus take a stand which, while not midway between the quantity theory and the balance of payments theory, is certainly not at either extreme.

There is, moreover, a third account. Presented in strong form by Joan Robinson (1938) and more moderately by Laursen and Pedersen (1964), this emphasises the role of wages, which, increasingly indexed to prices or the exchange rate in the later stages of the inflation, ensured that each external depreciation of the mark was ineffective in restoring payments equilibrium and thus brought about the collapse of the currency. By weakening Germany's trade balance and deterring the flow of speculative capital, excessive wage increases, in this view, also contributed to the very depreciation whose effects they were intended to alleviate. Particular note is taken of the summer of 1920 and the first half of 1921, our 'hiatus', during which wages remained buoyant even though other factors temporarily tended to lower the cost of living. On the whole, however, the wage-push thesis has found few to award it prime place, largely because wage rates lagged far behind prices through most of the inflation and seldom took a clear lead above other variables in the upward spiral.

Philip Cagan, in a well-known paper (1956), has attempted to demonstrate that the demand for money in the German and other hyperinflations was a stable function of expected inflation and that this in turn was determined as an exponentially declining weighted average of past inflation rates. The evidence is taken to demonstrate 'that domestic monetary factors alone explain hyperinflations' (p. 90) and to endorse the monetarist argument that, with the demand for money stable, changes in the supply can effectively be used to determine the actual money stock and so the rate of inflation.

These conclusions have been subject to considerable criticism. Carl-Ludwig Holtfrerich (1982) notes that, by Cagan's own admission, the model cannot explain the change in expectations which must have taken place to produce the sharp decline in money balances at the onset of hyperinflation. He takes the view (p.118) that 'It is almost a question of taste . . . whether [Cagan's] findings should be treated as exceptions to or refutations of the rule of a stable demand for money'. Holtfrerich's own account follows Heilperin, Hesse and other earlier writers in attributing the shift in expectations to realisation on the part of *foreign* holders of marks that their earlier expectations of a rise in the mark exchange rate had been mistaken – indeed, as Kindleberger (1984, p.320) argues, irrational. An ironical aspect of these expectations, in Holtfrerich's view, is that they seem in many cases to have been based on purchasing power parity theory; since external depreciation exceeded internal, a corrective appreciation of the exchange rate was to be expected. Irrationality thus appears to have resulted from a belief in orthodox theory.

Further criticisms of Cagan stem from R.L. Jacobs (1975), who argues that Cagan's estimation procedure is incorrect and that his empirical results 'are a direct result of the method used to solve' his models. Thus a chance rise in prices unconnected with the money supply is assumed to alter inflationary expectations while at the same time it reduces the real value of money balances, thereby providing all that is needed to yield a good fit for Cagan's data. Jacobs further takes the view that for consistency expectations should be specified as depending not adaptively on past price changes but 'rationally' on current changes in the money supply. When such a revised model is tested, however, the demand for money does not appear to be stable. Cagan, in a reply (with Kincaid, 1977), is willing to allow that expectations are determined by past price changes arising from any cause, including supply changes and balance of payments disturbances, but, as Kindleberger (op. cit., p.314) points out, by allowing the second of these he moves away from a pure 'monetarist' and towards a balance of payments theory of inflation.

Arising from the debate over Cagan's paper there has been recent discussion as to how far a single demand for money function (see Glossary) could be realistic when, according to many researchers (e.g. Bresciani, 1937, p.52; Holtfrerich, 1982; Nurkse, 1946, pp.44–5), the expectations of foreigners about the likely course of the exchange rate in the early stages of the inflation differed markedly from those of Germans. Hotlfrerich points to the McKenna Committee's finding that in 1919–23 an overall German balance of payments deficit of 9–10 billion gold marks was financed by foreign purchases of mark-denominated assets, and notes the sudden reversal of the mark premium which took place in June–July 1922 in the face of three events of largely *external* significance: the failure of the Cannes and Genoa Conferences to solve the reparations problem; the refusal of a committee of international bankers to recommend a long-term loan to Germany; and the assassination of Rathenau, who had advocated fulfilment of the country's obligations in the hope of securing abatement. Consistently with these observations, Holtfrerich finds that a model incorporating two distinct demand for money functions, domestic and foreign, yields a better fit. Debeir (1982, pp.132–6) argues that demand from foreigners, including branches of German banks and other organisations abroad, could not be distinct from demand from domestic sources, which included branches of foreign organisations situated in Germany. He also points to British-led recovery in 1922–3 as a factor attracting funds from Germany. Kindleberger, for his part, quotes Leonard P. Ayres' estimate that Americans who made speculative purchases of marks incurred losses of some 3.2 billion gold marks (cited in Holtfrerich, 1980, p.285), losses only possible if they sold (if at all) at prices lower than those at which they bought. The suggested conclusion is that a great many of them must at some stage have undergone a change in their expectations and in their demand for money, which a single function, aggregating their demand with that of Germans who had sold marks all along, would seriously misrepresent.

If the links between price increases and the demand for money are loose, other links do not seem to be much tighter. There is widespread support for the view that monetary growth, via excess demand, raised prices. Schacht, however, (1927, p. 25) emphasises government action in permitting, and even encouraging, the issue of private and municipal emergency monies which were to be acceptable by the Reichsbank and government departments, a step which could scarcely fail to make the money supply responsive to the rising price level and so reverse the usually assumed direction of causality. Moreover, a rising money supply in the hiatus of 1920–1 did not, on balance, raise prices.

Graham (1930, p. 39) and, for the period after the summer of 1922, Bresciani (1937, p. 62) discern a causal link running from the fall of the mark exchange rate to the growth of the budget deficit, via a rise in the prices and wages paid by government and not offset by any corresponding rise in tax revenue. Nurkse (1946, pp. 18–27), allowing that this link existed but deeming its effect in general modest, attributes its onset in mid-1922 primarily to the increasing degree of indexation of wages for public employees and to the depreciation of tax revenue, which by 1922 more than offset the diminishing effect of the decline in real interest payments on the public debt. There would, on the other hand, be strong and general agreement that budget deficits brought about exchange rate depreciation. The deficits, which arose substantially because business interests successfully opposed any alternative (Maier, 1978, p. 50), were too big to be financed by borrowing from the private sector and so gave rise to monetary growth, with consequent inflation and exchange depreciation. Just as between money supply and price level, so between budget deficit and exchange rate, the causal link seems to have worked both ways. Graham (op. cit., p. 149), as we have seen, similarly allows a two-way relation between the exchange rate and inflation, with the former affecting prices, regardless of the money supply, by changing the velocity of circulation. Bresciani, on the other hand, regards the effect as a direct one via import prices and describes it as being only 'immediate' or short term (e.g. p. 38).

Balance of payments theorists, for their part, have some scope for differences of view on exactly *how* the burden of reparations stimulated inflation. The problem here springs largely from the wide divergences between different estimates of the value of the reparations actually paid. The latter, though huge, were far below the figures discussed in contemporary Allied statements; those in cash, indeed, were begun only in the summer of 1921 and ended a year later. The German authorities valued the total paid up to the end of 1922 at 51.7 billion gold marks, an estimate well above any the Reparations Commission would accept. Charles Gide (cited Holtfrerich, 1986, p.146) estimated the value of payments up to April 1922 at 12–14 billion gold marks, while Keynes put forward a figure of 26 billion up to the end of 1922. Moulton and McGuire (1923) cite 25.8 billion to the same date. Reviewing the evidence, Holtfrerich forms the view that the value of reparations paid for the four years 1919–22, excluding the value of sequestrated property either belonging to the Reich itself or for which the Reich did not pay compensation, totalled about 13.2 billion – a figure broadly consistent with the estimates of Keynes and McGuire, who include the value of the above-named property. From 1923, payments fell to much lower levels. Holtfrerich concludes that 'during the inflation the Reich required sums equivalent to ten percent of national income to meet its Reparations obligations'. The enormity of the sum is undeniable. None the less, it represents only one-tenth of the total demanded in the Allied Ultimatum of May 1921, which, though it was in Sally Marks' (1969) view officially regarded as a mere public relations formula, greatly helped to foment resentment and panic among the German public. Of the total for the inflationary years, moreover, only a minority part consisted of cash payments, variously estimated at between 1.7 and 3.3 billion gold marks (Holtfrerich, pp.146–7). Since payments in kind, though they may have helped to create domestic shortages and were financed by monetary growth, did not directly depress the exchange rate, the calculation makes it possible to doubt whether reparation payments can have exercised, directly and persistently, quite the dramatic effect on the exchanges which has sometimes been claimed for them. For this reason, reparationists have tended to blame not only the actual payments but also, and principally, the psychological effect of their imposition, Holtfrerich himself comments: ' . . . between 1918 and 1923 uncertainty about the future level of reparations requirements was probably the principal destabilizing agent'.

## POLICY REGIMES AND THE VALUE OF GOVERNMENT LIABILITIES

Thomas J. Sargent (1986), in an interesting development of monetarist theory, has recently maintained the following propositions:

(a) A 'change of policy regime' of the kind experienced in the hyperinflations of the 1920s can change economic relationships dramatically and so achieve stabilisation at very low cost. In this view, inflation has no inherent momentum other than that created by public expectations, and these change rapidly once government provides good reasons for the change.

(b) The issue of new currencies in the course of stabilisations in the 1920s was unimportant in achieving price stability.

(c) In Germany and other countries the money supply did not, after stabilisation, vary proportionally with the price level. On the contrary, it continued to rise, sometimes fast, while prices remained at least moderately stable. These facts are, however, not inconsistent with a theory of inflation which maintains that the value of money is determined not merely by the quantity of money but also by the interpretation which can be put upon it. Thus, before stabilisation government notes were not 'backed' either by any assurance of convertibility into a stable-value currency or by any government commitment to raise future tax revenue; after stabilisation, they were. This, in Sargent's view, meant that the value of money was ultimately determined by the strength of public expectations that the government would in the future levy sufficient tax revenue to prevent overissue. In short, the value of the government's liabilities − money − was determined in much the same way as the value of a private financial organisation's liabilities is assumed, in neoclassical economic theory, to be determined in perfectly efficient markets: that is, by the present value of the organisation's expected surplus of future revenue over expenditure.

That changes of 'policy regime' can take place, and that such a change did take place in Germany in the way suggested under (a), is scarcely to be doubted. Furthermore, in the Europe of the 1920s, this could and sometimes did happen even when no new currency was issued − though to allow this is not to deny a disinflationary role to such issues in all cases. Nor does it seem open to doubt that any currency whose free convertibility into another stable-value currency is assured will itself *tend* to retain a stable value. The most controversial element in Sargent's argument is the assumption that the markets for goods, foreign exchange and assets alike always operate with extreme efficiency and without a time-lag. Thus if a country's money supply, backed by gold and foreign exchange, were for any reason to swell to the point where it gave rise to excess demand, the assumption must be that the latter would at once be reflected in additional purchases of goods or assets from abroad without raising domestic prices. Convertibility and free trade would thus ensure price stability. If the international goods market were not to behave with this degree of efficiency, a sound currency backed by gold would be insufficient to guarantee, at least in the short to medium term, freedom from inflation. Questionable, too, is the assumption, in relation to financial markets, that in the deliberations of market operators equal weight is given, for example, to the expectation of a budget deficit in the near future and to the equally confident expectation of an offsetting budget surplus in the more distant future. The belief that such an assumption will assuredly hold true may well be seen as requiring excessive confidence in the market's long-term foresight and monetarist convictions.

## THE INFLATIONARY WATERSHED AND THE ROLE OF SPECULATION

Some debate has centred on the phases of the inflation. Both the official figures of the *Statistisches Jahrbuch* (see e.g. Ringer, 1969, p.80) and those of Bresciani (1937, Tables I–VII, pp.25–36) make it clear that whereas monetary growth led the wartime inflation chronologically, the postwar inflation was led from an early stage by the plunge of the mark exchange rate. The only periods of exception to the general postwar rule that the exchange rate led were the hiatus of 1920–1, a brief period in the spring of 1922 and, probably, the last stages of hyperinflation. The period from the Armistice to February 1920 seem broadly to fit Nurkse's model (1946, esp. Chapter 6) of the early or 'moderate' stage of inflation, when inflows of speculative foreign capital tended, albeit somewhat weakly, to have a stabilising effect on the exchange rate and financed a deficit on current trade. During the 1920–1 hiatus the inflow continued more strongly, encouraged by government intervention in the exchange market together with improved terms of trade during the world recession (Laursen and Pedersen, 1964, p.62), helping to prevent the onset of cumulative inflation. The period after

June 1922, on the other hand, when the premium on the mark became negative as foreign speculators abandoned hope of an appreciation and the flight from the mark began, fits Nurkse's second phase of 'runaway' inflation, with the exchange rate leading.

Opinion largely agrees, too, on the date of the shift of expectations which pushed the economy eventually into hyperinflation, with Holtfrerich, Cagan, Kindleberger, Nurkse and Bresciani all favouring the months of June–August 1922. June 15 was, indeed, the date later chosen as the limit for revaluation claims made in German courts on liquidated debts, a further acknowledgment of its critical character (Maier, 1975, pp.359, 493). The few dissentients include Borchardt, who suggests May 1921, and Frenkel, who offers, in his selection of possibilities, the date of the assumption of power in France by the intransigent Poincaré in January 1922.

Whenever the watershed, the role of speculation in precipitating a slide from it is hard to doubt. Professor Friedman (1953, pp.157–203) has argued that speculation is, on balance, stabilising, in the sense of moving market prices towards their equilibrium market-clearing level; for only by buying cheap and selling dear can speculators make a profit, which, as a body of professionals, they are bound in general to do. Yet by buying cheap they raise prices and by selling dear depress them, thus in either case propelling prices towards an equilibrium level. The argument is, however, too general to be relied on. Even if professionals make a regular profit, an ever-changing body of amateurs may dominate the market in destabilising fashion, one group of loss-makers continually being replaced by another. Or professional speculators may *not* make a profit; on the contrary, if the value of a currency falls without limit under the influence of self-aggravating extrapolative expectations, then *all* sales of it may involve a loss. The German experience certainly provides evidence of speculation which drove the mark down far below the value which, but for the panic it itself engendered, would have been its equilibrium level. In an account of late 1921 Bresciani (p.97) writes: 'That German speculation exaggerated the exchange rates of the dollar is obvious from the fact that the dollar, which had been pushed beyond 300 marks . . . fell precipitously . . .

to 190. The result was an indescribable panic among the mass of small capitalists who had speculated on the fall of the mark . . .'

The destabilising effect of speculation in the later stages of hyperinflation is also hard to question. A believer both in the quantity theory of money and in Cassel's then current version of the purchasing power parity doctrine (see Glossary) might argue that, with the money stock soaring and prices therefore rising, the fall in the exchange rate merely restored purchasing power parity. Those who sold the mark were therefore driving it towards its Casselian equilibrium level, in accordance with both the orthodox theories. The problem here is to account for mark sales which took place on the many occasions when the exchange rate had already plunged out of proportion to the rise in internal prices. For not only did these not propel the exchange rate towards equilibrium at purchasing power parity. Their effect, by raising import prices, was to raise the domestic price level out of proportion to the supply of money – another departure from the equilibrium of orthodox theory. Furthermore, even if speculators' fears were, in the longer run, to prove justified, this was substantially because the speculators' own flight from the mark, by raising import prices, had justified the fears on which it was based.

Certainly, a more sophisticated version of purchasing power parity theory can present such sales in a stabilising light. The general rise in prices may, for example, be hypothesised as having consisted of two parts; a sharp rise in the price of tradeable goods and services, combined with relative stability in the price on nontradeables. In such a case the fall in the mark exchange rate necessary to bring about equilibrium in the sense of purchasing power parity in traded goods, would have been more than proportional to the internal rise in prices, so that even speculation which drove down the external value of the mark more than the internal might still have been, in that sense, stabilising. There is, indeed, some unsystematic evidence that the prices of goods did rise faster than those of services, which are usually less tradeable; and that the sellers of services – notably clerical and some professional workers – were, correspondingly, among those who suffered most from the inflation. The evidence needed to support the proposed argument is, however, so far lacking; and in the absence of more detailed information on relative price changes for tradeable and other goods over short time-periods the case for rejecting contemporary views that speculation against the mark was destabilising (in the senses named) remains as yet unsubstantiated.

## INFLATIONARY DISTORTIONS AS A WEAPON OF CLASS STRUGGLE

Some recent accounts of the German inflation have seen it as the product of a social conflict in which the sum of all claims to current income exceeded the total income available. The argument links with the older claim that inflation, which creates economic distortions to the benefit of some classes and the detriment of others, continues so long as the benefiting class is in a position to block stabilising measures. The problem is thus essentially one of class struggle.

In Germany, such distortions took many forms. Inflation distorted the pattern of employment as large numbers were taken into banking and other service industries to deal with the ever-growing volume of paperwork. The plunge of the exchange rate ahead of inflation also drew resources into temporarily profitable export industries. The search for 'real values' increased the number of people speculating in almost any physical object and reduced the flow of funds into housing, where rents were controlled. Share values likewise benefited at the expense of bonds. Mendershausen (1955, pp.41–2) argues, similarly, that the pattern of investment was distorted within an increased total. James (1986, pp.127–9), on the other hand, has recently expressed doubts on this score, arguing that long-term investment must have been rather little affected by an obviously temporary inflation. Only in 1922–3, moreover, does he observe the massive extension of bank credit which might be expected to have accompanied fixed investment intended to yield a 'speculative' profit by enabling borrowers to repay their loans in depreciated money.

Even if account is taken of these reservations, however, the inflation certainly distorted the distribution of labour, income and wealth. Relative gainers from the resulting redistribution included: many large businesses, the value of whose output often kept pace with inflation; farmers, who could repay their mortgages in worthless money; others with debts fixed in money terms; and all who had ready access to foreign currency. Losers included: those providing services, including the middle and upper ranks of the civil service; many workers; creditors; and rentiers. Even some relative gainers, deceived and demoralised by war and inflation, believed themselves to be losers (Moeller, 1982, pp.255–88).

Charles S. Maier, discussing such redistributive effects, (1975, p.358; 1978, p.50), sees the gains reaped by the business classes as their reason for withholding support for serious stabilising measures in 1921–3. Stabilisation meant recession, a loss of export advantage and even a danger of socialist revolution. The support of the business classes was necessary if heavier taxes on property and a tax on increases in the value of capital assets were to be introduced (Bresciani, p.58), so that parliamentary non-cooperation was sufficient to give them victory. Only when the disruption wrought by inflation (including, by November 1923, heavy unemployment, the threat of *coups* by political extremists and a widespread rejection of the currency) put entrepreneurial benefits at risk was agreement to stabilise forthcoming. The theory of inter-group conflict for economic advantage seems to fit the German case rather well.

## SHOCK TREATMENT VERSUS GRADUALISM

Many recent discussions of stabilisation policy have also focused upon the speed at which such policies should be introduced. In dealing with this question, some studies have confined themselves to proffering advice for one particular set of circumstances. Thus the British House of Commons Treasury and Civil Service Committee (1981) concluded from a lengthy study of available evidence that 'shock treatment' – a sudden reduction of public expenditure or increase in taxation, together with a sudden tightening of monetary conditions – was inappropriate in modern British circumstances. Other writers have not hesitated, however, to propound general rules to be followed by any stabilising government. The following convey the essence of the polar views expressed:

1 'The most important device for mitigating the side effects [of a stabilisation] is to slow inflation *gradually but steadily* by a policy announced in advance and adhered to so it becomes credible.' (Friedman and Friedman, 1979, p.323)
2 '. . . if inflation could really be controlled by monetary measures it would surely be preferable to bring the inflationary process to a halt suddenly . . . rather than slowly.' (Kaldor, 1970)
3 'The magnitude of unemployment caused by a cessation of inflation will increase with the length of the period during which such [stabilising] policies are pursued.' (Hayek, 1978, p.114)

What light does Germany's experience throw on the matter? The German stabilisation certainly proceeded quickly. Within a few days the new Rentenmark was introduced into circulation, the dollar rate stabilised and held on the Berlin exchange, the state required to balance its budget, and all Reichsbank offices forbidden to accept emergency money of any kind. True, other measures took longer to implement; fresh curbs on credit to private business were, for example, still being introduced five months later. Yet there can be no doubt that, by modern standards, the implementation of the new policies must, overall, be accounted 'sudden'.

Even so, it was not, on examination, sudden enough to account for observed events. The dramatic halt to inflation which occurred in mid-November after a precipitous rise in the preceding weeks was not, immediately at least, due to the stabilisation of the official money supply, for that did not occur. On the contrary, along with a steady increase in the number of Rentenmarks in circulation up to the prescribed limit, there went a continuing increase in the number of paper marks. These were issued via the discounting of commercial bills − a practice still permitted under the new arrangements and suggestive of an adherence to the Real Bills Doctrine (see Glossary) − which boosted the total number of paper marks in circulation by a factor of thirteen between 16 November 1923 and 31 July 1924. Furthermore, the new Bank Law of 11 October 1924 compelled the Reichsbank to buy gold and foreign exchange for domestic currency at a fixed price, thus preventing direct official control of the domestic money supply (Schacht, 1927, p.227). Actual changes in monetary growth cannot explain the stabilisation.

Neither was the *actuality* of a halt to reparation payments a sufficient cause of price stabilisation, for cash payments, the only type of payment to influence the exchange rate directly, had been halted long before, without halting the inflation. Nor, again, was the *existence* of a new payments plan for settling the reparations issue, for the Dawes Plan, which satisfied that description, was not announced until 9 April 1924 and not put into operation until 1 September. Nor did the proximate cause of stabilisation lie in the withdrawal of the old paper mark, which did not take place until 5 June 1925. Finally, the actuality of a balanced budget cannot have brought about the sudden stability, since this did not emerge until early in 1924 and was itself largely the *result* of the stabilisation, which led automatically to a huge rise in the gold mark value of tax revenues (Bresciani–Turroni, 1937, p.350).

The fact is that the German stabilisation resulted not from measures actually implemented but from faith in measures announced. Price stability returned to Germany because German and other holders of the mark suddenly began to trust their currency's future value. In consequence, they became willing to hold more marks, lowering the velocity of circulation of money, to curb their expenditure and to desist from raising the prices of their products. Thus they brought about the price stability on which they were relying. The fall in velocity was one major reason why stable prices were able to survive the ever-increasing flood of new money in the months after stabilisation. Others were the facts: that an acute shortage of money existed, in real terms, on stabilisation day; that substitute monies were withdrawn from circulation after stabilisation; and that a temporary revival of economic activity ensued, boosting supplies of goods. Of the last three factors, two arose only because of stabilisation. Confidence in the currency, which brought about stabilisation, thus helped to justify itself.

But what were the sources of that confidence? On one view, confidence returned with government intervention to stabilise the exchange rate. Such intervention had already achieved temporary success in curbing external depreciation during the hiatus of 1920–1, when it had attracted an inflow of capital from abroad and contributed powerfully to price stabilisation. This was all the more remarkable because at that time (Feldman, 1982, p.191) few people had considered stabilisation possible; both the Genoa Conference of April 1922 and the Paris Conference of the preceding year had regarded the settlement of Germany's debts as a necessary precondition for stabilisation. It was not, moreover, until a similar policy was again tried, between February and April 1923, that the exchange rate and with it the cost of living again became markedly more stable. For these reasons, it may fairly be argued, exchange rate intervention is likely to have contributed substantially to public confidence in the stabilisation, the more so as public attention had during the hyperinflation been centred increasingly on the dollar exchange rate.

A further explanation relates that Germans felt, out of sheer desperation, a *need* to trust their new currency. More guardedly, they may be said to have decided to act *as if* they regarded the currency's future value as assured. The crucial words are 'as if'. Whether most Germans really believed the inflation was over is not wholly clear. Schacht (p.110) writes: [In the last months of 1923] 'no one in the Rhineland believed in the possibility of stabilisation' and (p.152) [during the early months of 1924] 'The confidence of the business community in the stability of the currency was still only very slight.' Furthermore, although the dollar value of the Rentenmark might be fixed by government intervention and rationing on the Berlin Bourse, in other markets its value sagged heavily. Even so, the fact that price stability survived the dramatic increase in the quantity of money which took place after stabilisation was undoubtedly and primarily due to a general and new willingness to hold money. Individuals and organisations slowed their rates of disbursement of money towards pre-inflation levels and so prevented the continuance or reappearance of an inflationary level of demand. It was this act of faith in the Rentenmark which instantly 'valorised' tax revenue and so helped balance the Reich's budget; which contained the demand for goods and services at reasonable levels; which brought large sums of foreign currency out of hoards and into the hands of the

Reichsbank, thus strengthening its power to control the exchange rate; and which, in the course of 1924, enabled businesses to raise their productivity and real wages (Bresciani, 1937, pp.394–7).

Yet the question persists: if it was an announcement effect that triggered the stabilisation, which announcement did the trick? The time of stabilisation witnessed announcements not merely about the money supply and the end of government borrowing from the Reichsbank but also about the setting up of an international committee of experts to ensure that steps were taken to deal with the reparations issue; as a result of these the Dawes Committee first met in January 1924. All the main sources of inflation were thus attacked at once. The result is that our evidence is insufficient to distinguish between the possible different sources of renewed confidence. Possibly the similarity of the German policies to those which had succeeded the previous year in Austria was a crucial feature; but if so we have to explain the Austrian success in other terms – perhaps by reference to the League of Nations' guarantee of that country's existence and integrity. All that can be said with certainty in the German case is that, although in the longer term both fiscal and monetary measures were needed to bring stability, in the short term, psychological or 'announcement' effects of a kind not precisely definable played the crucial role. Furthermore, they greatly aided longer-term cures. The German stabilisation succeeded largely because of a mass act of faith. In what that faith was placed may not have been clear to Germans, even at the time.

## SUMMARY AND CONCLUSIONS

During World War I the main active sources of German inflation were the state deficit and the issue of money to finance it; from 1919 it was the plunge of the exchange rate, reflecting weakness in the trade balance and the severity of the proposed terms of the Treaty of Versailles. Thereafter, apart from a brief hiatus in 1920–1, exchange depreciation due to the payment and, perhaps still more, the fear of payment of reparations, together with governmental weakness which prevented any halt to monetary growth, led the way to hyperinflation. Stabilisation when it came was strictly orthodox but exacted a delayed cost in the form of recession. No one mechanism fully explains the inflation, still less the remedy, with its strange suggestion of faith healing.

As to the lessons that can be drawn, the German inflation has, above all others, left an enduring mark on opinion about the causes of and cures for inflation. In the United States, Argentina, Brazil and even in Britain, where the subsequent and more traumatic experience of the Great Depression has tended to outweigh earlier and weaker impressions, the legend of the German currency collapse continues many decades later to exert a powerful influence on popular, academic and governmental thinking.

One effect long evident in Germany and more recently in some British and American circles has been the tendency to view with deep suspicion any measures associated with inflation, such as currency devaluation, monetary accommodation or deficit financing. Along with this has gone heavy emphasis upon the costs of the inflation: the huge, unlegislated redistributions of income and wealth; the concentration of wealth alongside extreme hardship; the maldistribution of employment and investment; the spread of anti-social attitudes as speculation and financial manipulation came to dominate people's daily lives; and the subsequent long wrangles over the revaluation of old debts. The tendency is especially interesting in view of such arguments as Graham's (1930, p.321) to the effect that *in material terms* the inflation yielded Germany a net overall surplus of gains over losses. True, a material assessment neglects the episode's deplorable effects on morale and social cohesion, as well as the distributive injustices. It also overlooks any moral questions arising from the way in which Germany for a time financed her import surplus with irreparably depreciating marks. The likelihood that some gains were made because the inflation finally persuaded the Allies to relax their demands for reparations also involves certain moral issues. And of course Graham wrote before the rise of the Nazis, an event which many writers attribute in part to the effects of the inflation in ravaging the savings of the middle class. Even so, inflation may, in its early stages, have warded off the revolution which severely restrictive policies might well have evoked. The thesis that German governments were wrong to allow the inflation, assuming that they had the parliamentary power to curtail it, is one which requires demonstration. All that is certain is that the German experience gave inflation a bad name for many years and in many countries.

But Germany also gave 'shock treatment' a good name. Even in Britain in the 1970s high-level academic voices could be heard citing the effects of Hjalmar Schacht's policies in support of the claim that sudden stabilisation could be costless. As we have seen, in the short run a pure confidence trick – the false announcement of zero monetary growth – did curb demand enough to halt inflation but not so much as to prevent a growth of output and employment. The rise in the money stock, on the one hand, and the fall in its velocity, on the other, by good fortune combined to produce an ideal level and rate of growth of expenditure[2]. But the claim that such a trick could go on for long, or is even predictable initially, goes as far beyond the German evidence as does the claim that the stabilisation exacted no cost in the form of subsequent recession. At least three considerations seem, however, to suggest that a policy of shock treatment without price and wage controls is far more likely to succeed after extreme than after moderate inflation. One is that the dire effects of hyperinflation may increase people's willingness to gamble on the stability of the reformed currency and so to bring it about. A second is that in hyperinflation real tax revenue is more likely to be eroded by inflation between assessment and collection – a phenomenon which, once temporarily eliminated by an announcement effect, may give way to dramatic reductions in the fiscal deficit. Finally, hyperinflation often sees the disappearance of large amounts of foreign exchange into private hoards, from which it may reappear once confidence is restored. By all three mechanisms a temporary halt to inflation can render itself permanent.

Of the more misleading conclusions drawn from Germany, one has been particularly widespread. In the words of Milton and Rose Friedman (1979, p.329): 'Inflation is a monetary phenomenon, arising from a more rapid increase in the quantity of money than in output . . .' If inflation is defined in terms of the general price level (as, e.g., a persistent tendency for the general price level to rise) and if the general price level is defined in terms of money (how else?), then the initial assertion is true by definition. But what it is clearly meant to imply − namely, that money is the sole cause of inflation and always an active, as distinct from an accommodating cause − is untrue, as the German experience testifies. To some substantial extent the exchange rate, plunging under the burden of trade deficit, capital flight and reparations payments (actual and feared), was an active cause of the inflation, which monetary growth to that extent merely accommodated. When combined with political deadlock which prevented adequate fiscal retrenchment, it led, again as an active cause, to the issue of more money. Sometimes, as during World War I, monetary growth was an active cause; but no useful purpose is served by denying the roles played by many other factors in causing the German inflation.

## NOTES

1. Bresciani does not, however give the basis of his figures; and in any case estimates of what is presumably income velocity at a time of peak (but unrecorded) transactions in secondhand goods (as well as of numerous unofficial monies) seem likely to be of questionable value.
2. Tulloch G. and Campbell C. (1964) note the occurrence of this happy conjunction of offsetting factors in China during the 1940s.

# 3 Austria and Hungary in the 1920s

## *Austria*

### INTRODUCTION: THE EARLY POSTWAR YEARS

Austria's inflation was not, by the standards of its time, exceptionally grave. Retail prices rose less than in several other countries: by a factor of 150–200 (de Bordes, 1924, pp. 96–7; Young, 1925, vol. II, p. 293) during the twenty months before the main peak of September 1922, and about fifteen thousandfold (if housing is excluded) compared with prewar. The importance of Austria's experience lay mainly in two other facts. First, Austria was the first country in Central Europe substantially to achieve stability after hyperinflation. Second, the manner of its doing so, under League of Nations supervision, was taken as setting the norm for future stabilisation, a norm embodied in the phrase, 'the League of Nations method'. How far the policies used could prove efficacious in different circumstances constitutes one of the main questions underlying our enquiry.

The Austrian Republic, one of the first states to arise from the dissolution of the Austro-Hungarian Empire, proclaimed its existence on 12 November 1918. Like the other successor states, it found itself faced by formidable economic problems. Not only did the new country comprise little more than a quarter of the old Empire's territory and 23 per cent of its population. The internal balance of its industry was drastically changed, with almost one third of the population now living in Vienna. More serious still, its new neighbours restricted supplies of goods, and notably of food and raw materials, while at the same time obstructing access to many of Austria's nearest export markets. Coming on top of wartime disruption and privation, which had already in January 1918 provoked hunger riots in Vienna, the crippling of trade created shortages so severe as to lead to starvation. Inside the country, moreover, workmen's councils worsened the hardship felt in Vienna by shutting off food supplies to it. In the presence of such grave economic disruptions, political discontents simmered in April 1919 fifty people were killed during a leftwing demonstration in Vienna. Nor did the example of Hungary's Bolshevik revolution in March 1919, or the proclamation of Austro-German union — a step soon to be negated by the terms of the Treaty of St Germain — do anything to allay fears of national disintegration or catastrophe.

## PROBLEMS AND REMEDIES

In this situation the new government attempted to alleviate hardship by several means: by forbidding food exports; by maintaining, as far as possible, rations of virtually free food despite rapidly diminishing stocks; by extensive relief to the unemployed, whose numbers rose as high as 186,000 in May 1919, a level not to be reached again until 1925; by selling state enterprises' products, including tobacco and rail travel, at prices below cost; and by maintaining unnecessarily large administrative staffs. With its expenditure consequently far in excess of its tax revenue the government incurred budget deficits which it was slow to curb. From 67 per cent of state expenditure in the first half of 1919, the deficit fell only slowly to 40 per cent for calendar 1922. Indeed, it was only *after* the stabilisation of that year that it reached its peak, in nominal terms, in calendar 1923 before falling to a low level in 1924 and giving way to surplus in the course of the following year. The deficits were financed by the printing of new notes by the bank of issue, the Austro-Hungarian Bank, in payment for Treasury bills sold to it by the government; and to this expanding stock of notes were added others made available to the private sector through the discount of private and commercial paper at extremely cheap rates.

The inflation which accompanied these developments was severe. According to the index calculated by the Mixed Commission which was created in December 1921, the cost of living (including housing) rose from a base of 100 in July 1914 to 1326 in November 1918. Thereafter for nearly four years prices rose continually, accelerating dramatically in the course of late 1921 and especially in 1922, to a peak of 11,271 in September 1922. In the course of this increase many particularly sharp rises (above a smooth trend line) were noted; while even after the stabilisation of the early autumn of 1922, which was less than totally successful, moderately sharp price increases were observed in March–May 1923, September 1923 and January–February 1924.

As in the other central European hyperinflations of the time the Austrian was accompanied by, and contributed to, a number of grave economic disorders; These included:

1   The fortuitous redistribution of real income via changes in relative money incomes and prices;
2   Reductions in the ratio of cash holdings to income, as firms and individuals shifted into the holding of less liquid assets, which they expected to appreciate more nearly in proportion with the general price level;
3   A distortion of investment in line with short-term speculative demand for different types of asset rather than with a pattern of demand more sustainable in normal conditions;
4   Losses incurred by Austria as a whole, as assets were sold to foreigners at the low prices, expressed in foreign currency, to which a rapidly depreciating crown gave rise.

Alongside Austria's other problems there was, finally, a grave imbalance in overseas trade and payments. Austria's trade was, throughout the period under review, in heavy deficit. No figures exist for 1919 but for every year between 1920 and 1926 Pasvolsky (1928, p. 135) reports an adverse balance amounting regularly to more than half the total value of imports. Despite a substantial income from foreign investments, from tourism, and from the sale of property, including crowns, to foreigners, Austria was obliged to borrow in order to finance her imports,

the reparations payments imposed on her by the Peace Treaty
and the interest on the League of Nations' reconstruction loan
and on prewar debts inherited from the old Monarchy.

In these circumstances, the exchange value of the crown
declined dramatically. In the course of the war it had fallen to
less than one third of its pre-war parity in terms both of gold and
of the dollar; in the four years beginning 1919 the dollar
exchange rate rose further by factors of ten, four, eight and
twelve respectively. Falls in the crown's exchange rate were
especially marked in times of crisis. In the seven weeks following
publication of the terms of the Peace Treaty the dollar rose by 75
per cent. After the refusal of credits to Austria in December 1919
it doubled in less than two months. In the course of the entire
inflation, the value of the crown fell below one fifteen
thousandth of its pre-war gold parity, and it was only with
general stabilisation that the dollar rate itself stabilised and even
to some extent tended to fall.

Of the four main sets of remedies proposed for the country's
economic ills, two were of major importance. The first,
attempted by the government of Dr Renner in 1919, limited itself
solely to internal measures primarily designed to raise tax
revenue and so reduce the budget deficit. In the course of 1919
Vienna's municipal tariffs were indexed and the rates of
corporation tax raised to a theoretical maximum of 79 per cent.
The war profits tax for a time yielded large revenues; receipts
from the taxes on wages and the gross profits of hotels and
restaurants were also substantial. At best, however, the success
of tax-raising policy as an anti-inflation measure was not great,
as was clear from the continuing budget deficit.

After the rejection of two more proposed remedies for the
crisis (the 'Goode scheme' named after Sir William Goode in
1920 and the Loucheur scheme of 1921), a fourth proposal was,
in essentials, finally adopted, though only after prolonged and
difficult negotiations. Drawn up by the League of Nations'
Financial Committee and approved by the Supreme Council in
June 1921, the scheme proposed internal reforms but argued
that foreign loans, whose use should be supervised centrally to
guard against waste, were also necessary. Since Austria's credit
was believed at that time to be good, this would, it was thought,
provide a sufficient security for a private foreign loan, without

government guarantees, if only the 'lien' or mortgage upon Austria's assets provided for under the Peace Treaty were to be lifted. The following month, however, constitutional difficulties in the United States blocked progress, giving rise to panic sales of crowns on the Vienna exchange market, and not even the Austrian Finance Minister's visits to London, Paris and Geneva could obtain the credits envisaged.

From then on hyperinflation developed apace. During the first eight months of 1922 the collapse of the crown and the rise in Austrian domestic prices proceeded at an alarming and accelerating pace not visibly moderated by the formation in May, for the first time, of a reasonably strong governing coalition under the leadership of Dr Seipel. On 9 August the Austrian Minister in London addressed to the President of the Supreme Council a plea for a credit of £15 million, couched in extreme terms and asserting that in the absence of such a credit 'neither the present nor any other government is in a position to continue the administration of the state.' When the credit was none the less refused the dollar exchange rate rose to a peak of 83,600 on 25 August.

By this stage the critical state of Austria's economic and political life was evident to all, endangering as it did the continued existence of the country and possibly the peace of central Europe. It was the increased awareness of these dangers which finally drove the Allies to overcome their reluctance to provide further funds and to agree to a solution when in September Dr Seipel placed the problem once more before the League of Nations' Council. Referring the matter to its Financial Committee for advice, the Council received a reply stressing the necessity of balanced international trade for a permanent solution to Austria's problems but arguing that appropriate financial policies, including notably a balanced budget, would bring the economy to equilibrium by evoking 'an increase in production and the transfer of large classes of its population to economic work'; alternatively, economic pressure would 'compel the population to emigrate or reduce it to destitution'.

The plan of action adopted was set out in three Protocols signed in Geneva on 4 October 1922. In Protocol I the governments of Britain, France and Italy guaranteed the sovereignty, territorial integrity and independence of Austria in return for an undertaking by the Austrian government not to engage in any diplomatic, economic or financial activities which might in any way compromise the country's independence. Protocol II, which was signed only by Britain, France, Italy and Czechoslovakia, contained details of the reconstruction loan to be made to Austria, the conditions under which the money would be raised and the system to be used for supervising the administration of the loan, as well as the guarantee by the four governments of the payment of annuities under the terms of the loan. Protocol III was signed only by Austria and committed her to a programme of measures, to be carried out over a two-year period, designed to stabilise the currency and gradually to balance the state's budget. These included the enactment of a law giving any government coming to power within the period plenary powers for implementing its reforms without recourse to parliament; the acceptance of a Commissioner General, to be appointed by the Council, who would supervise and report on the working of the scheme; and the provision of securities necessary for the guarantee of the reconstruction loan.

In more detail, the scheme centred upon the need to balance the budget by the end of 1924. The Allied reconstruction loan would serve the purpose of bridging the budgetary gap until that date, thereby relieving Austria 'from the necessity of financing herself by the issue of paper and so causing a continuance of the precipitous fall of the crown', which, it was stated, had up to that date 'rendered all efforts at budget equilibrium futile' (League of Nations, 1926, p. 26). The League's report further called for the establishment of a bank of issue. It warned that the period of reform would be painful but asserted that to delay would be to make inevitable even harsher measures at some later date.

## STABILISATION AND ITS CONSEQUENCES

The first major step taken towards stabilisation was the establishment in November 1922 of a new central bank of issue, the Austrian National Bank, largely independent of government and forbidden to supply funds to government except in exchange for gold or other acceptable foreign assets (not

Treasury bills or bonds). A second measure halted increases in the uncovered note circulation, a step which, while not guaranteeing that the circulation was stabilised, ensured that future increases were after that date matched by increases in the Bank's holdings of gold, foreign assets and commercial paper. On 26 November the government took upon itself the extraordinary powers envisaged under Protocol III.

The effects of the mere announcement of the measures were strikingly similar to those accompanying similar announcements in other European countries. Prices stabilised, the plunge of the exchange rate was brought to an end and a change in the public's expectations and attitudes became instantly evident. During the two years which followed, steady progress was made towards achieving the objectives of the League's programme. Prices, after an initial halt, while not remaining completely stable, at least fluctuated within a far narrower range than any that had been seen over a comparable period since July 1914. Similarly, stability returned to the exchanges. The state's budget was reduced in 1924 and gave place to a surplus the following year. At the end of 1924 a new currency unit, the schilling, valued at 10,000 paper crowns or the equivalent in gold, and designed gradually to replace the crown, was introduced. It was not, however, redeemable in gold, though provision for such an event in the future was made. The Bank therefore maintained it at its gold parity by sales and purchases of foreign exchange, only permitting in 1925 small variations about the parity.

In balancing the state budget within the two-year implementation period, the government adopted far-reaching measures. More efficient methods of tax collection were introduced. Railway fares and the prices charged by other state enterprises were gradually raised in an attempt to cut or eliminate deficits. Some taxes were increased, other introduced. Partly as a result of these measures total revenue rose by almost 30 per cent between 1923 and 1925. In addition the government cut administrative staff, sacking over 23,000 officials in the last quarter of 1923, and reducing the country's bureaucracy to a size better suited to its reduced post-imperial functions. The projected reconstruction loan was also floated in 1923 during the summer, its success and that of the government in balancing the budget and stabilising the currency both externally and internally each constituting major elements in this, the League of Nations' first scheme for recovery after hyperinflation.

Two phenomena deserve special note as occurring during the League's period of control after stabilisation. The first was the ensuing period of recession. As we have seen, in the first quarter of 1923 unemployment rose sharply and then, after falling somewhat in the second half of the year, rose sporadically and with marked seasonal variations to unprecedented levels in the course of 1925 and 1926. The post-stabilisation slump in employment and output was therefore both severe and long delayed. Its counterpart was evident in the rise in the number of bankruptcies from 25 in 1922 to 448 in 1924 and in the continuing rise into 1925. It must, however, have been aggravated to some unknown extent by the need to complete the adjustment to Austria's changed boundaries and industrial structure, so that the effects of the reallocation of resources after inflation cannot clearly be distinguished.

The second noteworthy phenomenon, the stock exchange boom, was, on the other hand, both more immediate and of shorter duration. Prompted by the return of confidence in Austria's political integrity and economic prospects, the boom represented a reversal of the lag of share prices behind those of goods and services generally which had characterised the inflation – an exception to the 'rule' proposed by Irving Fisher (1911, p. 187) that at such times share prices rise more promptly than do prices generally. Between September 1922 and the end of 1923 the index of stock exchange quotations, exclusive of mining companies (de Bordes, 1924, p. 216), almost quintupled to a level 1631 times higher than the average for the first half of 1914. Since during that period prices generally were reasonably stable the gains made in the boom were huge in real terms and the real interest rates of 2–4 per cent *per week* which were paid to finance speculation accelerated greatly the repatriation of Austrian capital from abroad. A speculative flight out of the French franc, which at that time was undergoing a severe crisis of confidence, also swelled the influx, as did a widespread, though misplaced, belief in the doctrine of *Substanzwert,* which asserted that shares represented in some sense industrial assets so that their real value could not fall. This doctrine was also observed to be widely held during the German hyperinflation.

In January 1924 the Vienna stock exchange index peaked and for three months remained at a fairly constant high level. In March, however, in the wake of bank closures stemming from speculation in the franc, interest rates rose to levels as high as 17½ per cent and the country entered at once upon a severe financial crisis. The stock exchange boom came to an end; large cuts were made in the staffs of financial institutions; and the number of small banks fell from 260 at the peak of the boom to 195 in July 1925. By October 1924 the all-stock index had fallen from its January peak by over 60 per cent, and despite fluctuations was still at less than half the peak level when the financial crisis ended early in 1925. The industrial recession, however, persisted for a far longer period.

Despite its high degree of early success, the Austrian stabilisation did not quickly achieve all of its main aims. As late as the spring of 1924 the new central bank was faced by a severe crisis, with the collapse of the stock exchange boom and of banking and other businesses; and there were major delays before the requirements of the stabilisation plan were fully satisfied. Inflation, furthermore, was not dead. Retail prices, after an initial fall of 13 per cent from their peak of September 1922, rose fairly steadily, by 25 per cent to the end of 1923 and by a further 11 per cent to June 1924. In June 1925, however, stabilisation was completed when unrestricted transactions in dollars were established in Vienna and virtually complete stability restored to the external value of the currency, with the Bank's gold and foreign exchange reserves rising fast. In March the new schilling was introduced and various taxes reduced in response to the Financial Committee's recommendations. Thereafter the Commissioner General's control over the country's finances was gradually loosened and in June 1926 his office was at last discontinued. The first great experiment in financial reconstruction under the League of Nations' supervision was at an end.

## MECHANISMS OF THE INFLATION AND FISCAL DEFICIT

A number of basic questions arise about the mechanisms

involved in the Austrian inflation. Several of these concern causality. No measure of excess productive capacity exists for the most inflationary period and the best proxy, the number of unemployed receiving relief, is not easy to interpret. Even so, the trends they indicate are consistent with the view that, after a period of slackness in 1919, demand picked up in the early part of the following year and remained high throughout 1921, reaching a peak in the closing months. Conversely, unemployment in 1922, though much higher than in the preceding year, remained at only a small fraction of the high levels of 1919; and only after the stabilisation of August/September did it rise, to levels which eventually exceeded even the 1919 level. There seems, therefore, little doubt that excess demand, fuelled not only by state deficits and subsidised prices but also by the desire to hold goods rather than money, played an important part in furthering inflation, at least in the years 1920–2.

For 1919, however, it is not clear that excess demand can be invoked as a major cause, even when account is taken of the severe disruption of production which followed the breakup of the Austro-Hungarian Empire. Here, and especially in the latter part of the year (as well as in the closing months of 1918), the falling exchange rate seems likely to have played, at least proximately, a predominant role. For 1919 and 1920 it is impossible to check upon the accuracy of this claim since the available price indices do not afford sufficiently frequent readings; but for 1921–2 it is illuminating to compare movements in the Mixed Commission's price index (excluding housing, which might be expected to be slow to react to increases in the price of imports and import substitutes) with short term movements of the exchange rate. Table 3:1 gives the relevant figures.

The figures appear to yield support for at least a short-run balance-of-payments theory of the inflation. First, the correlation between price level and exchange rate is much closer than that between price level and note circulation. Second, whereas the note circulation *never* fell in the course of the two years in question, the gold exchange rate fell on several occasions: in March–May 1921 (by small amounts); in December 1921 and February 1922 (by large amounts); and

*Table 3.1: Economic indicators, Austria, 1921–2*

|  | Cost of living excluding housing (July 1914 = 1) | Index of note circulation, (crowns, mid-month, 1914 = 1) | Cost of gold crown in paper crowns Vienna, mid-month) |
|---|---|---|---|
| **1921** | | | |
| January | 92 | 69 | 132 |
| February | 100 | 77 | 146 |
| March | 112 | 82 | 140 |
| April | 111 | 90 | 134 |
| May | 119 | 91 | 122 |
| June | 119 | 99 | 146 |
| July | 125 | 108 | 194 |
| August | 124 | 117 | 219 |
| September | 151 | 140 | 511 |
| October | 238 | 182 | 882 |
| November | 374 | 241 | 1,726 |
| December | 661 | 348 | 1,069 |
| **1922** | | | |
| January | 830 | 454 | 1,494 |
| February | 980 | 520 | 1,287 |
| March | 989 | 608 | 1,517 |
| April | 1,089 | 693 | 1,608 |
| May | 1,364 | 796 | 2,249 |
| June | 2,339 | 1,100 | 3,830 |
| July | 3,308 | 1,572 | 8,581 |
| August | 7,422 | 2,707 | 15,663 |
| September | 14,153 | 4,555 | 15,037 |
| October | 12,965 | 5,942 | 14,903 |
| November | 12,158 | 6,836 | 14,467 |
| December | 11,737 | 8,160 | 14,189 |

*Source:* de Bordes (1924), pp 96–7. Figures rounded to nearest whole number.

again in the last quarter of 1922. Roughly corresponding with these periods of external stability for the crown were periods when the cost of living index stopped rising, however temporarily: in April, June and August 1921; in March 1922; and in the last quarter of 1922. The coincidence of the periods of stability in the two series is not perfect; nor can one draw firm conclusions from statistical correlations. Even so, the fact that the note circulation continued to rise throughout the periods of approximate and definite price stability is strongly suggestive of a greater *immediate and active* link between prices and the exchange rate than between prices and the note circulation, even though the latter may still have played a vital accommodating and permissive role. Support for this interpretation comes from the League of Nations' Survey on the Financial Reconstruction of Austria (1926, p. 75), which argues that 'it was impossible [in August 1920] to reform the budget while the currency was falling, for an estimate made one day was wildly wrong the next.' Since the plunge of the exchange rate could not fail to raise prices and so make the currency fall both in external and internal value, this amounts to saying that exchange stability was a precondition for budgetary balance, and that the fall of the crown was therefore an active and sufficient cause of the inflation, however far it might itself be ratified by monetary growth in the longer run. As in the case of Germany, this view is further supported by the fact that in the stabilisation both the internal and the external depreciation ended 'a full two months before printing [of new notes] stopped'.

Another feature of the Austrian inflation emerging clearly from the time-path of the crown's gold exchange rate is the rate's extreme sensitivity to economic or political shocks. This is evident throughout the whole of our period. Thus the periods of most dramatic increase in the rate coincide strikingly with times of panic or near-panic arising from fresh economic and political developments. In the long list of such times we may note: (a) the first half of 1919 (of which de Bordes remarks that during the whole of that year the price level seems to have been unrelated to changes *either* in the exchange rate *or* in the note circulation, attributing this to the drastic reduction in the supply of goods resulting from the breakup of the Empire); (b) late July 1919 to mid-February 1920, and especially at the time when the final text of the Peace Treaty was published; (c) end-January and early February 1921 (when the Goode scheme was rejected); (d) late July 1921, a time of constitutional problems in the United States; and (e) March to August 1922, especially 28 April and the failure of Italian and French credits. The periods of drastic depreciation again do not always coincide exactly with the political crises. None the less, it would be hard to explain most of them purely on grounds of coincidence.

There is, then, general agreement on the existence of a direct causal link between fears of Austria's imminent dismemberment or insolvency, on the one hand, and the fall of the exchange rate, on the other; and, somewhat less strongly, between the exchange rate and the general price level. The latter link arose, moreover, not only via increases in the prices of imported goods and through them of import substitutes and goods made with imported materials. It arose also from what became a fairly widespread habit, on the part of suppliers, of using the exchange rate as a price index, in the absence of any other such index, and of adjusting their own domestic prices accordingly. The net result of these influences is that for many short subperiods it seems safe to draw the same conclusion which de Bordes draws for 1922: ' . . . it was not the price level which determined the rate of exchange but the rate of exchange which determined the price level' (op. cit., p. 172).

The increase in the note circulation, on the other hand, which delivered into the public's hands the means of making its excess demands effective, arose partly from the central bank's practice of financing state deficits by the discount of Treasury bills and partly from its accompanying provision of loans and discounts to private organisations and individuals at nominal rates of interest. In this sense, under the conditions of low unemployment which prevailed for part of our period, it may well be suspected of being a major active cause of inflation as well as, for long periods, an accommodating cause. But in this latter role it is important to consider how far the issue of new money to cover budget deficits was a discretionary act on the part of government, how far quasi-automatic.

The link between inflation and the fiscal deficit is, in fact, about as well established in the case of Austria as in that of Germany. The following are among the chief mechanisms suggested:

(a) Expenditure fixed in foreign currency rose in crowns as the exchange rate fell, worsening the budget deficit and so necessitating further creation of money. The extent to which this process took place in Austria awaits precise measurement.

(b) Expenditure on the payment of reparations both created a budgetary burden and necessitated the purchase of foreign currency or gold on the exchanges, thus driving down the value of the crown. Compared with the German burden, however, Austrian reparations were small and the Allies were more lenient in allowing postponement. This factor was therefore in itself of small importance.

(c) Public expenditure on items, including labour, whose prices kept pace more or less fully with the general inflation tended to maintain the deficit. The spread of wage indexation in the postwar period helped to create this tendency. Such data as exist suggest that, after falling dramatically during the war, real wages went far towards attaining their prewar level once more in the early 1920s.

(d) Restraints upon the prices charged by public enterprises contributed towards increasing budget deficits as costs grew, thus swelling the note circulation as a means of bridging the budgetary gap.

(e) Similarly, lags in the assessment and receipt of taxes contributed to growing deficits and increasing note circulation as prices and the dollar exchange rose. (Conversely, when the foreign exchanges and the price level were stabilised, tax revenue began to rise unexpectedly quickly.)

(f) External depreciation and the ensuing inflation made precise budgeting impossible and so proved self-reinforcing. This, as we have seen, was the League of Nations' view.

In general, despite the lack of much firm evidence, we can venture three broad conclusions in this field. First, as in Germany, budget deficits were in part an accommodating cause of inflation which was often actively caused by exchange depreciation. Second, reparations, by contrast, played only a minor role in the plunge of the exchange rate; fear of continued budget deficits was itself a more powerful cause of the flight from the crown, as was the fear, especially in the last year of the inflation, that Austria might be unable to survive as an independent sovereign state. Expectations based on the quantity theory of money were thus supplemented by exogenous shocks and fears in the inflationary process.

Third, in the League's view, the exchange depreciation was

itself directly a cause, as in Germany, of budget deficits via one or more of the mechanisms outlined above – most probably (d), (e) and (f). In an economy without great unused resources and with expectations conditioned by the long series of wartime budget deficits, postwar demand was swelled by further deficits; and with political fears playing a large role here, as again in Germany, it is perhaps not surprising that, when stabilisation came, psychological factors played a strikingly similar role in (temporarily) halting inflation at a stroke, even before most of the substantive measures of stabilisation had been put into effect. It is noteworthy, too, that in both countries the sudden change in expectations at the time of stabilisation arose not only from steps taken in the direction of internal fiscal balance but also towards external balance.

The success of the mere announcement of remedial measures lends strong support to a 'psychological' diagnosis of the inflation. It may, however, also be consistent with the view of those (see e.g. T.J. Sargent, 1986, pp. 54–5) who argue that the value of currency unit is determined by the present value of the expected future revenue, net of expenditures, of the organisation issuing the currency – in this case the Austrian government. Such a view proves on inspection to be the quantity theory in revised form: people raise their prices, sell the domestic currency for foreign exchange and reduce their holdings of money (all forms of inflationary behaviour) because they expect inflation; and they expect inflation because they expect that there will be future budget deficits and that these will eventually be financed by the creation of money.

Such a view is held to explain the apparent refutation of the traditional quantity theory by the events of August 1922 to December 1924, when a sixfold increase in the Austrian note circulation was accompanied by only mild inflation. The reason, Sargent argues, is that stabilisation brought about a change in the interpretation of the money figures. Before stabilisation the Austrian currency was in effect unbacked, since the official backing of treasury bills signified no commitment to raise revenues through future tax collections. After stabilisation, on the other hand, the currency was backed by gold, foreign assets and commercial paper and ultimately by the government's resolve to collect tax revenue. At the margin, moreover, 'central bank liabilities were backed 100 per cent by gold, foreign assets and commercial paper as the deposits were created through open market operations in those assets.'

There are two strands of thought here. One, the view that a currency will retain a stable value so long as it is reliably exchangeable for another currency of stable value, is persuasive in proportion as those possessing the currency have and make use of ready and low-cost access to an efficient foreign exchange market. What is far less reliable is the link relating the currency's value to expected future budget surpluses. First, a growing debt whose interest cost rises no faster than the tax base may never give rise to the creation of money; tax revenue, at unchanged tax rates, will rise sufficiently to service it. Second, today's deficits, if financed by the creation of money in a time of full employment, may give rise to an inflation which, in the presence of asymmetrical factors like rigid wages, tomorrow's surpluses may fail to correct. For both reasons the link between expected budgets and inflation is weak. To this, moreover, must be added the reminder that even if expectations do affect the currency's value, as seems undeniable, those expectations may be shortsighted. Traders in the market, actual and potential, may care more about today's deficits than tomorrow's likely surpluses.

## SUMMARY OF EVENTS; AUSTRIA AND GERMANY

The Austrian inflation had its origins in excess demand fuelled by a state deficit, and in postwar supply shortages. It was, however, the plunge of the exchange rate, in which fears of political extinction as well as adverse external payments played a major part, which led the postwar inflation. Orthodox stabilisation, introduced under the auspices of the League of Nations and involving centrally budgetary balance and a foreign loan, brought with a dramatic though temporary halt to internal and external depreciation alike; but it took several years before long term price stability and monetary control were assured, and in the meantime the recessionary costs were substantial.

The Austrian and German stabilisations displayed marked similarities in that both involved a return to strict budgetary balance, a foreign loan (which in both cases took some time to materialise), postponement of reparations payments, and the presence of 'psychological' factors bringing about an instant halt to inflation and exchange depreciation on the very date on which the new policies were announced, even though the note circulation continued to soar thereafter. After stabilisation, moreover, the worst of the resulting recession did not materialise for three or four years in either country. In so far as one can, like the League of Nations, discern slower recuperation in Austria than in Germany, the cause may have lain in that country's greater geographical dismemberment at the end of the war.

The experiences of the two countries did, on the other hand, show some differences. First, the extent of the two inflations was very different, with prices rising by a factor of 14–15,000 (11,000 if housing is included) in Austria, compared with over a trillion (one million millions) in Germany. Austria, on the other hand, seems to have gained less respite from internal inflation during the brief but severe recession in world trade between March 1920 and mid-1921. As we have seen, reparations played a much smaller role in the Austrian case. In Austria the new currency unit, the schilling, was not introduced until more than two and a half years after *de facto* stabilisation, in what was almost certainly a declaratory measure, whereas in Germany the Rentenmark was introduced simultaneously, and the new Reichsmark within a year; the inference seems to be that in halting hyperinflation a new currency may not always be essential. The Austrian stabilisation, moreover, achieved a less complete success that the German, with prices still fluctuating substantially in the following years. Even in the 1920s 'shock treatment' in a free market could be a precarious business, largely a means of gaining time in which to curb budgetary excesses.

The two experiences were thus, in short, very different in extent, but otherwise differed only in a number of rather secondary respects. None the less, similar remedies were applied in both. The League's Financial Committee made, however, the explicit proviso, in the Austrian case, that 'the methods hitherto adopted constitute only the guiding experience, not a binding precedent, for any new case that may present itself.' It remains for us to consider, in the light of other countries' experiences, how far any set of remedies can be claimed as having more general application.

# *Hungary*

## INTRODUCTION; COURSE OF THE INFLATION

The postwar Hungarian inflation, which increased retail prices about 500-fold between July 1921 and April 1924, was similar in its total extent to Austria's and arose, like Austria's, from postwar disruption combined with uncontrolled public deficits. The crisis was, however, less fundamental than Austria's in that it did not threaten the new Hungary's political survival. Nor was the basic economy of the new Hungary so unbalanced internally or so weak externally as that of its neighbour. Yet the course of inflation and the subsequent stabilisation were in many ways strikingly similar.

War had imposed great economic and financial strains upon the former Empire. The conscription of farm labour and the drain of food to Germany had created food shortages and because the authorities had financed the war largely by the inflationary printing of new notes, credit transactions had almost ceased. With Allied victory assured and nationalist rebellion breaking out throughout the Empire the Hungarians on 22 October 1918 declared their independence. When the borders of the new Hungary became stable the country had lost 72 per cent of its territory and 63 per cent of its population, and its economic condition was ruinous.

Political upheavals followed, involving the overthrow of two governments and a temporary invasion by Romania; and it was not until 1920 that the Treaty of Trianon was signed which officially ended the war, while providing that Hungary should pay reparations, to which at that date no ceiling was fixed, to the Allies. Even after the signing, however, the government of Admiral Horthy was by no means secure. On the contrary, it had to withstand, in April and October 1921, two attempts by the former Emperor, who had also borne the title King Charles of Hungary, to regain the Hungarian throne. Economically, too, the country suffered gravely from the disruption of industry and agriculture, a severe trade deficit, and inflation accompanied by large and, after 1920–1, growing budget deficits.

Some steps towards stabilisation were, however, taken during the years 1919–21. The Austro-Hungarian Bank was liquidated, its Austrian and Hungarian sections respectively forming the nuclei of new national banks. All Austro-Hungarian notes in circulation in Hungary were stamped and half of them retained in exchange for 4 per cent bonds – in effect a forced loan. In addition crown notes were issued in exchange both for the stamped notes and for several other kinds of note in circulation. In this way the currency was, up to a point, regularised.

In December 1921, moreover, the financier Dr Roland Hegedüs, entrusted with wide powers upon becoming Finance Minister, raised the rates of existing taxes and introduced new ones, notably a capital levy on property, in an attempt to balance the state budget. In this for a time he succeeded; inflation temporarily halted and the exchange rate of the crown rose rapidly. Success was, however, short-lived. Inefficient administrative procedures delayed tax collection and much of the revenue from the capital levy was allowed to finance increases in officials' salaries, with the result that the budget remained in deficit. The foreign trade balance, too, was persistently, though diminishingly, in deficit and could not be covered by foreign loans so long as the Allied reparation claims and the associated mortgage, or 'lien', on all Hungary's natural resources prevented the country offering any security for overseas borrowing. This situation, together with uncertainty about Hungary's political future, made the exchange rate permanently unstable and so posed a grave threat to price stability. The outcome was that from June 1921 both inflation and the depreciation of the crown accelerated and by September, when Hegedüs resigned, both were deteriorating.

The following year saw a substantial recovery in Hungary's exports which to some extent reduced the trade deficit. The fundamental problem of currency instability persisted, however, with the budget deficit persisting at a high level, external confidence low and prices soaring alarmingly. Early in 1923 the government applied formally to the Reparations Commission for permission to raise the lien on Hungarian property as a necessary preliminary to floating a foreign loan which would bridge the fiscal deficit until stabilising measures could be put into effect. The chances of success for such a venture were much increased in July, when Hungary's neighbours, Czechoslovakia, Romania and Yugoslavia, agreed at Sinaia not to raise any objection to Hungary's application provided that Hungary − now a country strongly influenced by irredentist claims − pledged itself not to disturb the peace. In October the Reparations Commission agreed to the Hungarian request and in January 1924 a reconstruction scheme drawn up by the League's Financial Committee was finally approved. The following month the Commission raised the lien on Hungarian property and in March the reconstruction scheme was launched by the signing of two protocols.

*Table 3:2 Hungarian prices and exchange rate, 1921−4*

|      |           | Index of prices* | Exchange rate (cents per crown, New York) |
|------|-----------|------------------|-------------------------------------------|
| 1921 | September | 6250             | 0.1944                                    |
|      | December  | 8250             | 0.1512                                    |
| 1922 | March     | 9900             | 0.1256                                    |
|      | June      | 12900            | 0.1079                                    |
|      | September | 26600            | 0.0423                                    |
|      | December  | 33400            | 0.0430                                    |
| 1923 | March     | 66000            | 0.0289                                    |
|      | June      | 144500           | 0.0140                                    |
|      | September | 554000           | 0.0055                                    |
|      | December  | 714000           | 0.0052                                    |
| 1924 | March     | 2076700          | 0.0015                                    |
|      | June      | 2207800          | 0.0011                                    |
|      | September | 2236600          | 0.0013                                    |
|      | December  | 2346600          | 0.0013                                    |

* Until November 1923 the index embodies retail prices of 60 commodities, with 1914 = 100. Thereafter, it is based on wholesale prices for 52 commodities, with 1913 = 100.

## THE RECONSTRUCTION SCHEME AND ITS CONSEQUENCES

In the first Protocol Britain, France, Italy Czechoslovakia, Romania and Yugoslavia agreed to respect the independence, sovereignty and territorial integrity of Hungary while Hungary undertook to keep its commitment to preserve the peace of the region. In the second, Hungary undertook to devise and carry out a programme of financial reconstruction which would include balancing the budget and stabilising the value of the currency. A League of Nations Commissioner General would supervise the operation of the programme.

The reconstruction scheme was implemented rapidly. A law of 26 April established a new bank of issue, the Hungarian National Bank, which took over the functions of the former Note Issuing Institute and assumed the power to control foreign currency transactions, for that purpose maintaining a stock of gold and foreign currency. The new Bank opened its doors on 24 June.

Even more important than price stabilisation, in the general view, was the successful floating of a foreign loan which would provide the country with hard currency or metallic reserves. After protracted but unsuccessful negotiations for an American loan, the government finally obtained a credit of £4 million from the Bank of England on the condition that the crown should be stabilised with respect to the pound sterling, the value of which was not at this stage fixed in relation to gold. Thus, after an initial attempt at stabilisation at a rather lower rate, the crown was at last stabilised at 346,000 to £1 on 31 July 1924. The consequence was that when, in 1925, Britain returned to gold at a somewhat higher sterling rate of exchange the Hungarian crown followed the pound upwards on the exchanges. It was in 1925, too, that a new currency, the pengo, was introduced at an exchange rate of one to 12,500 paper crowns or 17.45 US cents. It thus had a value fixed in terms of gold but was not itself directly convertible into gold.

The other main provisions of the scheme, which in many respects drew on the League's earlier experience during the Austrian stabilisation, were strictly orthodox. The new central bank was to make loans to the government only on the security of gold or foreign bills of exchange. The ratio of the Bank's reserves to its circulation (less the government's debt to the Bank) was to rise in planned stages from an initial minimum of 20 per cent to one of 40 per cent upon the eventual intended resumption of specie payments. There were to be no more issues of paper money to cover budget deficits and the state budget must be balanced within two and a half years. State enterprises, including most notably the railways, were to be instructed to cover their costs and to raise capital for their own needs. The role of the reconstruction loan in all this was, as in Austria, to cover the budget deficit until its planned elimination in the second half of 1926.

The scheme succeeded with unexpected rapidity. Indeed, the mere signing of the protocols produced a marked check to both internal and external currency depreciation. From March to July (Young, 1925, Vol. 2, p. 323) the price index rose by less than 10 per cent, compared with 44 per cent in January, and thereafter rose to a peak in December only some 6 per cent above its level when the new central bank began operations in June. By March 1925, moreover, it was down to its level of a year earlier. The dollar rate reached bottom still earlier, in June itself, falling only from 0.0015 cents per crown to 0.0011 and rising slowly from July well into the following year.

Fiscal developments were yet more dramatic. The budget deficit was eliminated even in the first six months of the reconstruction period (July–December 1924) and in the following six months it was replaced by a sizeable surplus. The turnabout arose to some extent because expenditure fell below its forecast level, with the number of the government's administrative employees being cut by over 38,000 between 1924 and 1926/7, but the main reason was an unexpectedly sharp rise in tax revenue, notably in that from turnover tax, custom duties and other consumption taxes. This was in marked contrast with the course of events envisaged by the planners, who expected direct taxes to play the principal role in achieving balance.

Some immediate loss of employment seems to have followed, with the number of members of the Union of Socialist Workers out of work rising from 22,000 to 23,000 between April and May, and thereafter to 37,000 in the first half of 1925; but by October of that year the total seems to have fallen to its pre-stabilisation level and its peak the next winter, at 29,000, was well below its level of the previous year. The trade balance, for its part, remained in deficit (which was reduced but not eliminated during the good harvest of 1925) and payments abroad in the form of reparations and debt interest remained heavy, the cost being met by extensive foreign borrowing on the part of firms, banks and municipalities, together with a return flow of foreign-held paper crowns. The general economic situation was, none the less, deemed sufficiently favourable to permit the League in June 1926 to withdraw its control, according to plan, upon the same date as its similar withdrawal from Austria. The step was facilitated by the scheme's provision for resuming the suspended reparations payments at an annual average rate of 10 million crowns for the following ten years.

Despite this happy outcome, severe economic problems remained – though neither then nor during the inflation had these been on anything approaching the Austrian scale. The adverse balance of payments has already been mentioned. Pasvolsky (1928, p. 351) presents evidence that industrial capacity, which had grown substantially during the period of inflation, was inadequately used, with output at only about 80 per cent of its 1913 level. Furthermore, the banking system had suffered severely from the inflation. Since fewer people had been willing to maintain large sums in the forms of bank deposits, the gold value of those deposits had fallen dramatically; the value of companies' operating capital was correspondingly much reduced. The advent of stabilisation brought, however, a substantial though gradual improvement in this last respect, with bank deposits once more beginning to increase. Even so, as late as at the end of 1926 a shortage of liquid capital still persisted, impeding the maintenance of production substantially. One favourable side-effect, however, was that as deposits increased throughout most of the reconstruction period the authorities felt able to lower interest rates, thus discouraging inflows of volatile capital from abroad.

## HUNGARY AND AUSTRIA

In the Hungarian statistics available for the period of inflation, as in the Austrian, the main perceptible relationship is that between the foreign exchange value of the crown and the domestic price index. When, for example, in November 1921 the crown exchange rate reached a temporary trough the price index rose sharply, falling back again in the following two months. The sudden plunge of the exchange rate in July–October 1922 was accompanied by a rise of 155 per cent in the price index, and when during the last quarter of the year the exchange rate more or less stabilised, so did the price index. The inverse correlation was by no means perfect. Though it seems to have held in the summer of 1923 the stabilisation of the crown during the last five months of that year did not bring about price stabilisation. None the less, when the reconstruction scheme was agreed both variables responded visibly; the exchange rate steadied immediately in March and moved little thereafter, while prices, after some fluctuations, reached their peak, not much above their July level, in December, before going into decline. The implication widely drawn for Hungary, as for Austria, has been that the exchange rate, under the influence of many factors such as political shocks and territorial loss unconnected with the money supply, often became, as it depreciated, the main active cause of inflation, not merely reflecting monetary growth but leading it. Available unemployment statistics, on the other hand, are inadequate to permit any firm conclusions as to whether they are correlated with inflation or not.

Other marked similarities between the Hungarian and Austrian experiences are not hard to find. The extent of the inflations was similar: Austria finally stabilised at 14,400 crowns to the prewar Austro-Hungarian crown, Hungary at 14,500 krone. In both countries the government was granted plenary powers and was committed to the implementation of a reconstruction scheme which was essentially an indivisible unity involving three key elements: budgetary balance, reorganisation of the central banking system and the flotation of a foreign loan. In both countries these goals were achieved rapidly and without undue difficulty.

In both countries, too, stabilisation preceded the balancing of the budget and helped powerfully to bring it about. Similarly, in both cases, the absolute size of the budget exceeded the size planned for, since it proved harder to curb public expenditure than to raise more tax revenue in the new and easier conditions of stability. In both countries the large-scale repatriation of foreign-held funds quickly swelled the gold and exchange reserves. Confidence was in both cases the key to success, even before the budget had been balanced.

Differences are scarcer and on the whole small. The Hungarian foreign loan, unlike the Austrian, was floated without any governmental guarantee, which the League's Financial Committee regarded as impracticable and unnecessary. Again, the Austrian reconstruction scheme contained no specific provision about the payment of reparations, since the guarantors of the loans were themselves reparations recipients, who were therefore unlikely to demand their reparations and so activate the guarantees on the Austrian loan. The Hungarian arrangements, on the other hand, did include a specific plan for payments. There were also some minor difference in the central banking reorganisations, though both involved abolition of the *Devisenzentrale* and transfer of its function to a new bank of issue.

More fundamentally, the plight of Hungary was at no stage as perilous as Austria's. There was never much doubt, for example, that Hungary would survive as an independent sovereign state, whatever its precise borders, whereas fears of Austria's dismemberment were widespread at home and abroad. Hungary was better balanced in its internal economy and better fitted for survival than the new Austria. In both countries, however, the post-stabilisation recession was severe, a delayed readjustment both to the new frontiers and the newfound stability of prices and exchange rates.

## IDIOSYNCRASIES OF THE STABILISATION

Several idiosyncrasies in Hungary's stabilisation deserve note. First, the introduction in February 1924 of the 'savings crown' or sparkrone is of interest as a weak example of that approach which attempts to neutralise the ill effects of inflation by the use of a parallel and indexed money. The extent to which the sparkrone was such a money was, however, very limited. It was never issued as a currency; it never served as a means of exchange or even a store of value. Its sole use was as a means of measuring value in broadly constant terms, its own value being fixed daily by the Note Issuing Institute by reference to the foreign exchange rate. Thus, a contract expressed in sparkrone would be payable in paper crowns but the number payable would rise in proportion to the depreciation of the paper crown on the foreign exchanges. Pasvolsky (1928, p. 313) comments that the introduction of the new money served to some extent to curb inflation. Michel Mitzakis (1926), on the other hand, reports that the effect was to reduce confidence in the paper crown and so to increase speculation against it.

Some defence of the sparkrone may be possible. In so far as lenders insisted on indexing their loans by its use, inflationary uncertainties and the scope for speculative borrowing would be reduced. Yet it seems entirely credible that an inflationary rise in the velocity of circulation of paper crowns also resulted. Certainly, the slowing of inflation in February 1924 seems more plausibly attributable to the approach of agreement on a stabilisation plan, such as was to be reached in Geneva shortly afterwards, than to the creation of the sparkrone.

The stabilisation package itself, like its counterparts in other countries, also deserves note, including as it did a fascinating assemblage of elements, some highly conservative, some novel or even radical, many to be applied in subsequent inflations. On the conservative side, public enterprises were to minimise investment and cover their costs fully. The central bank was to be totally independent of political influence. It was also to be free to discount normal trade bills without limit, though not accommodation bills or government paper – a modern version of the subsequently unfashionable Real Bills Doctrine.

On the other and more radical hand, the capital levy which had been proposed, with unfortunate effects on capital flight, in France, was in fact introduced in Hungary, where, even before a somewhat imperfect execution, its announcement alone brought a temporary (though only a temporary) halt to internal and external depreciation. The tying of the domestic currency to a major foreign currency, in this case sterling, also has a modern ring about it, providing an omen of subsequent similar times, such as the Chilean link with the dollar after June 1979. In the Hungarian case, as to some extent in the Chilean, a subsequent rise in the general exchange value of the anchor currency brought additional difficulties to its satellite. The episodes were thus of a kind where mechanical rules prove worse guides to economic policy than reasonably well-exercised discretion.

## SUMMARY AND CONCLUSIONS

Hungary's inflation, arising initially from currency issue unrelated to the war-depleted volume of output, continued in the postwar years as a result of weakness in external payments. One method used in an attempt to curb it involved the introduction of a parallel money, but with no marked success. Stabilisation when it came involved a combination of orthodox and radical elements and as in other countries initially involved dramatic reversals of expectations and attitudes; as elsewhere, budgetary balance emerged as a result rather than as a cause. As elsewhere, moreover, recession followed. In particular, the decision to tie the currency to an anchor currency, sterling, proved, when the latter returned to its prewar parity, to have marked disadvantages for Hungary.

# 4 France in the Twenties –
## A Crisis of Confidence

The French inflation of 1918–26 has evoked a volume of literature much greater than have most of the central European inflations of that time. Yet at no stage was its extent enough to warrant the name 'hyperinflation'. Retail prices increased less than threefold between the Armistice and their peak of late 1926. The inflation lacked most of the dramatic and novel features of other inflations; and in some respects its moderate nature concealed interesting tendencies which were clearly visible in more extreme crises elsewhere. Yet its importance was great, arising not only from its persistence and unusual causal origins but also from the influence which it was to exert on the economic policies of later French governments. For convenience we divide the narrative into phases chosen on financial rather than general economic grounds.

## THE WAR PERIOD AND POSTWAR BUSINESS CYCLE

During the war French government expenditure was not financed to any important extent by increased taxation. Not until 1917 was any addition made to the prewar level of taxation and then the extra payments merely offset tax reductions granted to the families of servicemen early in the war. Instead, the government borrowed to finance wartime expenditure, incurring additional wartime debts of some 144,000 million francs. Of this, 15 per cent was borrowed from the Bank of France, giving rise to monetary growth; 29 per cent by sales of National Defence bills and other short-term paper to the nonbank public; 36 per cent by means of permanent or funded loans from the market; and 20 per cent by means of foreign loans. As from September 1914 the government suspended the convertibility of notes into gold and so opened the way for an ever-recurring issue of inconvertible paper money at a time when national resources were so fully used that there could be no possibility of a corresponding increase in the output of goods and services.

Many prices were controlled, as was the exchange rate; some important goods – notably sugar, coal and petrol – were rationed. None the less, prices rose steadily throughout the war, by a factor of about 3.5 (Dulles, 1929, p. 107) and wholesale prices by one of about 4 (Federal Reserve Bulletin, 1921, p. 842; Jèze, 1927, p. 110). To the mounting domestic debt were added large and growing sums owed to the United States. The end of the war saw the country's finances in what was regarded as a highly unsatisfactory condition relieved only, in French eyes, by firm confidence that fully recompensing German reparations would be paid within a short time.

The signing of the Armistice in November 1918 introduced a new phase in the country's economic life. In March 1919 price controls were much relaxed and the franc unpegged on the foreign exchange market. There followed a sharp fall in the exchange rate, which was variously ascribed to the market's readjustment to the end of British and other credits, to the shortage of private credits and to proposals being made for a capital levy. In the course of the year the dollar moved from a value of 5.45 francs to one of over 10.50. Even so, under the influence of a temporary downturn in world economic activity wholesale prices during the first half of that year sagged somewhat. Retail prices, on the other hand, continued to rise sporadically at about the wartime rate until in 1920 they accelerated, despite the dramatic international slump which began in about March, and only turned down at the end of the year.

The government's budget was throughout this period veiled by an obscure method of presentation involving an 'extraordinary' as well as the 'ordinary' budget; and after the former's abolition in 1920 a budget for 'recoverable expenses' was substituted to include items which, it was believed, would ultimately be met from German reparations. Despite these complexities, however, it was clear that the increase in income tax and inheritance duties introduced in 1920 were progressively reducing the fiscal deficit. Indeed, even in 1920, when this process still had far to go, the deficit's persistence occasioned little concern, a widespread assumption being that before long prewar conditions and exchange rate parities would be restored. In addition, the receipt of German reparations was relied on.

Throughout the years 1919–22 the course of the French economy broadly resembled that of other western industrial nations. A boom in the second half of 1919 and early 1920 gave way to a short but severe slump. with sharply increased unemployment, in the following year. Wholesale, and to a lesser extent retail prices fell to a low point early in 1922. Throughout the recession successive governments expressed their intention of reducing public deficits. On 31 December 1920 a law embodying that intention was enacted on the basis of an agreement, the so-called Francois-Marsal Convention, between the Finance Minister and M. Robineau, the Governor of the Bank of France. This provided for the state to begin, in one year's time, repaying to the Bank two billion francs of its outstanding debt in each year. In the event, however, the full planned repayment proved impossible to make in the second year of the scheme, and throughout both the first and second years the cut in note circulation resulting from the scheme was fully offset by an increase in government borrowing, notably borrowing via the 'floating debt', which consisted largely of National Defence bonds (most of them actually short term bills) sold to the general public. Even if the government had adhered strictly to this non-inflationary method of finance, it would have encountered grave problems in redeeming the debt when, bunched as it was into a few critical years like 1925, it came to maturity. In the event, however, as we shall see, the government's facade of financial orthodoxy was spurious and the loss of confidence in governmental competence and probity to which the public revelation of that fact gave rise played a substantial part in the external and internal depreciation of the franc which was to follow.

## MILD DEPRECIATION, 1922–3

Despite an unpromising financial situation, the French economy, once the short slump had been weathered, showed many favourable features, which persisted right through the period of inflation. First, from the beginning of 1922 until stabilisation in 1926 national production rose almost continuously. Unemployment, curbed as a result of heavy wartime losses of manpower, seems to have been low by any standards. The current trade balance, after showing a heavy deficit for the first two postwar years, improved sharply in 1921 and subsequently moved into rising surplus. The recession of 1920–1 itself improved the balance, cutting visible imports by more than it reduced exports; while during the recovery exports rose the more sharply of the two. Inflation, which resumed its course after the upturn of 1922, and the accompanying fall in the exchange rate constituted the only major economic problems of the day.

Early 1923, bringing with it Franco-Belgian occupation of the Ruhr in retaliation for Germany's alleged non-payments of reparations, saw an intensification of public concern at the country's financial position. The suspension of cash reparation payments the previous summer had been followed by a fall in the franc on the exchanges and from now on the effect of political actions and announcements on the franc's external value began to be dramatic. The time is generally seen as marking the realisation, first by professional exchange dealers and then by the general public, that reparations from Germany might never be received. It also marks the appearance of another persistent feature of the inflation – the systematic inverse relationship of prices and the exchange rate. With growing awareness of both these factors the flight from the franc began.

In June and November further depreciations followed as the possibility of hyperinflation became evident through the example of Germany and as the expense of the Ruhr occupation mounted while reparations prospects worsened. The government's failure to make further payments under the Francois-Marsal Convention was also associated with the spread of pessimistic financial expectations, and of distrust of government, as evidenced by the public's failure to take up the eighth loan of Crédit National, an institution launched in 1919 to raise loans for the benefit of war victims. Meanwhile, a succession of weak and short-lived governments failed to take any adequate steps to halt either the inflation or the fall of the currency.

## DEEPENING CRISIS, 1924–6

In mid-January 1924 the Bank of France raised its discount rate in an attempt to halt the drift; but by then confidence in the authorities' will or ability to correct matters was so weak that the move was seen as a sign of weakness rather than of strength and the fall of the franc accelerated. The following month, however, the government of M. Poincaré introduced severer measures in the form of legislation to abolish a large number of civil service posts, to control the export of capital and to raise tax rates generally by 20 per cent (the *'double décime'*); and with funds borrowed from J.P. Morgan of New York and Lazard Freres of London it intervened successfully to support the franc on the foreign exchanges. Speculation subsided, the franc rose, even though in the event the *double décime* was never enforced nor, at the time, the budget fully balanced, and for a few months after March retail prices fell. Much of the success was attributed to the effect upon confidence of Poincaré's determination and orthodoxy, both of them fully evidenced during his long prewar career in a succession of high offices.

In May 1924 a general election was held, at which the *Bloc National* which Poincaré led lost strength in the Chamber of Deputies. It was succeeded in government by the *Cartel des Gauches,* a union of socialists and radical-socialists. Unhappily, the radicals, who were (Clough, 1939, p. 297) normally a necessary constituent of any stable coalition government, were not easily persuaded to give their support in either legislative chamber to measures which were also acceptable to more leftwing groups. For this reason a period of governmental instability now began which lasted until July 1926, with no fewer that eight different administrations taking office before that date. Dispute centred on whether the budget should be balanced by raising direct taxes, as favoured by the left, or indirect, as favoured by the right. Usually the dispute was settled by agreement to increase the note circulation by raising the ceiling for which the Francois-Marsal Convention provided. Proposals to do this were, however, commonly rejected by the Senate.

In this situation fiscal control was scarcely possible and in April 1925, with retail prices rising fast, it became known that the government had persuaded the Bank of France to break through the ceiling on note issue, issuing bonds discountable at the Bank of France which therefore led to additional note issue, and concealing its illegal practice by falsification of the Bank's balance sheets. Although Prime Minister Herriot defended his government's actions on the ground that they had merely followed in the path of other governments since 1920 – a defence unlikely to to restore public confidence in government generally – the scandal forced his resignation.

The successor government of M. Painlevé, though committed to ending inflation, found itself within six months asking the Assembly for a further increase in the note ceiling. The government's need to redeem maturing debt, even given the bunching of redemptions in 1925, would not have mattered had the government been able to raise the necessary funds by further sales of new bonds. Lack of public confidence made this impossible, however, and the bonds had to be repurchased with cash. Attempts to make the new bonds more attractive by indexing their value to sterling failed (indeed, Wolff (1943, p. 131) argues that it worsened matters), while proposals for a capital levy inspired further panic in the exchange market.

By this time, with the budget deficit for 1925 reduced to only about one ninth of its 1919 level, the franc's exchange value had clearly become the dominant factor in the inflation. Loss of hope of receiving German reparations, the experience of currency collapse in nearby countries and the long history of ineffectual government combined to spread alarm to the general public. It became common to value all transactions in pounds or dollars, and to buy goods wherever possible rather than to hold money. The velocity of circulation of money rose. Above all, the outflow of funds from France accelerated. In response, the Bank of France raised its discount rate to the crisis level of 7½ per cent and the government implemented a wartime law to enforce a degree of exchange control. The latter, however, was widely evaded and both exchange depreciation and inflation continued unchecked.

## THE PATH TO STABILISATION

In July 1926 the report of a Committee of Experts set up to advise on the crisis recommended the following action:

(i) The 'ceiling' system should be abandoned and replaced by a percentage gold reserve requirement to serve as 'cover' for the note circulation.

(ii) An independent bureau should be created to manage the issue of short-term bonds.

(iii) France should revert to the gold standard and the franc's prewar parity be restored, not immediately but as soon as the budget could be balanced, adequate exchange reserves accumulated, calm restored to financial markets, the balance of payments normalised, and inter-Allied debts (i.e. non-commercial debt arising out of the war) 'adjusted'.

(iv) Indirect taxes should be raised and public spending cut.

(v) Bond maturities should be staggered.

(vi) The government should be granted plenary powers to achieve these ends without recourse to parliament.

The government in power, that of M. Briand, accordingly sought the plenary powers indicated; but an attack from Herriott, who claimed that these could lead to dictatorship, brought about the government's downfall. On 25 July Poincaré was asked to form a government of 'national unity' including ministers from almost all parties but most importantly from those of right and centre.

Poincaré's reputation for honesty and austerity, recently evidenced by his actions while briefly in office in 1924, produced an immediate effect on confidence. Speculation against the franc stopped. From a 'high' of 49.22 francs to the dollar on 20 July, the rate had fallen to about 35 francs by 4 August, where it remained with only small variations throughout the month before subsiding in the last quarter of the year to its stabilised level of just over 25.25 francs. Wholesale prices followed quickly and by autumn retail prices too. The note circulation likewise peaked early in August and then fell to a stable level by the year's end (though there were further rises late in 1927). All the immediate stabilising changes of the summer were thus due solely to psychological factors, to expected rather than actual changes in policy.

Poincaré's policies, when announced, supported the image of austerity. He announced, first, his intention of implementing the recommendation of the Committee of Experts by extending the business turnover tax to all business transactions, by raising the luxury tax to 12 per cent, and by increasing import duties slightly. Against this, he lowered the rate of tax on the highest incomes from 60 to 30 per cent, thereby rejecting the left's preference for higher direct taxation. The measures, notably the business turnover tax, proved highly successful. Before the end of 1926 the budget had moved into surplus.

A second feature of policy was the establishment of a special *Caisse d'Amortissement* whose functions included management of the National Defence bonds and amortisation of the public debt. As a means of gaining public confidence it was declared to be 'independent' of the Treasury. It was to have at its disposal specially earmarked funds from the government's tobacco monopoly, inheritance duties and the newly-introduced tax on first transfer of real estate, and was to use these to redeem each issue of short-term bonds as it fell due. This duty it performed over the next year with outstanding success. By the end of January 1927 Defence Bonds of up to six months' maturation had vanished from the market and in June the number of one-year bonds began to be reduced.

At the end of 1926 the newfound stability of the exchange rate was formalised at an announced level of 122.25 francs to the pound. A law of 7 August further provided:

(i)   that the Bank of France could, for the first time since 1916, buy foreign bills of exchange; it could also buy gold and currency on the open market;

(ii)  that the Finance Minister could conclude agreements with the Bank about Treasury loans and the limits of note circulation; and

(iii) that the Bank could issue notes in payment for newly acquired reserves without counting them for the purposes of the 'ceiling' established on 22 July 1926; in this way the Bank was enabled to prevent unwanted rises in the franc's foreign exchange value, though at the expense of a higher note circulation.

From the date of Poincaré's accession to office, funds began to flow into the country. In pursuance of its aim of stabilising the exchange rate the Bank intervened in the market to purchase large quantities of gold, to the point where the Bank of England, anxious over its gold losses, had to persuade it to desist. Initially, therefore, Poincaré's aims were achieved quickly and without much apparent cost. Inflation and exchange depreciation halted at once; the budget, aided by the success of the extended business turnover tax, completed its move into balance; external payments, which had not been a ground for much concern since the immediate postwar period, remained favourable enough not to jeopardise the new stability.

Production, however, fell − according to the official index, by some 20 per cent − to a low point in April 1927, while 'unsatisfied demands for employment', which stood at 7682 in July 1926, rose by the following February to a peak of 96,670. Yet the recession proved to be short-lived. Long before the time of *de jure* stabilisation on 25 June 1928 the Poincaré government could claim to have achieved all the main objectives − stable prices, external balance and a high level of activity − towards which economic policy is normally directed.

## OPINION ON THE FRENCH INFLATION

Explanations of the wartime and immediate postwar French inflation have on the whole, over six decades, shown a high degree of agreement in allotting the main causal role to demand (Rogers, 1929; Dulles, 1929; Wolff, 1943; Kemp, 1972). Independent cost-push played little part, and with British and American funds helping to support the exchange rate there was until March 1919 little scope for the import of inflation through that medium. For some considerable time after the Armistice, moreover, state deficits were the predominant cause of the malady. Thereafter, business borrowing and in particular the discounting of commercial bills become more important

*Table 4.1: France, 1920–7*

| Year & quarter | | Retail prices (July 1914 = 100) 1st month of qtr. | Note circulation 000m francs start of qtr | $ exchange, francs per $ daily av., 1st month of qtr | |
|---|---|---|---|---|---|
| | | | | Low | High |
| 1920: | 1 | 290 | 37.7 | 10.75 | 13.41 |
| | 2 | 358 | 37.3 | 14.74 | 17.08 |
| | 3 | 373 | 37.8 | 11.60 | 13.09 |
| | 4 | 420 | 39.6 | 14.85 | 15.76 |
| 1921: | 1 | 410 | 38.6 | 13.93 | 17.18 |
| | 2 | 328 | 38.7 | 12.90 | 14.33 |
| | 3 | 306 | 37.7 | 12.45 | 13.16 |
| | 4 | 331 | 37.8 | 13.66 | 14.13 |
| 1922: | 1 | 319 | 37.4 | 11.97 | 12.60 |
| | 2 | 304 | 36.2 | 10.72 | 11.08 |
| | 3 | 297 | 36.8 | 11.78 | 12.70 |
| | 4 | 290 | 37.5 | 13.10 | 14.61 |
| 1923: | 1 | 309 | 37.4 | 13.55 | 16.89 |
| | 2 | 320 | 37.8 | 14.73 | 15.52 |
| | 3 | 321 | 37.7 | 16.75 | 17.38 |
| | 4 | 349 | 38.5 | 16.31 | 17.47 |
| 1924: | 1 | 376 | 39.1 | 19.88 | 22.49 |
| | 2 | 380 | 40.2 | 14.82 | 17.95 |
| | 3 | 360 | 40.1 | 19.26 | 20.10 |
| | 4 | 383 | 40.5 | 18.83 | 19.38 |
| 1925: | 1 | 408 | 40.9 | 18.38 | 18.77 |
| | 2 | 409 | 40.9 | 18.91 | 19.56 |
| | 3 | 421 | 43.8 | 20.93 | 22.38 |
| | 4 | 433 | 46.4 | 21.12 | 23.82 |
| 1926: | 1 | 480 | 52.0 | 25.90 | 26.99 |
| | 2 | 503 | 52.1 | 28.62 | 30.49 |
| | 3 | 574 | 53.9 | 36.61 | 49.22 |
| | 4 | 624 | 56.0 | 31.80 | 35.74 |
| 1927: | 1 | 592 | 54.3 | 25.14 | 25.38 |
| | 2 | 580 | 53.4 | 25.53 | |
| | 3 | 557 | 54.0 | 25.55 | |
| | 4 | 520 | 55.9 | 25.47 | |

*Source:* Dulles (1929), Statistical Appendices I, II and VII.

(Rogers, 1929, p. 191). At a time of low unemployment and extensive expenditure on postwar reconstruction, excess demand powered by monetary growth was thus the main active cause of the rapid price rises which, beginning in 1914, continued until the peak of the postwar international business cycle early in 1920.

At the end of that year, however, retail prices began to fall. This happened despite the state deficit, continuing advances from the Bank of France to finance that deficit and a persistent high (though now no longer rising) level of note circulation. Prices on international markets were falling and with production beginning to decline in May and unemployment rising, it is hard to sustain any longer a diagnosis of excess demand.

The country passed the lowest point of its production cycle in October 1921 and by March 1922 was operating at a higher level of output than at its pre-recession peak. The year 1922 as a whole has justly been called one of brilliant recovery; but it was then that inflation recommenced. The discounting of commercial bills was an important factor aggravating the difficulties encountered by the government in borrowing to meet its (declining) deficit and to refinance maturing debt. The efflux of capital from France was, moreover, also becoming more marked.

From the latter source there soon arose a continuous depreciation of the exchange rate which itself became the chief active cause of the inflation. On this explanation, as on that relating to wartime inflation, there is an impressive amount of contemporary and subsequent agreement. Thus Allyn Young (cited Dulles, 1929, p. 37) writes: 'Inflation has been the result rather than the cause of the depreciation'; while Eleanor Dulles, writing of the years 1921 and 1922, notes that 'there was a very slight reduction of the note circulation but this followed rather than preceded the decline in prices of this period' (1929, p. 138). She concludes that 'it was the exchange value of the franc which led to internal depreciation and the quantity theory cannot account directly for this aspect of money value' (p. 274). Martin Wolfe (1951, p. 39) emphasises how in 1925 and 1926:

Every groceryman was considering the effect of the exchange rate on coffee . . . [and] could hardly make a purchase without some discussion of the exchange rate with the result that there emerged a simultaneity of exchange depreciation and price inflation not easily explainable in quantitative theoretical terms . . . . From the resignation of the Herriot government in April

1925 to just after the *de facto* stabilisation at the end of 1926, the correlation of French wholesale prices and exchange rates was almost perfect.

## Similarly, Robert Wolff (1943, p. 147) writes that:

. . . in a modern country, the 'engine' governing prices does not reside in the note circulation: the main 'motor' is the foreign exchange market; prices and wages adjust themselves of their own accord more or less closely to the 'parities' created by the foreign exchanges and for a given pace of industrial activity a certain total of notes is necessary: if an increase in the note circulation takes place, it produces a corresponding growth in advances [from the central bank to the state].

The final sentence, with its clear implication that the note circulation (taken here as a measure of the stock of money, since cheques were little used in France at the time) is determined by the *demand* for notes, also reflects a common suggestion in the literature of the period.

The financial crisis did not, then, arise from an excessive increase in the note circulation, which constituted overwhelmingly the main part of the money supply, for no increase took place between 1920 and late 1923, in striking refutation of the claim that monetary growth alone causes inflation. True, the national debt rose moderately, but Dulles (op. cit., p. 140), rejecting some contemporary reports, asserts that the use of short term government bonds (the bulk of the 'floating debt') as money was 'almost negligible'. Nor was crisis caused by the current budget deficit, which declined steadily from 1919 onwards and could normally have been financed without difficulty by sales of government debt to the public. Wolff indeed records that from 1925 the British floating debt was far bigger.

The crisis arose partly from the large debt carried over from the war and early postwar years. Even in 1913 interest payments on government debt had amounted to 27.3 per cent of total budgetary expenditure, of which part was still due to payments on account of debt sales made in order to pay the reparations exacted by Prussia after the war of 1870; some aspects of the transfer problem of that time thus persisted, even forty years later. Another and perhaps more serious cause of the postwar public's loss of confidence in the franc's future value arose,

Table 4.2: *Budget Deficits and National Income in France, 1919–26*
*(francs, billions)*

|  | Budget Deficit (1) | National Income (2) | (1) as percent of (2) |
| --- | --- | --- | --- |
| 1919 | − 42.6 | . . . | . . . |
| 1920 | − 38.0 | 110 | 11 |
| 1921 | − 28.0 | 115 | 15 |
| 1922 | − 24.7 | 119 | 11 |
| 1923 | − 18.1 | 134 | 9 |
| 1924 | − 9.1 | 155 | 5 |
| 1925 | − 4.7 | 172 | 3 |
| 1926 | + 0.2 | 208 | 3 |

Source: Nurkse (1946), p. 34.

however, from justified scepticism of successive governments' ability to control the size of its debt. To these problems must be added the variable rate at which outstanding bonds matured, bunching in 1925.

The effect on the public finances was clear. From early 1924 the public refused to purchase new issues of debt as old issues matured. To finance the budget deficit, advances to the state from the Bank of France, and with them the note circulation, began to rise. Sales of goods and services were stimulated, with the velocity of circulation rising, an important element in the inflationary process; and funds fled the country in search of stable currencies abroad, driving down the exchange rate, raising export demand and boosting import prices. From 1922 Dulles notes a link between the exchange rate and government bond prices as funds for purchase or sale flowed to and fro across the exchanges.

A rising level of business activity further contributed to the inflation. Not only was the pressure of demand correspondingly greater. As business borrowed more and held more transactions balances, fewer funds were available for the purchase of government bonds, so that the financing of the debt without increasing the money supply became more difficult. In so far as commercial bills were discounted at the Bank of France, as happened on a large scale from late 1922 until the end of 1924, the note circulation tended to be prevented from falling (Dulles, op. cit., p. 157). The 'debt problem' at the centre of the inflation thus sprang from excessive government spending in the past, together with unconvincing financial management (rather than a large or rising deficit) in the present and expected future. The version of the quantity theory widely accepted at the time did not fit the facts. The note circulation never, between 1922 and 1927, moved as closely in line with prices as did the exchange rate; the velocity of circulation, though not precisely measured, is agreed to have risen a good deal (Nurkse, p. 36); and in the later stages of the inflation psychological forces were certainly dominant (Dulles, p. 52).

What were these forces? In general they may be said to have arisen from the fear that money would permanently lose its purchasing power. Fears on this score, minor in the early postwar years, grew as hope of receiving German reparations faded; but this would have mattered little if the government had been able to curb more promptly the expenditure, largely for postwar reconstruction and the servicing of past debt, which it had incurred when reparations payments seemed in prospect. It was the combination of weak government and disappointed expectations about postwar receipts that chiefly brought about the flight from the franc; announcements about reparations and the failure to balance budgets or to restrict the note issue within the permitted ceilings seldom failed to produce sudden depreciations of the exchange rate. Among writers on the subject there is also near unanimity in attributing great importance to political and international factors as causes of speculative capital movements and so of exchange rate depreciation. The quantity of money had, by comparison, only a minor active influence on the price level during the later years of the inflation.

## RATIONALITY, SPECULATION AND PURCHASING POWER PARITY

In a longer-term perspective, however, Thomas J. Sargent (1986, pp. 142–3) has argued that the *prospect* of monetary growth powered the inflation. Sargent cites with approval the doctrine of classical financial policy which asserts that current real government deficits are inflationary if, but only if, they are unaccompanied by expectations of offsetting government surpluses in the future. Prospective budget surpluses constitute, in short, a form of backing for a country's currency, and it was the disappearance of such expectations in France — a rational change of outlook, in Sargent's opinion – which brought about the fall of the franc. On this view, the fall of the exchange rate, far from being an independent cause of inflation, merely represented one facet of an overall process of depreciation which was due to expected monetary growth.

The argument is a more sophisticated version of quantity theory. Changes in the value of money are asserted to reflect changes in the present value of expected net surpluses or deficits accruing to the government issuing the money, since deficits will eventually, it is assumed, be met by the creation of money and this is taken to be inflationary. The process thus works in much the same way as, according to neoclassical theory, is the case with private organisations' liabilities.

In the French case the general argument carries considerable force; distrust of governments did indeed play a vital part in the inflation. As in the case of Austria, however, doubts arise at a more detailed level. The absence of any measure of public expectations at the time prevents a convincing or direct test being made. In its absence, moreover, the claim that foreign exchange markets will reflect in a stable and reliable manner the degree of public confidence in governments' future financial rectitude may be thought rather fanciful. Will not some, but a varying proportion, of the people trading on the foreign exchanges have short-term time horizons, so that the weight exerted by expectations for the near and distant future will vary unpredictably, except on quite implausible assumptions about the foresight of actual and potential market participants?

Hardest of all to accept is the recent claim that market behaviour in France reflected rational beliefs on the part of market agents. Thus, the actions of those who disbursed francs to buy durable goods or foreign currencies have been cited – because they arose from the belief that monetary growth would lead to inflation – as an example of rational behaviour. As we have seen, the quantity theory is by no means so secure as to make its identification with rationality obvious. If we allow, however, that the ultimate causes of the inflation of 1924–6 were the pre-existing state debt and the danger that weak governments would renege on it by inflationary finance, it might seem at first sight arguable that speculators' behaviour in this case was in fact rational. The chief objection is that the flight from the franc worsened as the budget deficit shrank. By the time the worst inflation arrived the budget was close to balance. Moreover, the panic in financial markets was clearly self-aggravating, not tied to rational calculation. This appeared clearly in the headlong rush to sell francs which occurred when a fall in the outstanding value of Defence Bonds was announced, the fall being interpreted as a bad portent, a sign that people were not willing to buy bonds. Because of panic fears ill-justified on underlying economic or financial grounds, a government on the brink of balancing its budget was unable to sell bonds; a flight from the currency was thus provoked, bringing about inflation which further lessened the willingness to hold bonds. The vicious circle was complete. Interestingly, a few years later, as Born (1977) points out, a reduction in the public debt would be given the opposite interpretation, as a sign of stronger government finances – an example of the treacherous nature of economic statistics when used as a guide to mass psychology. No doubt the term 'rational' is adaptable enough to be applied to each of these occurrences; but if so, we may doubt whether it is precise enough to be very helpful.

Even given the weakness of French governments, the size of postwar deficits and of the public debt were not such as to lead to inevitable inflation but for the panic fears, mentioned above, of a multitude of small property-holders who, for fear of losing their savings, refused to purchase new government bonds as old ones matured. This class based its fears on unrealistic parallels with events in Germany and was clearly overinfluenced by the unusualness of the French inflation, following as it did more than a century of price stability. It may, indeed, be rational for any one market operator to take account of the exaggerated or otherwise irrational fears of others. There must always remain, however, some original irrationality to explain. Had market operators all been rational all the time, there would, after 1924, have been little or no inflation rationally to fear.

Contemporary evidence supports doubts such as these as to

the effect of speculation upon exchange and price stability. Dulles (op. cit., p. 46) is certainly in no doubt that the intervention of many non-professional traders in the foreign exchange market increased the amplitude of fluctuations there, while even Leland Yeager (1966, p. 283), who denies that exchange speculation was disequilibrating, nonetheless notes that 'by July 1926 speculative "overshooting" had brought the franc lower than the fundamentals justified.' A belief in overshooting – a form of destabilisation due to speculative behaviour – thus continues to be generally held.

In this connection, it is worth emphasising the full extent to which, despite obvious similarities, the French experience of inflation differed from the German. France's external debts were certainly very onerous, reaching a peak of 36,743 million francs in 1926, as much as the total budget. Even so, they could scarcely compare with the German reparations debt, as initially threatened, which was publicised as 132 billion gold marks in May 1921 (whatever the sum which officials may actually have expected to be enforced – see S. Marks, 1969).

Furthermore, the extent to which the depreciation of the franc directly swelled the state's deficit, thus necessitating the issue of new money and ratifying the higher level of prices which devaluation had brought about, was far smaller in France (Nurkse, 1946, p. 37). Several reasons for this emerge. Much government expenditure took the form of wages and indemnity payments, which in France were not immediately affected by rising prices; indeed, a large proportion of these items could not very well change in the course of any one year. Military and naval expenditures were likewise invariant with inflation in the short run. Few of the state's requirements were imported; and superior ability to forecast changes in the exchange rate enabled the Treasury to avoid some of the price increases which did emanate from that source. Furthermore, tax revenue rose fairly promptly with inflation and the postwar boom. As a result, exchange depreciation did not automatically swell the budget deficit. Causality led rather from public lack of confidence to the state's inability to borrow and thence to monetary growth and inflation. It was the dubiously rational *fear* of budget deficits rather than the deficits themselves that prompted the inflation.

Purchasing power parity theory is another traditional theory to have fared ill in France. The theory (see Glossary) has more than one variant but in one of its more popular forms it may be said to assert that in the absence of pegged exchange rates or obstacles to trade, if a unit of one currency − say, £1 − spent in one country (Britain) will buy twice as many goods as a unit of another currency − $1 − spent in the United States, then the rate of exchange will tend to more towards: £1 = $2. The crux of the whole matter rests, however, on the 'basket' of goods which is assumed to be bought; for unless the selection or 'basket' has the same composition in both countries the comparison is meaningless. If the basket consist only of goods traded between the two countries and in the proportions in which they are traded, then the theory comes close to tautology.[1] If, however, the basket includes all goods, traded or untraded, then the evidence of France's experience in the 1920s is far from supporting it. The exchange rate between the franc and other currencies, individually or collectively, did not move in any close or parallel relationship to the ratio of French prices to those abroad. On the contrary, until the closing stages of the inflation the exchange rate remained consistently lower than the relevant price ratio; that is, French goods were cheaper, in relation to the general price level, for foreigners to buy than for French residents. In this respect the French inflation resembled many others in the Europe of the 1920s.

The theory's failure adequately to account for the observed facts could in principle have been due to differences or divergent trends in the prices of *untraded* goods in France and abroad, which could have prevented the price ratio equalling, or indeed having any firm relationship with the exchange rate. In fact, however, the theory was largely invalidated by its failure to take account of capital movements. The 'flight from the franc' in 1922−3 and, in the following year, the 'attack on the franc' by foreign speculators as well as by large numbers of Frenchmen did much to drive down the exchange rate, while internal prices rose more slowly until the final stages of inflation. The conclusion remains, therefore, that 'the purchasing power parity doctrine was not useful in explaining the value of the depreciated franc' (Dulles, op. cit., p. 20). Indeed, if the theory is interpreted as implying that the exchange rate adjusted itself so as to reflect the ratio of the respective currencies' purchasing powers, then it seems for most periods to have reversed the true causal relationship.

The failure of the two central orthodox theories of inflation is worth emphasising for it draws attention to the scarcity of clear, consistent relationships between pairs of variables in the French economy during our period. During the last three or four years of the inflation only one such relationship regularly emerged – a marked correlation between the dollar exchange rate and wholesale prices; even when the extent of their respective changes differed the direction was almost always the same in any given month. Apart from this, however, no clear bivariate relationship emerges among; note circulation, Bank advances to the state, exchange rate, retail prices and wholesale prices. Nor is the search more conclusive if more than two variables are taken; for many of the main divergences from regularity are clearly due to particular political events in the short run, while in the long run too many influences have changed for us to be able to allot causality with any confidence on statistical grounds.

The problem is not, however, simply one of indeterminacy between the *extents* to which different variables changes at any given time. Even the *direction* of change could be, and often was, indeterminate. The effect on expected inflation of reductions in the public debt has already been mentioned. The effect of changes in the central bank's discount rate also affords an example. Thus, a rise in a central bank's discount rate can normally be taken as a sign of determination to check monetary expansion at home or the decline of the exchange rate abroad. Yet when the Bank of France raised its rate to curb the inflationary flight from the franc in mid-January 1924 the step was interpreted as a panic measure, with the result that the franc fell even faster on the exchanges. In a word, dealers had extrapolative, not regressive expectations.[2]

This general indeterminacy applies with particular force to V, the velocity of circulation of money. According to the neoclassical monetary theory of the years before 1918 this variable could be assumed to remain roughly constant in the short run, but, as is now widely recognised, in practice V can be subject to important and rapid variations. Figures from which adequate estimates could be calculated are not available for

France in the 1920s but Dulles (p. 18) offers the judgement that velocity showed striking cumulative increases, especially in the years 1921, 1924 and 1925, 'because of the exchange crises in those years and in spite of fairly steady means of payment'. Her conclusion is that the importance of changes in V and of factors influencing it was so great that 'politics played a larger part than did paper notes' in the inflation. Further, confirming the remarks we have made above, she adds (op. cit., p. 19) the comment that changes in V, being subject to shifts in public confidence, represent 'the unknown and uncontrollable factor and, in the case of extreme depreciation, the most important element' in the inflation.

## LESSONS OF THE POINCARÉ STABILISATION

At first glance one might be tempted to conclude that the *de facto* stabilisation of 1926 demonstrated the possibility of halting an inflation at low cost in terms of unemployment and lost output, provided only that the stabilisation is rapid and carries immediate conviction to financial markets and the general public. This, some have argued, was achieved in France by convincing all concerned that the budget would soon be balanced, the money supply frozen and the franc made convertible once more into gold. The example seems to count, therefore, strongly in favour of sudden 'shock treatment'.

The full facts, however, only partially support such a conclusion. For, as noted above, the French stabilisation was not costless. In the two months to February 1927 unemployment more than quadrupled, while production fell by about 20 per cent between its October peak and its April trough. Even so it must be admitted that unemployment was still low and the recession brief. A number of factors helped to produce this result. First, unlike Germany in November 1923, France in July 1926 enjoyed full, perhaps overfull, employment and a high and rising level of production. The very large profits which firms had made in 1925 and 1926 also greatly helped them to surmount the difficulties of the following year. The extent of the inflation had been much less than in Germany; it has even been argued that the moderate rise in prices encouraged the growth of entrepreneurship at the expense of less venturesome activities (Dulles, op. cit., p. 50). That it facilitated postwar reconstruction and growth, while assisting the trade balance and cutting the real public debt, is widely acknowledged (e.g. Clough, 1939, p. 318; Wolfe, 1951, p. 53). Since wages had been largely unindexed throughout the inflation the problems of post-stabilisation wage adjustments was less acute than in the case of a partially indexed economy. The low exchange value of the franc after stabilisation helped to sustain foreign demand. Domestic unemployment was kept down through the refusal of visa extensions for immigrant workers. Good harvests, rent control and restrictions on the charges made for state-provided services helped the industrial working class to begin the stabilisation period in a much more prosperous condition than that of German workers in 1923. For all these reasons the consequences of stabilisation were less grave in France than in any country of Central Europe. Yet the outstanding fact about the abating factors is that almost all were fortuitous, almost none due to policy. The most important variable in this, as in many economic models, emerges as luck.

Much emphasis has been given to the role of governmental weakness and its connection with a system of proportional representation in fostering the French inflation. Weakness there was, though it did not spring from any system of proportional representation for none was in operation. On the contrary, at the 1924 elections the *Bloc National* actually won fewer seats than the *Cartel des Gauches,* though winning more votes – a direct failure of proportionality. The central problem, which well may have sprung from the need for coalition government, lay in the Cartel's difficulties in maintaining agreement among its own supporters. More deeply, its division, like the continual deadlocks produced by Senate blocking tactics, reflected the deep divisions of the nation as a whole. Whether an electoral system still less proportional than the 'semi-proportional' one used (Clough, 1939, p. 300) could have fostered stronger government at an earlier stage by ignoring popular opinion still more blatantly remains an unanswered question.

Whatever the causes of governmental instability, the central fact should be noted. Political conflict between two almost equally-balanced groupings both prompted and perpetuated an inflation which effectively redistributed income and wealth in the community; and no solution was implemented until a government with a solid parliamentary majority was invested with the plenary powers which only two years earlier the lower house had regarded as unacceptably dictatorial, enabling it to impose taxes primarily upon one section of the community in order to end the budget deficit.

Many of the other characteristics of stabilisation elsewhere were lacking. The currency was not recalled or replaced. No loan was extended or guaranteed by foreign governments at the time of stabilisation. It was, however, the familiar 'announcement effect' at the time when Poincaré took office which by itself arrested inflation and exchange depreciation alike; and this was rapidly followed by the balancing of the budget. The central point is that the uneasy, almost equal balance of power ended. The observation is important in the debate as to whether inflation should be viewed as a weapon in, or a means of concealing the outcome of, a class or sectional struggle.

Several details of the French experience are noteworthy. Poincaré's success in halting inflation, depending crucially as it did upon the success of an 'announcement effect', has been termed a 'change of policy regime' of a kind which can, and in the French case did, alter basic macroeconomic relationships. Such an effect depends, however, on public belief in the efficacy of the policies now likely to be adopted. To convince the public of the need for such policies and then fail to implement them can be worse that to fail to convince in the first place. In such an event the old inflationary pattern may be positively reinforced. In France this appears to have been what often happened: the failure of governments before Poincaré to keep within their financial ceilings, when discovered, stimulated fresh flights of capital abroad and so worsened the inflation.

That the French stabilisation was conservative in character, with major regressive tax changes and no overt capital levy, probably owed something not only to the entrenched self-interest of the political right (Shirer, 1907, p. 136) but also to the fact that France's was a capitalist economy with no ready means of introducing a truly watertight system of exchange controls. Moreover, a great part of the financial crisis sprang from, or at least was channelled through, exchange depreciation and this is generally agreed to have been worsened by the socialists' threat of a capital levy. The French government's problem has been widely encountered both before and since: whether, in a market economy with extensive international financial linkages, stabilisation can be carried out in combination with a progressive redistribution of income without provoking a capital outflow or a financial crisis. In Hungary in 1921, and in Poland in 1924, this seems to have been achieved, if only temporarily (Nurkse, 1946, pp. 25–7, 60; I. Spigler, 1986); in France the greatest measure of progressive redistribution that proved possible – no radical transformation – was the introduction of a tax on first sales of real estate or businesses.

Finally, the stabilisation incorporated another 'orthodox' feature widely supported at the time but much less popular today. By the law of 7 August the Bank of France was to be entitled to issue, without limit under the new 'ceiling', new notes against purchases of foreign currency. 'Sterilisation' of reserve inflows was deemed unnecessary, since such note issues were not regarded as inflationary. On orthodox gold standard lines, prices could be allowed to rise when reserves flowed into the country, thus tending to erode the payments surplus and restore external balance. It was not a doctrine to weather well the widespread observation of later years that prices, once raised, were not easy to coax down again when the flow of funds into the country was reversed.

## SUMMARY AND CONCLUSIONS

Excess demand largely accounted for wartime and immediate postwar inflation. By the time this disappeared and budget deficits began to dwindle, panic fears took over. These operated largely through flights of capital abroad, depressing the exchange rate, and through the public's refusal to purchase new government bonds when old issues matured. National disunity and in particular extreme suspicion of governments on the part of business and small property-holders lay at the heart of the refusal to lend to government. In the event, Poincaré's mere accession to office restored confidence and solved the problem at a stroke by dispelling fears of future governmental extravagance. How far the franc's depreciation was stably, let alone rationally, related to expectations about the present value of future net government deficits (a version of the quantity theory) is much more debatable. The intense fears of the time certainly seem to have given undue weight to the analogy with German hyperinflation and to have ignored the far smaller and diminishing extent of French monetary growth and budgetary debt. What can be said with certainty is that no other, less ingenious version of the quantity theory can even begin to explain the French inflation.

## NOTES

1.  Thus, if the exchange rate is assumed to adjust promptly in such a way as to restore trade balance, e.g. to make the value of American exports to Britain in dollars equal the value of British exports to America in pounds, then it necessarily follows that either country's total exports can be bought for the same sum of money (in pounds or dollars); the exchange rate exactly reflects relative purchasing power over traded goods.
2.  When prices are rising extrapolative expectations predict a continued rise, regressive a fall.

# 5 Postwar Inflation in the Soviet Union and Poland

## *The Soviet Union*

### EARLY POSTWAR INFLATION

The World War of 1914–18 was to Tsarist Russia and its successor state, the Soviet Union, even more than to other European countries, both a source of massive disruption bringing the country close to economic collapse and at the same time a major cause of inflation. The upsurge which resulted raised the prewar price level by a factor of 157 by December 1918 and of 650 million by October 1923 and was accompanied by conditions of the most extreme and widespread hardship. Perhaps the main interest of the episode, however, springs from the policies which were designed to end it, which involved the introduction, in combination with generally orthodox fiscal policies, of a parallel currency, the chervonetz, in an attempt to bring about stabilisation gradually.

The preconditions for inflation were created at the war's onset. The gold standard and the payment of gold for credit notes were suspended. The State Bank was enabled to issue 300 million roubles' worth of notes unbacked by gold and thus the practice of raising the note issue ceiling, already begun in 1906, was extended, partly in order to prevent the loss of the country's gold reserves abroad, but partly to bridge the gap between government expenditure and revenue. It was a gap which was to grow by half in the course of the war and again by more than seven hundredfold thereafter.

Until 1917 not all of the budget deficit was financed by note issue, part of the necessary finance being raised by borrowing, by means either of long or short term Treasury bills. By 1918, however, virtually the whole deficit had come to be met by the issue of notes. At first the effect of this method of finance on prices was to some extent offset by the withdrawal of gold coins into hoards and by the public's slow realisation of the risk involved in saving notes, but before long inflation soared dramatically.

By the beginning of 1917 the war, waged with reckless incompetence and at enormous cost, had reduced the Russian economy to chaos; and in November of that year, in the wake of strikes, mutinies and a brief liberal interregnum, the small Bolshevik faction seized power and the era of Soviet rule began. On 3 March 1918 under the Treaty of Brest Litovsk Russia left the European war.

Departure from the war was not followed by an easing of economic pressures; rather the reverse. For the next three years of 'War Communism', the government tried not only to introduce socialism but also to wage the civil war which now developed. On the first count, many goods were distributed at 'fixed' prices, or, as in the case of housing, in exchange for tickets rather than money; the output of state enterprises was distributed free of charge; payment of salaries and taxes was often in kind; and free trading in grain and other commodities was prohibited. In consequence the rouble became largely unnecessary.

State expenditure, on the other hand, boosted by the cost, first, of civil war against the 'White' armies of the old regime aided by foreign armies, and then of war against invading Polish forces, rose sharply — fourfold in 1919, fivefold in 1920 and more than twentyfold in 1921. By the time peace was restored, at the cost of a settlement which shifted Poland's border several hundred miles eastward, the Soviet policy of confiscating peasants' crops had produced its inevitable response: the peasants' refusal to plant and the slaughtering of cattle. By the beginning of 1921 privation to the point of starvation was widespread and the unbacked issue of notes, which by March 1921 had risen by a factor of over 870 compared with prewar, had produced massive inflation.

*Table 5.1: Soviet economic indicators, 1916–23*

|  | Price index in Soviet roubles (1 December, Russia) (1913 = 1.0) | State deficit as % of expenditure | Note issue (preceding 12 months) (million roubles) |
|---|---|---|---|
| 1916 | 2.87 | 76.0 | 3480 |
| 1917 | 18.05 | 81.7 | 16403 |
| 1918 | 157 | 66.6 | 33500 |
| 1919 | 1790 | 77.3 | 164200 |
| 1920 | 12600 | 86.9 | 943600 |
| 1921 | 138000 | 84.1 | 16.4m |
| 1922 | 17226000 | . . . | . . . |
| 1923, Oct 1 | 648m . . . | . . . | . . . |

*Source:* S.S. Katzenellenbaum (1925), pp. 69, 74–5.

The inflation resulting from this combination of acute supply shortages and soaring money issue is graphically reflected in the Gosplan price index. Between 1913 and February 1922 the index for Russia rose by a factor of some 545,000; the course of the years 1921 and 1922 saw rises by factors of 11 and 125 respectively. With the rise in the note circulation went other familiar phenomena. The quantity of money proving inadequate for trade at the new price level, the government authorised other types of paper to be used; Yurovsky (1925, p. 29) records that in all some seventy eight different issues of money came to be used. The chief function of the State Bank, before its amalgamation with the People's Bank and subsequent suppression in 1920, changed from the discount of private and commercial bills to that of Treasury bills. By mid-1917 the state's debt to the Bank vastly exceeded all other debts. The rouble's exchange rate, after a period of temporary relative stability during 1916 and early 1917, began in May 1917 to plunge, the speed of its erratic fall varying in response to Russian victories and defeats.

During the period of War Communism the exchange rate inside Russia remained a matter of minor importance because of the small scale of foreign trade. On foreign money markets values were heavily influenced by the prospects of the old regime being restored, as well as by military and political developments. With the introduction of the New Economic Policy (NEP) in 1921, however, government policy on exchange operations, as on many other economic matters, was for a time relaxed. A State Bank was once more established. Foreign trade revived, carried on not only by state trading organisations but also privately. With continuing inflation the demand for foreign currencies to hold as a store of value increased; and money markets began to operate openly in the big cities. More generally, NEP reverted, albeit temporarily, to reliance on private profit as a stimulus to production, permitting peasants to sell their output, after taxes had been paid in kind, on a free market and restoring commercial incentives in trade and industry.

The resulting economic revival was inevitably accompanied by a growing demand for money. Moving away from earlier statements to the effect that money could and should be abolished, the government now took steps towards a permanent restoration of the money economy. In May 1921 restrictions on the holding of paper money were removed, to be followed by those on holding foreign currency and precious metals and stones. By February 1923 the buying and selling of gold and silver bullion, of foreign currencies and of cheques and bills of exchange denominated in foreign currency had similarly been legalised. For a country thus increasingly dependent on money, prompt action to end the continuing hyperinflation was clearly essential.

## THE CHERVONETZ

There now existed, moreover, an additional reason for effecting an early stabilisation. By issuing new notes the authorities were pre-empting real resources at the expense of currency holders, whose holdings depreciated in real terms as prices rose. The 'inflation tax revenue' or 'seigniorage'[1] thus gained was, however, now falling in value. This was for two reasons. First, much of the note issue was held by state institutions, so that the state was levying the 'inflation tax' upon itself. Second, the loss of seigniorage occurred because, as prices rose, ever greater issues of new money were necessary to procure successive *equal* gains in real resources. The returns to inflationary finance were therefore falling sharply.

The government's response was initially to introduce 'gold accounting' – in effect an indexation of business transactions. The latter were to be expressed in gold roubles but actual payments were to be in paper roubles to the agreed gold values; the calculations involved thus made use of the current, and ever-changing, exchange rate between paper roubles and gold.

The new system spread quickly from commercial transactions to everyday personal uses. It was followed by further measures of reform. At the end of 1921 the new State Bank was established and on 27 November 1922 a new currency, the chervonetz, was issued. The latter was a parallel currency, designed to circulate alongside the rouble but at a floating rather than a fixed exchange rate. Covered to the extent of one quarter by precious metals and hard foreign currencies, the new notes were intended eventually to become convertible into gold and to this extent could be regarded as extending the functions of the gold accounting rouble, hitherto only a unit of account and store of value, so that it now served also as a means of exchange. The chervonetz was also designed to facilitate the development of the Bank's operations, particularly the discounting of bills and the making of advances.

One of the government's reasons for thus introducing the new currency in parallel lay in its uncertainty as to how quickly the public would come to accept the chervonetz. A second, however, was the desire to avoid immediate withdrawal of the old currency, since, had that occurred, the government would have had to finance its deficit by issuing new chervonetz notes, thus dooming them to instant depreciation. By introducing the notes through the Bank's discounting operations and initially in highly restricted quantities it was hoped to avoid, or at least moderate, that tendency.

In this attempt the government was largely successful. The chervonetz did depreciate but far less rapidly than the Soviet rouble, which was used to finance the remaining budget deficit. The result was that, after a phase in which prices rose faster than the stock of money, the country began to witness, even before the beginning of 1924, a renewed and rapid rise in the real value

*Table 5.2: Exchange rate of the chervonetz (Moscow exchange, beginning of each month)*

|  | In Soviet roubles (1923 issue) | In $s (parity: 1.057) | In $S (parity: 5.14) |
|---|---|---|---|
| 1922 | | | |
| December | 117 | 1.170 | 5.087 |
| 1923 | | | |
| January | 175 | 1.219 | 5.426 |
| April | 302 | 1.168 | 5.206 |
| July | 760 | 1.020 | 4.662 |
| October | 4000 | 1.066 | 4.878 |
| 1924 | | | |
| January | 30000 | 1.064 | 4.545 |
| April | 500000 | 1.196 | 5.141 |
| July | — | 1.189 | 5.141 |
| October | — | 1.152 | 5.141 |

*Source:* S.S. Katcenellebaum (1925), p. 111.

of the money stock. This represented success for the new policy of reintroducing money, part of it reasonably stable in value, into general use, and in consequence the old Soviet rouble could before long be withdrawn from circulation, to be replaced by a new and stable note issued by the Treasury and with a value bearing a fixed relation to that of the chervonetz. The hyperinflation had thus been ended not at a stroke, as was the case in certain other countries, but by gradual replacement of the eroded currency, first by the more stable chervonetz, and finally by the still stabler Treasury note.

Currency reform was completed in February–March 1924. It was not, however, carried out costlessly. On the contrary, the system of parallel currencies had been attended by serious disruption of the money markets. One reason for this was that the majority of businesses tended to fix the rate of exchange between the two currencies for any given day at the rate which had been quoted on the Moscow Exchange *the day before,* whereas the uncontrolled market allowed the rate to fluctuate continuously. The result was that demand for one or other form of note tended to vary erratically, creating persistent and unpredictable shortages or surpluses. Often these took the form of small-change famines, (or, less often, gluts), since only the

Soviet rouble was available in small denominations. When, moreover, in October 1923 the persistent tendency to such famines was allayed, the advantages of holding chervontsi were so great that there developed a flight from the Soviet rouble, with consequent disruption of ordinary commercial transactions. Institutions holding large quantities of the Soviet notes suffered huge losses, and business was interrupted daily while holders of these notes rushed to dispose of them as quickly as possible. The introduction of current bank accounts at the State Bank and other credit institutions provided only a limited and belated remedy for this situation. Like all currency crises, the crisis arising from the system of parallel currencies encouraged mass speculation and exchange losses, and prevented accurate calculation or prediction of real values in the future, despite the fact that by that time more than half the currency consisted of reasonably stable chervonetz notes. The Soviet stabilisation thus stands alone among successful stabilisations of the 1920s in that its introduction was followed, as well as to some extent preceded, by a panic flight from the old currency.

In many respects, however, the stabilisation followed remarkably orthodox lines. The chervonetz's value was fixed in gold. The old currency was, eventually, withdrawn and replaced by new Treasury notes. The issue of other, substitute monies was prohibited. The foreign exchange rate of the chervonetz was supported by intervention on the foreign currency market. Vigorous efforts were made to balance the state budget.

The result of the stabilising measures quickly became evident. After March 1924 prices expressed in terms of chervontsi stopped rising and in the course of the next few months, with some minor fluctuations, fell somewhat. The average monthly exchange rate of the chervonetz rose from a low point in late 1923 to a slightly higher stable level. The total amount of currency, including both chervontsi and Treasury notes, continued, however, to rise – another common feature of contemporary stabilisations. The government aided disinflation by reducing the prices of goods in the hands of state and cooperative organisations, by cutting wages and by reducing the State Bank's credits to industry.

Budgetary retrenchment constituted a crucial element in the

disinflation, since without it confidence in the currency could not be restored and the private sector of the economy, now reviving under the NEP, enabled to do its work efficiently. From 1922 substantial reductions had already been made in the projected state deficits. Now the number of state employees was cut. New taxes were introduced and the proportion of tax revenue received in money, as distinct from kind, grew as the budget approached balance. With the currency reform of 1924 a tax on private and state enterprise was introduced, while the tax in kind was phased out at an increased pace. There was a compulsory sale of state bonds. By early 1924 the budget had moved into balance and in the financial year 1924/5 it showed a surplus. Despite the shortcomings of the available statistics, it is generally agreed, moreover, that from 1923 industrial production both of consumer and of producer goods rose sharply (Clarke and Matko, 1972, pp. 10–11), that aggregated agricultural production rose, though less quickly, and that, compared with the earlier years of War Communism and hyperinflation, those immediately following 1924 showed increased general growth and prosperity.

## OPINION ON CAUSALITY

On the basic cause of the inflation of World War I and early 1920s there has been little dispute. It was a classic example of profligate government expenditure financed by the printing press. Certain features, however, marked the Soviet inflation more than most others of the period. Foreign trade fell to an exceptionally low level so that the influence of the exchange rate on inflation was small. No organised internal market for gold continued throughout the period (Yurovsky, 1925, p. 80) so that fluctuations in the metal's value were increased and stabilisation made more difficult. The degree of privation and disorder, extending to a state of anarchy, which accompanied the hyperinflation was exceptional.

Notably, too, some of the worst financial disruption occurred not before but after the new chervonetz was introduced – indeed, after that currency had gone far in displacing the old paper rouble. Again, although parallel currencies were not at the time widely used as a means of stabilisation in Europe, the obvious alternative, sudden stabilisation or 'shock treatment' of the kind used elsewhere, was from the start rejected as unworkable because of the need for an interim period during which the budget could be balanced and the peasants could become familiar with the new currency. Again, the effects of inflation on town and countryside respectively probably differed more than elsewhere. Not only was use of the chervonetz slow in spreading to the countryside; the marked opening and closing of the so-called 'scissors' — the ratio of agricultural prices to the prices of manufactures — added a further complication to tendencies sometimes found elsewhere in milder form. Peasants, unwilling to receive more of the fast-depreciating paper roubles than they could spend immediately, reduced their sales of produce, creating shortages (Yurovsky, 1925, p. 118).

In other respects, however, the Soviet inflation resembled quite closely those further west. The public's initial slowness in realising the extent and irreversible nature of the wartime inflation fits Nurkse's model (1946, pp. 6–9). Typical, too, were: the initial growth, then decline of the real value of the money stock; the government's willingness, in the face of a scarcity of money, to allow additional monies to be issued; the public's introduction of other, illegal ones; and the withdrawal of gold and foreign exchange into hoards, from which they were withdrawn only when confidence in future price stability was restored.

Did stabilisation in the Soviet Union, as elsewhere, exert a depressing effect on the economy? On the whole, it seems, probably not. During 1923 industrial output rose with the spread of the chervonetz, though the bad harvest of 1924 was a severe setback in a predominantly agricultural country. In the next few years industrial growth was still faster, aided, in a statistical sense, by the very low initial levels of output and foreign trade. To argue that stabilisation worked in the direction of economic recession would be to imply that in its absence growth would have been still faster. The claim would be hard to sustain, especially in view of the fact that even the revival which did take place could not have occurred but for the existence of a sound currency — the result of stabilisation. The interesting conclusion seems to be that the regular tendency of stabilisation to produce recession can be outweighed by the effects of particular circumstances — in this case the upsurge of entrepreneurial effort accompanying the NEP and the restoration of a trustworthy currency. The episode also yields further support for the view that sudden — or, in this case, fairly sudden - stabilisation produces the higher ratio of benefits to costs when it follows extreme hyperinflation.

How successful was the experiment in using parallel currencies? The hyperinflation ended and a considerable degree of price stability was achieved. Furthermore, the method, as intended, did yield time in which the state budget could be balanced and the chervonetz gradually accepted in rural areas.

Even so, not *much* time was gained — little more than a year between the chervonetz's introduction and the decrees of early 1924, which introduced the new, stable rouble and redeemed the depreciated roubles; and the price paid for success was high. The chervonetz fluctuated substantially in value during the period of parallelism. This was partly because of the time-lag involved in the system of indexation, partly because the price of gold (in terms of which the chervonetz was defined and in theory ultimately redeemable) itself fluctuated. The expected rate of depreciation of the paper rouble varied, moreover, so that demand for chervontsi rose and fell, causing large shifts between the two currencies. Speculation in chervontsi was widespread and destructive of genuine economic effort. The unavailability of chervontsi in small denominations also caused exchange rate fluctuations. Furthermore, upsurges of unofficial note-issuing took place. Yurovsky, noting these various trends (p. 119), comments that in late 1923 and early 1924, 'The quantity of depreciating currency in proportion to the total was insignificant, but its presence was sufficient . . . to reduce the national economy to a state of havoc.' Meanwhile, the 'inflation tax', the continuance of which was a major object of the gradualist or 'parallel' approach, fell mainly upon state enterprises, and so failed to shift the budgetary burden on to the private sector's shoulders. The Pyrrhic nature of the victory thus won has to be remembered later when we consider more recent proposals for parallel currencies (see Chapter 13).

## SUMMARY

More than any other European inflation of the 1920s, the Soviet one was due overwhelmingly to domestic factors: disrupted supplies of goods and services and excess demand stimulated by budget deficits and monetary growth. External depreciation of the currency, so powerful in many other countries, exerted scarcely any influence. Stabilisation was in many ways strictly orthodox. One of its less usual but central features, the introduction of parallel currencies, constituted a fascinating and pioneering attempt to gain time in which to end inflation gradually. Though ultimately successful, however, it did not buy much time and its costs in disruption and destabilising money flows were high.

# Poland

## THE COURSE OF THE INFLATION

Inflation came to Poland in the familiar way, following in the wake of wartime devastation and, in particular, of the continuing war with Russia and the resulting boundary changes. These left the country with at least four different currencies corresponding to former occupying powers, as well as with three uncoordinated railway systems, each of them in grave need of improvement. Supply shortages and budget deficits financed by the printing press raised the postwar currency circulation, according to Nötel (1986, vol. II, p. 175), more than 25-fold by March 1921 and produced rapid inflation which successive governments failed to check. Two main attempts at stabilisation were necessary before the upsurge was at last curbed, and in the end the measures adopted were largely orthodox. The main interest of the episode lies in Poland's not having used, immediately, foreign loans as a means of stabilisation − a policy whose significance has given rise to differing interpretations.

After the early postwar convulsions and boundary changes the first step taken was to unify the currency, and early in 1920 the Polish mark was declared the sole legal tender and all other notes withdrawn. This, however, did not itself halt inflation. With the state budget gravely unbalanced, the volume of banknotes and the state's debt to the bank of issue continued to soar, while the exchange rate slumped. The fear of heavy unemployment, and possible revolution as a result, argued strongly against measures to curb demand, but early in 1921 the government tackled the problem by market intervention to peg the exchange rate, and for some months wholesale prices were held. Difficulties in borrowing to finance imports led the government to change policy in the summer, however, with the result that the exchange rate fell back. The government then addressed the problem by fiscal measures. A capital levy announced late in 1921 temporarily achieved its aim of covering state expenditure and for a while the external depreciation slowed − only to be resumed, however, after a subsequent change of government. Attempts to secure foreign loans failed and the proceeds of domestic loans were inadequate to finance the state deficit.

*Table 5.3: Polish exchange rate and index of domestic prices, 1913, 1919–23*

|  | 1913 | 1919 | 1920 | 1921 | 1922 | 1923 |
|---|---|---|---|---|---|---|
| Exchange Rate | 23.82 | 0.91 | 0.18 | 0.031 | 0.006 | 0.00002 |
| Wholesale Prices | 1 | . . | 169a | 571 | 3464 | 1423007 |
| Cost of Living | 1 | . . | 112 | 467 | 2310 | 1196567 |

*Source:* R. Nötel (1986), p. 178.
Exchange rate: December, US cents per mark.
Wholesale price index: December; 1913 = 1.0.
Cost of living: December; 1913 = 1.0.
a: estimated.

Many of the inflation's features mirror those found elsewhere. External depreciation, which often preceded internal, was driven on by a large trade deficit, the hoarding of foreign exchange and widespread speculation against the currency. Wages lagged behind prices, cutting workers' real incomes, and for a time output expanded, with industrial employment rising by 135 per cent between 1920 and 1922.

By 1923, however, the German hyperinflation had spread panic to Poland and a wave of strikes and protests was followed by the fall of the latest in the country's succession of short-lived governments. Inflation was at its peak, with prices in the eleven months to January 1924 rising by a factor of about 700, and by the following month the exchange rate had plunged to 2.2 millionths of its original parity. In these dire circumstances the new Grabski government introduced a further, and temporarily successful, attempt at stabilisation. First, the value of all taxes was indexed on a gold basis and administrative reforms were set in hand to improve tax collection. As a result tax revenue rose sharply and further note issues to cover budgetary expenditures became unnecessary. At the same time, despite the very low level of gold and foreign exchange reserves, the government intervened successfully to stabilise the exchange value of the Polish mark. By restoring confidence in the currency in this way it evoked both an inflow of capital from abroad and a widespread dishoarding of foreign banknotes at home, which swelled its reserves in the way familiar in many central European stabilisations of the time.

Further progress followed, this time again through the medium of fiscal policy. A new property tax was temporarily successful in securing fiscal balance, covering over one eighth of government expenditure. This was accompanied by a banking reform involving the creation of a new central bank with strictly limited powers of making loans to government, and the issue of a new gold-basis currency, the zloty, which had existed since 1919 but only as a unit of account. Cover for the new currency included, however, commercial bills, as in other central European countries, on the theory that notes so backed exerted no inflationary influence. In 1924 the budget went into surplus; but despite the reforms a bad harvest in 1924, together with the relaxing of government controls over foreign trade, produced a worsening of the trade balance and a fall in the reserves, which compelled the Bank of Poland to withdraw its support for the zloty. Property tax revenue, too, fell to disappointing levels as people delayed payment in expectation of further inflation, and the resulting budget deficit was financed once more by note issue.

It seems likely (Nurkse, 1946, p. 61; Mlynarski, 1926) that, given greater international currency reserves, Poland could have weathered the temporary storm without further exchange depreciation. As it was, the two main inflationary factors — external weakness and monetary growth — reappeared at once. A foreign loan might well have counteracted both weaknesses, which were transient, but an American loan actually proposed fell short of expectations. The attempted stabilisation, like that of 1921, thus proved only temporarily successful. To make matters worse, a tariff war broke out with Germany, in the course of which over half of Poland's exports to that country were banned. As a result the Bank of Poland proved unable to support the zloty, and both external and internal currency depreciation resumed their course. In May 1925 restrictions were reimposed on imports, while the year's harvest proved abundant. Even so, fears of further depreciation persisted until the following April, when a new government imposed fresh and severe measures. New taxes were introduced, old ones subjected to a 10 per cent surcharge. The prices of goods and services supplied by government monopolies, including railway fares, were raised. The result, due without doubt to the same kind of announcement effect as occurred in other countries, was the immediate disappearance of the budget deficit and stabilisation of the exchange rate. Inflation was thus halted initially by purely domestic measures, though when the new exchange rate was legally formalised the following year the country did avail itself of a foreign loan of $72 million. In the course of the inflation, however, the value of the zloty had fallen to 0.6 per cent of its original parity, while the currency as a whole, over the entire inflation to October 1926, had depreciated to about 3.8 millionths of its original value.

## CONCLUSIONS ON THE ROLE OF FOREIGN LOANS

The chief lesson which Nurkse (1946, pp. 25–7) draws from the Polish experience is the predominant influence of fiscal policy — rather than, for example, of foreign loans — on the exchange rate and the price level. The effects of the property tax and tax increases of 1924 constitute, in his view, overwhelming evidence for this thesis. Even so, the issue remains debatable. Moves towards fiscal balance were no doubt vital but they were themselves facilitated by, and in the medium run dependent on, the restoration of confidence in the currency, towards which a foreign loan could have, and finally did, contribute. The 1924 stabilisation was, after all, accompanied by intervention to stabilise the exchanges; so were the fiscal measures of 1926. The failure of the 1924 measures arose chiefly from the weakness of the trade balance; and in the end foreign loans were arranged to support the legal stabilisation of 1927. Nötel (1986, p. 206), indeed, notes that the loans were essential to permit the Bank of Poland to observe its minimum reserve requirements. Announcement effects and changes in confidence played, moreover, a crucial role throughout; and these resulted from the introduction of whole packages, including not only fiscal but also exchange rate policies. A more cautious judgement would be that the Polish inflation was a tenacious problem in the cure of which more than one type of policy is likely to have been essential.

## NOTES

1. In this case the seigniorage would be the difference between the cost of creating money and the value of what the state could buy with it.
2. See, however, our references to the Hungarian sparkrone (Chapter 2) and the Polish zloty (this chapter).

# 6 Lessons from the 1920s: an Interim Summary

What had been definitively learned by the eve of World War II about the causes of and cures for inflation? We make no attempt here to repeat the conclusions emerging for particular countries. A few general and central points may, however, be made.

First, the early stages of wartime inflation seem everywhere to have been prompted initially by budget deficits and the creation of money to finance them. Almost everywhere, plunges in the exchange rate became serious only later; and though the time lag was certainly due to the enforcement of wartime controls, there are no signs that in the absence of controls ordinary balance of payments weaknesses would by themselves have produced such dramatic deteriorations on the exchanges.

Even so it cannot be said that the evidence supports the widespread belief that the quantity of money was the sole cause, and always an active cause, of inflation. Orthodox theory *could* be borne out in practice, with uncovered budget deficits swelling the money supply, boosting expenditure and creating excess demand. But equally, accelerations of the inflationary spiral once it had begun could, on many particular occasions, be more plausibly said actively to result from a plunge in the exchange rate. This could, moreover, be due to balance of payments burdens, rising costs or, more generally, public loss of confidence either in the state's continued existence, in the government's financial competence or in the future external burdens to be imposed on the country. Possible links between the extent of an inflation and fiscal deficits, actual or in reasonable prospect, might, but need not, be close. Money might, furthermore, passively accommodate inflation rather than actively stimulate it. Again, it was clearly possible, as in the years following stabilisation in Austria and Hungary, for prices to remain tolerably stable even while the money supply was soaring; and, as in France 1920–3, for prices to rise sharply while the money supply remained no more than level. Similarly, purchasing power parity theory, as we have seen, likewise either proved tautological or failed to fit the facts. The exchange rate in many countries fell more than the theory in any of its contemporary forms would predict, thus creating inflation which tended in the long run to appear to justify it.

Nor did the 1920s bequeath an assured cure for inflation, though the impression that it had done so was, and long remained, widespread. The League of Nations' Finance Committee was at pains to emphasise that no 'binding precedent' for such a cure existed. The essence of the success of the so-called 'League of Nations method' lay in its psychological effect, the restoration of confidence in the currency via an announcement of orthodox, confidence-creating policies. This alone usually evoked foreign exchange from hoards, enabling governments to stabilise their exchange rates. Furthermore, it cut the velocity of circulation, bringing price rises to a halt, and thereby boosted real tax revenue, restoring budget balance with a rapidity which could be startling. But for such a method to succeed, a psychological transformation had to take place which to this day is not fully understood. There is certainly ample scope for doubt as to how far such a transformation could be relied upon in different circumstances. On the whole, it seems likely that the effect depends crucially upon the initial existence of *extreme* inflation, which makes the recessionary effects of stabilisation acceptable (or, if hyperinflation has already led to recessionary anarchy, unimportant) and evokes public willingness, through desperation, to put its faith in the stabilised currency.

The success of the stabilisation of the 1920s should not be overstated. In France, Poland, Austria, Czechoslovakia and, on a small scale, Germany initial measures had to be repeated or subsequently reinforced. The psychological effect of sudden stabilisation could not be relied on to last unless the initial confidence trick was followed before long by measures justifying the confidence. Monetary and fiscal orthodoxy, when they worked, ultimately did so over a lengthy period of time, even when the immediate effects seemed at the time to be all that was required. In this respect, the initial boost to confidence gained time for the government to take action, much as the introduction of a parallel currency was intended to do in the Soviet Union. Furthermore, orthodox stabilisation exacted a high cost. Post-stabilisation recessions were severe, except in the Soviet Union and to some extent France, despite their often being abated by the presence of an international trade boom and an influx of capital from abroad. Moreover, this occurred at a time when trade unions and wage indexation were less generally evident than was subsequently to be the case. Yet in the two cases mentioned there was little or no recession. In France the existence of numerous expansionary factors offset any such tendency, which in any case was not dramatic after only a moderate inflation; and in the Soviet Union the initial chaotic starting point and the offsetting effects of NEP and the reintroduction of money produced a similar outcome. Again, it may be fair to conclude that the greater the extremity the greater will be the willingness of workers and employers to adapt their behaviour promptly to a changed pattern of demand and employment, so that the post-stabilisation recession will be less severe.

Our case studies lend considerable support to the traditional view that inflation exacts high costs, not only via additional transactions costs and widespread economies in the use of money balances, but also via the unlegislated redistribution of income and wealth. More significantly, we may note the loss of the ability to judge accurately whether one has gained or lost; some gaining classes in Germany, for example, were demoralised enough to regard themselves as losers. This fact alone could exacerbate any underlying struggle for income shares.

Two possible clues to the basic nature of inflation emerged from the 1920s, though not with the force necessary to impress them on collective consciousness. First, it was common for inflation to be ended only after it had become so extreme that groups previously benefiting from it had become willing to withdraw their opposition to stabilisation. Inflation was, moreover, commonly accompanied by weak or divided government while, conversely, a precondition of stabilisation almost everywhere was the granting of plenary powers to governments. The preliminary hypothesis suggesting itself is that governments unable to impose a solution upon a divided country permit or foster inflation, while stronger governments are needed to end it. We return to this theme later.

Second, the hiatus in inflation during 1920–1 affected internationally trading countries so generally as to cast doubt on the many proffered explanations specific to individual countries. The episode seems to lend support to the view that improvements in a country's terms of trade can often check inflation, while deteriorations tend to remove the check. Improvements and deteriorations of this kind can be regarded as shifts in the distribution of real income and wealth between nations, not unlike the imposition of reparations. The question here is: how far are such attempts to transfer wealth associated more generally with the onset of inflations? Again, we pursue the theme below.

Finally, it has long been standard doctrine that 'orthodox' stabilisations on the model of the 1920s are politically conservative, involving deflation, unemployment, a return or approach to budgetary balance and a belief in the efficiency of markets, with prices and wages adjusting to changes in the money stock, not vice versa. The evidence of the 1920s endorses such a view, although it must be added that progressive taxes could and sometimes did show themselves capable of playing a vital role – notably, for a while, the property tax in the 1924 Polish stabilisation.

One particular conservative feature of the interwar stabilisations has, however, escaped widespread notice. It lies in the willingness, after stabilisation, to allow central banks to discount commercial bills without limit – the traditional 'Real Bills Doctrine'. O'Brien (1975, p. 151) defines this as the doctrine 'that so long as notes were issued in payment for bills of exchange which were related to real transactions in goods and services they could not be overissued', i.e. could not create inflation. The reason given for this claim was that, since receipts from the bills in question would by definition be used to finance the production and distribution of goods and services, it followed that an increase in the supply of goods could not fail, before long, to follow the discounting of the bills. Additional supply would therefore quickly follow the additional monetary demand. Furthermore, the quantity of money would be reduced as the bills matured and were redeemed.

The doctrine is no longer widely held. Objections cited by O'Brien include the following:

(i)  The central bank may be unable to distinguish 'real' from other bills.

(ii)  'If extra notes are issued then the price level will rise and the notes will then be required to support the same number of transactions as before'. In more modern language, an objection along these lines could be expressed in terms of a 'ratchet effect': extra money raises prices but its disappearance, when the bills creating it are redeemed, may not lower prices; inflation therefore results.

The decline of belief in the Real Bills Doctrine affords only one example of a general trend. In many other respects, too, the relevance and truth of the underlying assumptions of orthodox policy were even by 1939 coming to be doubted, as the efficiency of free markets was questioned and the increasing number of collectivist governments evinced a growing reluctance to rely upon the traditional assumptions of theory. With the outbreak of World War II and its ubiquitous state controls and planning, the question came to asked how far stabilisation of the future could and should be accompanied, at least temporarily, by controls over wages and prices. The signs as of 1939 were, however, still hidden in a mass of as yet only half digested hypotheses. The 1940s were to afford more evidence on the subject.

# 7 Suppressed Inflation In and After the Third Reich

The inflation which was extinguished by the German currency reform of June 1948 and which marks the beginning of the dramatic economic recovery of the postwar years had its origin not merely in World War II but also in the prewar financial policies of the National Socialist government. In extent it was correspondingly mild – milder, in fact, at least in the controlled sector, than any other inflation we shall investigate. Its interest lies in the fact that, unlike all the inflations we have so far discussed, it was not an open but a suppressed inflation, giving rise to different effects and problems.

## INFLATION IN THE THIRD REICH

The economy of the Third Reich was from the outset highly regulated. Despite earlier promises, the Nazis did not abolish private ownership of the means of production; yet state intervention in privately-owned business was so extensive and detailed that the effect was similar. In the course of two Four-Year Plans large-scale public works were undertaken to reduce unemployment; young men were conscripted into a Labour Service for such purpose as roadbuilding, agricultural work and land improvement; and in 1935 general military conscription was introduced. In every branch of activity trade associations or parallel bodies were organised to allocate supplies of raw materials, to approve investment plans and to determine the prices, profits and sales which were to result from any planned category of output. Access to foreign exchange was strictly controlled according to national priorities and as a result barter came to play an increasingly important role in the country's foreign trade, with exporters and importers entering into elaborate 'compensation deals' designed to circumvent the shortage of foreign exchange (Guillebaud, 1939, pp. 68–70). The effect of the controls was to restrict the supply of basic raw materials internally and so to necessitate their being rationed. There were also strict controls upon the financial sector. In fixing charges, interest rates and reserve ratios, commercial banks and credit institutions were closely supervised and if necessary made subject to the rulings of a Credit Supervisory Board.

One of the main aims of Nazi policy was to prevent inflation and in the early years of the regime market intervention by monopoly boards, as well as orders to firms to build up or reduce stocks, were used for this purpose. As the level of demand and employment rose, however, the danger of general inflation grew and late in 1936 a Price Stop Decree was announced which forbade all price increases above the level of 17 October without special permission. Rises due to increases in the import content of goods were permitted when unavoidable but a Commissioner for Price Formation had the right to lower any price at will.

Price control necessitated wage control. Officials known as Trustees of Labour were accordingly empowered to fix minimum wages and set about revising many wage rates with the aim of making them more orderly. The effect was to produce virtually no overall increase in average wages, though increases in working hours and in overtime meant that average earnings rose substantially.

The total effect of these policies was to produce a remarkably stable price level, despite the strong pressure of demand which had arisen by 1936. Between 1933, near the trough of the depression, and 1938 the general index of wholsesale prices rose only by about 16 per cent (Guillebaud, op. cit., p. 218), much of the rise originating abroad. The cost of living index for the period is less than wholly reliable. None the less, its rise from 118.0 for 1933 to 125.5 for March 1938, about 6 per cent, is thought to afford a reasonable general estimate of the true trend. This occurred despite the fact that, by March 1938, a state of full employment had, on any definition, been reached, most of the country's main industries were working to capacity, and the curtailment of imports in pursuit of national economic selfsufficiency had created inflationary scarcities of many imported materials. Pressure on prices was, moreover, aggravated by the drive to produce synthetic domestic substitutes for imports, often at much increased cost.

The achievement of near stability of prices is all the more remarkable in view of the way in which the high and rising level of public expenditure was financed. In the 1930s and during the war alike, the state, limiting its increases in taxation largely to two small rises in corporation tax, resorted increasingly to inflationary methods.

Had the Reichsbank simply extended direct credit in financing its plans for German self sufficiency, full employment and military victory, it would have contravened its statutes and awakened popular memories of hyperinflation. Instead, the government, using a technique not unlike that of French governments in the early 1920s, issued in exchange for its purchases a variety of ingeniously devised instruments which either were ultimately rediscountable at the Reichsbank (Nathan, 1944, pp. 276–331) or which could be used as collateral against advances from the Reichsbank (Lurié, 1947, pp. 32–3). Among these were tax remission certificates paid to individuals and special employment creation bills paid to firms. Later in the 1930s the government shifted somewhat from reliance on credit expansion by these and other means to an increased attempt to borrow funds out of institutional and personal savings. Even then, however, the creation of money still continued, unrestricted by any statutory limitation. Lurié (1947, p. 36) reports the Reichsbank's note circulation as slightly more than doubling between the ends of the financial years 1933/4 and 1938/9.

The annexation of Austria and Czechoslovakia and finally the outbreak of war brought with them an increase in extraordinary sources of finance. In part these were at the expense of occupied countries, in part at that of the Jews, who suffered large-scale expropriation. In part, too, taxes were increased. In September 1939 inessential public spending was cut, a surtax levied on personal incomes, and alcohol and tobacco taxes raised. As a result total tax revenue rose sharply, a trend strengthened by subsequent measures such as the dividend tax introduced in 1941, the war surcharge on corporation tax, and increased taxes elsewhere.

Even so, Stolper estimates that taxation financed less than a third of the Reich's wartime expenditures. To some extent noninflationary borrowing met the remainder. Forced savings resulting from the strict rationing of consumer goods were channelled to the state through a variety of credit institutions; and late in 1941 the public was offered an incentive to personal saving in the form of the promise of tax reliefs at the end of the war. During the first three and a half years of war, however, no attempt was made to issue war loans to the general public, probably, in Nathan's view (op. cit., p. 295), for fear of arousing memories of similar actions during World War One. Heavy borrowing through the issue of rediscountable bills therefore remained necessary.

The result of policies of this kind as the war proceeded was a dramatic increase in the Reich's official debt, which rose by over 50 per cent in 1942 and again in 1943. The total in March 1943 was estimated at about sixteen times its level a decade earlier. Between the pairs of fiscal years 1939/41 and 1943/5 the debt rose almost fivefold. With massively inflationary government finance held in check by the strict enforcement of fixed wages and prices, the inevitable result was suppressed inflation. By mid-1945 this, reflected in huge unspent money holdings by firms and individuals, threatened, the minute controls and rationing ended, to break out into hyperinflation. The situation was worsened by the disintegration of the German economy as the war ended. The breakdown of the transport system in the wake of the fighting produced a mass of barely connected local economies, in many parts of which production has ceased altogether, and where millions were homeless. Economic collapse was, moreover, worsened by Allied policy, in accordance with which, for two years after the notorious Joint Chiefs of Staff Directive of April 1945, the western Allies dismantled several hundred German factories, despite the already widespread shortages and destitution.

Monetary reform was generally admitted to be essential for recovery but for three years after the war's end the Soviet authorities in the eastern zone of Germany refused to cooperate in any reform which would involve treating the country as a unified currency area. Since unilateral action almost certainly meant the creation of a permanently divided Germany, the Allies hesitated to move and it was not until the Soviet Union withdrew its cooperation from the Allied Control Council in March 1948 and began increasingly to interrupt traffic between Berlin and the West that the western Allies finally decided to proceed with their own independent currency reform.

## THE ECONOMY BEFORE REFORM

The economies of the three western zones on the eve of the reform were aptly described by Ludwig Erhard, the German Director of Economic Administration in the United Economic Region (the Anglo-American Bizone formed in January 1947 and only subsequently augmented by the addition of the French zone), as being gripped by 'a price-frozen inflation'. The policies perpetuating this situation had the merit of attempting to ensure for everyone a minimum standard of living (albeit one which for a time was less than that calculated as necessary for sustaining life). None the less, they failed altogether to provide incentives which might stimulate workers to produce higher output. On the contrary, because everyone knew that a currency reform would eventually replace the depreciated currency by a better, firms kept part of such output as they produced in stocks, worsening the market shortage, while those many individuals who possessed, in an economy bloated with money, enough to buy their rations, were unwilling to expend energy earning additional sums which, because of high black market prices, would buy them little more.

In this situation money became increasingly unacceptable. Dire necessity, and the relaxation under the Allied administration of the previously draconian penalties for 'economic crimes', drove people to barter and to the black market. In the latter, prices were from fifty to one hundred and fifty times as high as the official legal prices. Commonly, prices were paid not in Reichsmarks but in cigarettes; and in many cases where the price legally chargeable for a product did not cover its costs firms took to producing a wide range of inessentials such as ashtrays and dolls, for which prices were uncontrolled, despite the widespread shortages of essentials. Such goods were bought as safeguards against inflation and possible currency confiscation. Despite some rise in black market prices just before the currency reform, there was no open hyperinflation. The economic stagnation caused by suppressed inflation was, none the less, a source of grave impoverishment and demoralisation to the general population.

## THE CURRENCY REFORM OF JUNE 1948

One possible course of action was to remove the suppressed inflation simply by abolishing controls and allowing prices to rise to market-clearing levels. A second was to accompany decontrol, as in many interwar stabilisations, by the confiscation, through taxation or otherwise, of any money in the public's hands in excess of that needed to finance trade at existing prices. The two solutions would no doubt have produced unpredictably different distributions of real income and wealth. It can also be argued that the first would have been more likely to trigger a wage–price spiral. Whatever the merits of the case, it was in the event the second which was chosen.

The reform confiscated a large part of the liquid funds then held throughout the economy. The method chosen was complex and evolved in stages. Its broad effect, however, was to convert currency and deposits in banks and savings accounts, at present valued in Reichsmarks, into a new unit of currency, the Deutsche Mark, at a rate eventually fixed as 100: 6.5. The effect was thus to impose a tax of 93.5 per cent on money holdings. Twelve million small savings accounts were wiped out altogether. As the first step in introducing the new currency and as a source of ready cash during the transition, individuals were given an allocation, first of 40, then of another 20 DMs, in exchange for the same number of RMs. Firms were also allowed 60 DMs per employee for their immediate cash needs, while public authorities were granted allowances equal to one month's revenue. Since liquid assets were thus being written down in value, debts had to be treated similarly. These were therefore scaled down, most of them in the ration of 10:1. In some cases the scaling down of long-term debt, such as mortgage debt on undamaged property, could have given rise to huge windfall profits for the mortgagee. In consequence, such profits, rather arbitrarily assessed, were in December made payable into a special find for the compensation of victims of war damage.

Along with curtailment of the stock of liquid assets went steps towards price and wage decontrol. In the weeks following the currency reform all goods except essential foodstuffs and basic materials were freed both from rationing and from price controls. Most of the remaining goods were before long similarly treated, while the wage freeze was abolished in November. The reform period thus not only introduced a stable currency into use; it also, and at least as importantly, restored incentives to produce goods corresponding with consumers' demands.

The effects of the reform package were immediate and striking. The following day, goods previously almost unknown reappeared in the shops. The black market declined dramatically. Barter disappeared; so did the earlier mass migrations of townsfolk to the countryside in search of food. Productivity and output soared, and with it public morale. So great was the boost to output that despite cuts in tax rates (to which some of the credit for the policy's success is widely ascribed) tax revenue rose quickly, restoring the budget to balance and even surplus. German commentators of all political viewpoints were almost unanimous in regarding the reform as an outstanding success; and though for some years English and American comment was markedly less favourable (see Hutchison, 1979), this too underwent a marked change in time.

Even so, some inflation did follow. Perhaps because the reform had failed to adjust money holdings exactly to the volume of supplies, basic material prices rose during the second half of 1948 by 21 per cent, factory prices by 14 per cent and the cost of living by 14 per cent. Wallich (1955, pp. 70, 75) mentions the excessive allocation of liquid reserves to banks as playing an important role here. Most of the price increases took place, however, by October and with wages remarkably stable it was clear by early 1949 that the rise had been halted. The measures instrumental in bringing this about included some designed to make firms run down stocks of previously hoarded goods and a wide range of tight money policies. Wallich (p. 74) doubts, however, whether these measures alone would have been sufficient to curb inflation, as bank credit rose, during the second half of 1948, from almost zero to 5.2 billion DM, and the (narrow) money supply by 16 per cent between September and December. Probably the most important single factor was the stability of wages, to which may be added the end of currency conversion and the emergence of budget surpluses as tax revenues rose with national income.

The short-lived inflationary boom was not followed by a recession in any sense in which the term would now be used. Throughout 1949 industrial production and national income continued to soar and the rise which took place in unemployment resulted more from the influx of refugees from the Soviet zone than from any slowdown in demand accompanying the emergence of budget surpluses and the general slackening in world trade. Table 7:1 gives evidence of the general trends at work.

*Table 7.1: German economic indicators, 1948–50*

|  |  | Industrial production (1936 = 100) | % Unemployment | Cost of living (1950 = 100) | Currency & demand deposits DM bill. |
|---|---|---|---|---|---|
| 1948, | June | 54 | 3.2 | 98 | n.a. |
|  | Sept | 71 | 5.5 | 107 | 12.3 |
|  | Dec | 79 | 5.3 | 112 | 14.3 |
| 1949, | Mar | 83 | 8.0 | 108 | 14.6 |
|  | June | 88 | 8.7 | 107 | 15.6 |
|  | Sept | 94 | 8.8 | 105 | 16.4 |
|  | Dec | 98 | 10.3 | 105 | 19.6 |
| 1950, | Mar | 99 | 12.2 | 100 | 17.3 |

*Source:* Wallich (1955), pp. 74–5, 80–1.

Even so, early in 1950, with two million workers unemployed, policies were initiated to stimulate economic activity and with the outbreak of the Korean War in June the danger of worse depression disappeared. On the evidence of subsequent events, it became hard to dispute the view that the currency reform had been almost totally successful.


## 1948 AND 1923

The difference between the currency reform of 1948 and the stabilisation of 1923 were sufficiently marked for comparison to be illuminating. The central difference lay in the natures of the two inflations, the earlier being overt, the later, apart from a few months just before the currency reform, suppressed. In 1923 the government's task was to stop a runaway inflation already far advanced, in 1948 to eliminate an 'overhang' of *potential* purchasing power before the controls restraining it either broke down or, as was inevitable, came to be dismantled. In the one case, a cure was called for; in the other, prevention.

Along with this fundamental difference went corresponding differences in the causes, nature and effects of the two inflations. In 1923 the excessive growth of the money stock was inextricably linked with current budget deficits, the growth of central bank credit to private business, the fall of the exchange rate, the payment of reparations, the extensive indexation of wages and the political deadlock which prevented governments taking firm remedial action. The problem of 1948 was conceptually simpler. After an initial issue of occupation money in 1945 there was no marked growth in the volume of money in the Allied zones, while at the same time production had already begun to rise. The authorities enforced what amounted to budgetary balance. Foreign trade scarcely existed, and payments involving foreign countries were limited to a small number of general categories, notably those covering ERP (Marshall Aid) and relief sent by the Allied aid agency GARIOA. Wages were still frozen under Nazi controls maintained by the Allies. Finally, the political regime, far from being weak and unstable, was authoritarian and, for Germans, immutable. The causes of the inflation were therefore entirely historical: a drastically reduced level of output combined with a huge reservoir of unspent money issued by the Third Reich.

Correspondingly, the characteristics of the two inflations

were also different. A few central illustrations may be cited. In 1921–3 prices soared at an ever-increasing pace. The velocity at which money circulated, in so far as this has been estimated (Bresciani, 1931, p. 168), rose sharply. The inflation was broadly homogeneous, affecting all goods (apart from controlled property rents) almost equally except in so far as they were affected by changes in relative supply and demand. A flight into 'real values' – any physical object which might form a hedge against inflation – was widely evident, but not the hoarding of newly produced goods by firms. Finally, in the later stages of the inflation, the costs and uncertainty resulting from the inflation became so great that chaos resulted, producing mounting unemployment.

In the 1940s almost none of the above characteristics was present. The cost of living index for legal, controlled prices rose by only 26 per cent between 1945 and the first half of 1948. Likewise, black market prices, after an initial increase to a high level, are not reported to have risen steeply. The velocity of circulation of money seems not to have risen but on the contrary (Mendershausen, 1955, p. 37) to have declined, partly perhaps because overt inflation was not a continuing phenomenon, partly because hopes of salvaging much real value from money may have faded at an early stage. The inflation was far from homogeneous, with price and wage controls creating a wide divergence between free and controlled levels. As in the 1920s, people did their utmost to exchange money for physical objects, in this case because currency reform and the confiscation of a great deal of wealth were confidently expected; but on this occasion, unlike the earlier one, firms also hoarded newly produced output, being unwilling to exchange it for largely worthless currency. Finally, unemployment, far from arising only in the weeks immediately preceding stabilisation, was heavy throughout the pre-reform period of the 1940s.

As to the remedial policies adopted, some broad similarities are perceptible, despite dominant differences. Both stabilisations involved foreign loans or other aid, though in widely differing ways and at different stages. Thus, in the earlier case it was not until the summer of 1924 after the Dawes Committee had reported that a start could be made in realising the proposed Dawes Loan; in the latter case, payments in the form of Marshall Aid and relief from GAROIA were in process long before stabilisation and currency reform. Again, both stabilisations worked well but neither worked perfectly. It was not until April 1924 that measures supplementary to the first stabilisation finally dispelled rumours of further inflation; nor until the end of 1948 that prices on the second occasion stopped rising and began a temporary gentle fall.

There, however, similarity ends. A consideration of some of the overall macroeconomic effects of the two episodes illustrates this clearly. As Mendershausen (1955, p. 42) says, writing of the respective effects of the two inflations in lowering the level of investment and distorting its pattern: 'On balance, the greater extent of the misinvestment in the open inflation [of the 1920s] may well have more than offset the greater rate of investment.' In short, the first inflation damaged the volume of investment less, its quality more. As for the distribution of costs and benefits between different classes of society in the two episodes, a detailed comparison is beyond our scope here. At the end of an examination of the two, however, one is left with an overall impression that if, putting aside the effects of wartime devastation, we were to compare the evils of the overt inflation of 1923 with those of the frozen inflation of 1948, we might arrive at the conclusion that for the great majority of Germans the first were greater. In the 1940s, official controls and rationing, combined with relief payments, spread the burden of hardship more evenly and removed a vast amount of uncertainty, injustice and panic, albeit at the price of widespread loss of incentives and initiative. Nor was it only the inflationary malady which was, in all probability, worse in 1923. The costs of stabilisation, in the form of subsequent unemployment and lost output, were also greater. Perhaps the most that can be said is that the severe phase of the 1923 crisis was at any rate shorter than the three-year stagnation of the 1940s. Hyperinflation has at least one merit: it can scarcely fail to provoke some early and sudden attempt at a remedy.

## STABILISATION WITHOUT RECESSION?

Did the events of 1948 constitute an exception to the general rule that successful stabilisations are achieved only at the price of subsequent recessions? To pose the question in this form is to assume that no recession followed – that, in other words, the slight slackening of demand in 1949 was not a result of currency reform but arose from other causes – an assumption which could be questioned. More fundamentally, however, the question demands a closer understanding of the nature of post-stabilisation recessions. Their causes, as we saw in Chapter 1, are primarily three. First, with the return of price stability people feel less obliged to spend quickly; the velocity of circulation of money therefore falls, bringing about a slackening of demand. Second, a prolonged period of inflation may have led firms and individuals to invest in forms of capital designed to produce fast-appreciating or speculatively promising goods rather than those which correspond with consumers' real long-term wants. When price stability returns the demand for such goods falls and those employed in making them become unemployed. A third possibility is that during the inflation individuals and firms, acting in the expectation that money will rapidly depreciate in real terms, have contracted money debts so large as to be, in normal times, unrepayable. A halt to inflation thus produces numerous insolvencies. Recession in such a case arises from the continuing extension of credit right up to the last stages of the inflation.

In the 1945–8 inflation the velocity of circulation played no major role; it is not recorded as rising drastically or continuously, nor does it seem to have changed dramatically at the time of reform. Certain distortions of the pattern of output did take place, notably because price controls discouraged the production (or at least the sale) of those goods which were in strongest demands. Similarly, the expectation of monetary reform and confiscation distorted the pattern of expenditure by shifting it into 'real values' – any chattels or physical objects likely to escape confiscation. On the whole, however, investment, in so far as it occurred at all, took place in vital basic national industries. Moreover, there were no reports of widespread speculative ventures or the massive extension of credit. The grounds for expecting a post-reform recession, as Erhard did (1963, p. 50) when he wrote of 'a mild deflationary purge', were therefore not strong. The preconditions for such a recession did not exist.

## SUMMARY AND CONCLUSIONS

Suppressed inflation built up continuously during the Third Reich in response to inflationary methods of finance and strictly enforced price controls. When, under the Allied occupation, penalties were relaxed a huge black market developed. Controls were, however, effective enough to stifle enterprise and distort the pattern of production, so that economic stagnation ensued until, in June 1948, a new currency was finally issued in limited quantities and most price controls removed. The curtailment of the currency ended, except for a brief period, general inflation; the removal of controls ended distortions in relative prices. Once a small amount of subsequent inflation had passed, the outcome was a dramatic upsurge of economic growth combined with a remarkable degree of price stability.

How far can the events of 1948 afford any general guidance to policies for ending suppressed inflations? More particularly, which played the more important role – the introduction of the new Deutsche Mark or the decontrol of prices and wages – in launching the upsurge of German economic growth which was to ensue? The answer seems likely to be that both decontrol and currency reform were essential to the process. Until the summer of 1948 the growth of Germany's output was held back chiefly by two factors: the reluctance of producers to accept payment in a currency which might soon be partially confiscated; and the fact that the cost of producing many goods equalled or exceeded the controlled prices at which they had to be sold. Currency reform removed the first of these obstacles, decontrol the second. Reform without decontrol would have created, and for certain goods did temporarily create, an incentive for firms to run down at least some of the hoards of goods which they had accumulated; at the same time distortions of relative prices and output due to the controls would have persisted. Decontrol without reform, on the other hand, would have allowed prices to soar to much higher levels, eliminating distortions in the pattern of output and releasing some goods from existing hoards; but it would have involved some risk of triggering a wage–price spiral and also, especially if accompanied by the end of rationing, might have increased hardship among the least well off. The currency reform acted as an equaliser as well as a stabiliser.

In general, then, it seems safe to conclude that to secure the twin abolitions of the monetary overhang and of price distortions the mixture of reform and decontrol actually chosen was well judged. No student of the period claims more than the roughest justice for the package of measures. Several writers have also commented that such measures could in all probability only have been introduced under authoritarian rule. None the less, there is general agreement, with only a few dissenting voices (e.g. that of E.F. Schumacher, in Prittie, 1979, p. 120) that, given Germany's ready supply of skilled labour, its still substantial remaining capital stock and its urgent need for higher output, the taxation of liquid funds and the decontrol of prices were both necessary and vital steps towards the forthcoming economic revival.

# 8 The Greatest Hyperinflation: Hungary, 1945–6

## BEGINNINGS AND EARLY COURSE OF THE INFLATION

The Hungarian hyperinflation, the greatest in the world's recorded history, was also an exceedingly short one. Between mid-1939 and 31 July 1946 – the total inflationary period, including its moderate phase – the cost of living index increased by a factor of 125,720,000,000,000,000. Between 15 July 1945 and 31 July 1946 – the period which may be termed the hyperinflation – the corresponding factor was 1,366,521,740,000,000. When a new currency unit, the forint, was finally introduced it was worth $4.10^{29}$ pengos, a figure with 29 noughts. This compared with a corresponding equivalence of 1 trillion to one in the German stabilisation of 1923. Table 8:1 illustrates.

The inflation began in the familiar way with World War II. In the course of the war government expenditure more than doubled to nearly half the gross national product but because tax revenue and borrowing from the public did not keep pace a steeply rising proportion of expenditure – 70 per cent by 1944 – had to be financed by the creation of money. The money stock rose sharply; money in circulation increased fifteenfold between 1938 and 1944. The exchange rate fell; in 1944 the pengo had less than a sixth of its prewar dollar value.

Hyperinflation, however, may be said not to have set in until close to the end of the war. By then the country had suffered a series of catastrophic shocks. In November 1944 Szalasi, the leader of Hungary's Nazi Party, seized power. In January the

*Table 8.1: Cost of living (without rent), 1938–46*
*(mid-1938 = 100)*

| | |
|---|---:|
| mid-1939 | 100 |
| mid-1941 | 139 |
| mid-1943 | 217 |
| 15 July 1945 | 9,200 |
| 31 August | 17,300 |
| 30 September | 38,900 |
| 31 October | 250,000 |
| 30 November | 1,545,700 |
| 31 December | 3,778,000 |
| 31 January 1946 | 7,089,000 |
| 28 February | 45,854,300 |
| 31 March | 205,060,000 |
| 30 April | 3,575,600,000 |
| 31 May | 1,076,400,000,000 |
| 30 June | 470,300,000,000,000 |
| 31 July | 12,572,000,000,000,000,000 |

*Source:* Ausch (1958), quoted in Falush (1976), p. 49.

country surrendered to invading Russian troops, though fighting continued until April. Devastation was extreme. In addition, the Soviet Union along with other East European countries exacted heavy reparations, usually in the form of agricultural output or capital goods. Food shortages were widespread.

Into this situation of acute supply shortage the continuance of the governmental policy of running large and rapidly increasing deficits financed by monetary growth injected the final condition for hyperinflation. Already in 1944 barter was widespread; the following year saw inflation so extreme that loss of confidence in the currency led to its widespread abandonment. In the first four months of 1945 alone the cost of living rose fifteenfold, after trebling in the preceding year. This, moreover, occurred at a time when, because of damage to printing works, the supply of money was for a time curbed. This effect was, however, in part offset by the return of pengos from Austria and the Romanian-occupied parts of Transylvania, which accelerated the fall of the exchanges and swelled demand for goods and services.

By the autumn, with the government deficit growing at an ever-accelerating rate and the note issue having increased tenfold in three months, the familiar signs of inflationary crisis were evident: a fall in the real value of the money stock as the price level rose faster than the soaring nominal money supply – in short, a scarcity of money; and a sharp increase in the speed with which people got rid of any money coming into their hands. The velocity of circulation is estimated (Falush, 1976, p. 52) to have risen, by 1946, about 300-fold. External trade was at a very low level and the purchasing power of the pengo abroad is thought to have fallen to less than one hundred million million millionth of its prewar value.

On 18 December 1945 the government published a decree calling in all pengo notes for stamping; since the stamps which now had to be attached cost three times the face value of the notes, this measure in effect confiscated 75 per cent of the notes in circulation. There was, however, no similar reduction in the volume of bank deposits and of other credits and liabilities. Money flows such as wages were similarly unaffected. The consequences of the stamping were in the main unsurprising. After a few days of immediate uncertainty, the cut in note circulation was followed by a steep fall in prices, variously estimated at between 40 and 80 per cent, in apparent accordance with the predictions of a simple quantity theory of money. Since, however, only the stock of notes was cut, not the flows of income in the economy, a resumed rise in prices could not be long delayed; a once-for-all cut in money balances was simply not enough to end inflation, since the budget deficit and the growth of money remained. The long-run trend towards hyperinflation therefore resumed its course, with individuals and businesses borrowing from the banks to replace liquid funds lost through the stamping, and banks meeting the increased demand by lowering their reserve ratios (Nogaro, 1948, p. 535). The stock of money was thus, at least for a time, demand-determined, as in other inflations (e.g. that of Britain in 1980–1). In the longer run, however, the Hungarian government's deficit must certainly have been a predominant influence on the money supply.

## INTRODUCTION OF THE TAX PENGO

On 1 January 1946 a second measure designed to restrain inflation was introduced. As in other hyperinflations, the real value of tax revenues, depleted by inflation during the time lags between assessment and receipt, remained at extremely low levels, eliminating any possibility of balancing the budget. In an attempt to solve this problem the government introduced, initially only as a unit of account, a new currency unit, the tax pengo. Thus, a tax assessed at 10 pengos could, when the date of payment arrived, be paid in regular pengos, but the number of the latter payable would be calculated as the number specified in the original assessment increased in proportion to the increase in a price index since assessment. Tax receipts were thus indexed and their real value to the government guaranteed.

Almost immediately, however, the government began to encourage the extension of the new tax pengo to other fields. In particular commercial and savings banks were encouraged to open 'valorised' accounts expressed in tax pengos (but from which and into which payment was made in regular pengos), in an attempt to cut the demand for dollars. The dollar, as a stable currency, had during the inflation been in great demand as a store of value and was continually invoked for comparison with the pengo, to the point where employers were reported to calculate their costs in dollars. The valorisation of savings accounts was designed to check these tendencies. One consequence of the measure provides a good, but by no means the only, illustration of the way in which measures of indexation can spark off a chain reaction: since banks' liabilities were now expressed in real terms, the credits they extended had to be similarly expressed if the banks were to avoid bankruptcy.

The final step in extending the use of tax pengos came on 1 June when tax pengo notes were issued and the new currency unit became not merely a unit of account and a store of value but also a means of exchange. Since to hold tax pengo notes was like having a valorised bank account except that no notice need be given before making withdrawals, it was not surprising that their use spread rapidly, soon apparently controverting Gresham's so-called law that bad money drives out good. The volume of money deposited in valorised bank accounts also grew at a rapidly increasing rate as firms and individuals shifted out of depreciating regular pengos into valorised accounts.

In the early stages of inflation the government had made gains in the form of 'seigniorage' or 'tax revenue' from the inflation. The gains were made by buying goods and services with newly created money at the cost, before long, of raising prices and so inflicting upon the public a reduction in the value of its cash holdings. The resemblance to a tax was clear: the government gained goods and services while the public lost them through inflation.

Two mechanisms now arose, however, which tended to reduce the 'inflation tax revenue'. One, a regular feature of inflations stimulated by fiscal deficits and excessive monetary growth, was that, as prices rose, successive equal issues of new money secured control over progressively *diminishing* increments of real resources. The returns to inflationary finance tended, in fact, to fall ever more sharply, an arithmetic progression in the issue of new money producing real gains which fell in geometrical progression.

The second limit to governmental profit from inflation (Bomberger and Makinin, 1980) stemmed from the fact that the shift out of regular pengos into valorised bank deposits also eroded the base of the 'inflation tax'. This constituted another reason why ever greater issues of money were needed to enable the government to pre-empt successive equal increments of real resources. Because much personal wealth was now protected against inflation, the rate of the 'inflation tax' (i.e. the volume of new money issued) had to be increased to maintain the required level of 'revenue'. With inflationary policies thus rapidly ceasing to yield gains, it could no longer be said that the inflation was working to any marked extent in the interests of the government. The incentive to stabilise was therefore strong and growing.

## EFFECTS AND LATER COURSE

Nor was this the only incentive. Many other ill effects were evident throughout the economy. About the state of employment and output in relation to the much reduced productive capacity of the country little is known. But barter was general and the results of this must have been to waste time and to lower productivity on a huge scale; even taxes were made lawfully payable in kind. Wages, though they had moved from a system of monthly to one of weekly and then of daily payments, lagged far behind prices. A sliding scale introduced in February 1946 making them partly payable in kind under the calorie-money system may have safeguarded workers' real incomes to some extent in the later stages of inflation, though not all firms were able to comply with the requirements of the system. Again, the freeze on rents and some basic prices also helped to shield many families from the effects of inflation. Even so, the other side of the indexation debate was already evident. Vargas (1947, p. 4) argues that over-provision of the real wage through indexation at too high a level itself worsened inflation by increasing the amount of excess demand in the economy. The observation was to have more general relevance, as becomes clear in later chapters.

As elsewhere, inflation redistributed real income. Among the classes which seem to have benefited, at least relatively to the nation as a whole, we may note in particular: the peasants, who sold produce for which demand was inelastic; the state; successful speculators; and some firms, notably in the export sector, which gained because for much of the time the pengo exchange rate plunged faster than domestic prices rose, thus making Hungarian exports cheaper to foreign buyers. Those who had access to hard currency, a stable store of value, also gained obvious benefits. Other classes, including many industrial workers, suffered severely.

To speak of excess demand in such chaotic conditions, where money had ceased to fulfil any of its three additional functions, may be to apply an inappropriate label; but prices were not, for most of the period, pushed up by rising wage costs nor to any great extent by rising import prices, which in the straightened circumstances of foreign trade at the time were of minor importance. Supply was certainly curtailed by a wage system which linked reward with need rather than effort (Vargas, 1947 (I), p. 4); but, more importantly still, the momentum of inflation stemmed from a rise in the velocity of circulation, which, if estimates are even roughly correct, was of a quite different order of magnitude even from that which occurred in Germany in the 1920s, and from the effects, described above, of the valorisation of bank accounts.

As we have seen, the tax pengo issued to alleviate some of the ill-effects of the inflation was designed to maintain a constant real purchasing power. At first it more or less achieved this objective; but not for long. It had, of course, been foreseen that its value would rise in relation to that of the regular pengo, and in fact during the month of January the rate of exchange between the two currencies moved from 1:1 to 1:1.7. What was not foreseen was the depreciation of the tax pengo itself. On 19 April, for administrative reasons but also, it is suggested, because the government feared that the indexed tax pengo might be aggravating inflation in terms of regular pengos, the index number used for converting regular pengos into tax pengos was changed to that which prevailed at the end of the *previous* day's business. At a time of astronomical and rapid inflation this time-lag came to be of great importance and the tax pengo, though at an ever-increasing premium in relation to the regular pengo, itself began to depreciate in relation to the dollar. Rumours that the tax pengo was to be withdrawn and uncertainty about the exchange rate at which, in that event, it might be convertible into any new currency had a similar effect; further falls in the tax pengo's dollar value thus reflected not merely conditions of spot trading but expectations about possible future losses. By June the regular pengo had disappeared from circulation and the tax pengo became the only official currency. Since its value was indexed only in terms of the old pengo, not in terms of goods and services, there was now nothing to stop it depreciating with overissue; and this it did at an ever-accelerating pace. By 27 July one tax pengo might still, for the purposes of purely academic calculation, be worth two octillions of the former regular pengos. More pertinently, it was by then worth only an infinitesimal fraction of its own original value.

## CURRENCY REFORM

The very speed of the inflation made early reform inevitable; and on 1 August this was duly introduced. On that day the coalition government, in which the Communists played a minority role, put into circulation a further new currency unit, the forint, and formally withdrew the regular pengo (though not the tax pengo). The forint was defined as equal value to 75.7 milligrams of gold, 400 octillions of regular pengos and 200 million tax pengos; there were 11.47 forints to the dollar. No commitment to maintain the exchange rate was made, though Nogaro (op. cit., p. 535) regards its deliberate maintenance as certainly having taken place.

The new notes were to be strictly limited in amount. Prices, wages and property rents were re-fixed, and strenuous efforts made to balance the budget. The stabilisation, though in many ways similar to those of the 1920s, did not, however, involve any foreign loan or any foreign government's guarantee of a loan raised on the open market; nor did it rely on market forces to fix prices under the new regime. During the interim period before internal and external balance could be fully restored, any funds necessary for supporting the forint on the foreign exchanges were (Nogaro, pp. 538–9) provided by additional inflows into the National Bank's dollar reserves. In part these took the form of repatriations of capital held abroad by domestic residents, as in the stabilisations of the 1920s. In part they arose from the Bank's massive purchases of dollars held within Hungary by residents who had bought them as a safeguard against recent inflation. In total the reserves which the Bank was able to accumulate in these ways amounted, according to Nogaro, to some 517 million forints.

The currency reform worked promptly. Prices stopped rising and even began to fall well before the necessary fiscal and monetary reforms were actually implemented. Goods were brought out of stock for sale. The hordes of black marketeers disappeared. In the first fortnight after stabilisation, firms and individuals sold, according to Kaldor (1946(I), p. 331), some $10 million dollars in notes to the National Bank in exchange for forints. The entire existing note circulation was redeemed for 14 million forints, little more than 0.1 per cent of the national income in terms of the new currency. Goods long since in short supply appeared on the market in quantity; only plentiful demand was lacking. Unemployment began to rise.

There, however, any resemblance to interwar stabilisations

ended. Wages and prices in the new currency, as in the old, far from being determined by the market, were governmentally settled in advance of stabilisation. Starting with an arbitrarily chosen price for wheat, the authorities proceeded to fix other prices in relation to it. They then fixed wages, salaries and rents in relation to prices. The value of the new forint in terms both of dollars and tax pengos was the last thing to be announced. As a planned package of measures involving detailed control of all the main variables and values in the economy, the Hungarian stabilisation represents an alternative model to the model of stabilisation followed in the 1920s, and one which was in turn to be followed in other countries, notably – though not necessarily consciously – in the attempted Argentine and Brazilian stabilisations of the mid-1980s.

One further related effect deserves mention. Because of its extreme nature, the inflation provided the occasion for the huge extension of state control and ownership in the economy, which had been postponed in the first four months after Soviet occupation because of the extreme problems facing the country. Coalmines and power stations were nationalised in December 1945, banks firmly regulated, and by the date of stabilisation the state controlled about half of all output, with food rationing and price and wage controls legally enacted, if not always enforced. Because of its accompanying divergences in wealth and income and its widespread speculation, the inflation also went far towards discrediting capitalism in the public mind. In both ways it thus seems to have helped to speed up the inevitable takeover of the country by the Communists.

## EXCEPTIONAL CAUSES AND DEPOSIT INDEXATION

The special interest of the Hungarian inflation arises chiefly from three aspects of that country's experience. Two of these – the tendency of partial indexation to set up pressure for its extension, and the possible inflationary effects of wage indexation – have already been mentioned. A third, however, is of interest because it seems to yield an answer to the most obvious and main question to preoccupy subsequent students of the period: why was the inflation so severe?

First, the balance of payments seems unlikely to have played a major part. With trade at about 4 per cent of its prewar level (Falush, 1976, p. 54), any deficit incurred by the end of the war seems to have been inadequate to account for more than a small part of the hyperinflationary explosion. Capital movements across the exchanges likewise evoke little emphasis in contemporary accounts. The role of chief originating cause of the inflation seems certainly to fall to money creation. Why should this have been so exceptionally rapid?

Convincing reasons are not hard to find. The budget deficit, which was financed through the printing press, can largely be explained by the huge expansion of the burden of public spending due to wartime devastation, the need to pay heavy reparations and the costs of the army of occupation, along with the problems of raising real tax revenue when money was depreciating fast. As we have also mentioned, there can be little doubt that the attempt at wage indexation further worsened matters (Kaldor(I), 1946, p. 299; Vargas, 1947(I), p. 4). The hypothesis that memories of the inflation of the 1920s made the velocity of circulation rise with exceptional rapidity also receives apparent support from several econometric studies. Even when all these circumstances are invoked, however, the unprecedented rise in velocity recorded still demands additional explanation.

The contention of Bomberger and Makinen (1980) is that because the indexation of bank deposits in and after January 1946 greatly narrowed the base of the inflation tax, the government, unable at once to curb its deficit, was obliged to resort to the printing press more rapidly than it would otherwise have done, and so greatly worsened inflation. Put otherwise, the argument rests on the fact that deposit indexation made a large part of the public's wealth immune from erosion by inflation. As a result the government, in its desperate struggle for greater control over resources, was obliged to issue ever-growing quantities of regular pengos and so worsen the inflation tax on the remaining part of the public's wealth − namely, the part consisting of those pengos and the (unindexed) assets denominated in terms of them. In terms of regular pengos, inflation therefore worsened dramatically.

The argument divides into two parts. First, figures of the

deposit-to-note ratio for four European hyperinflations of the 1920s are presented to show that these exhibit no trend over time which could be regarded as a 'source of the 17-fold to 7 billion-fold increases in broadly defined money over the periods in question.' Then the Hungarian figures for 1944–6 are examined, showing how, in contrast, from approximate stability during the later months of 1945, the deposit/note ratio for that country rose at a fast and quickly accelerating pace from February 1946 until the date of stabilisation. The inference is that this feature of the Hungarian experience explains much of its exceptional severity. Table 8:2 illustrates.

*Table 8.2: Ratio of bank deposits to outstanding notes*

| Month | Deposit/note ratio |
|---|---|
| December, 1944 | 0.28 |
| June, 1945 | 0.22 |
| July, | 0.24 |
| August | 0.19 |
| September | 0.15 |
| October | 0.09 |
| November | 0.08 |
| December | 0.08 |
| January, 1946 | 0.09 |
| February, | 0.21 |
| March | 0.35 |
| April | 0.81 |
| May | 1.67 |
| June | 2.70 |
| July | 5.1billion |
| August | 0.14 |
| September | 0.18 |
| October | 0.20 |
| November | 0.26 |
| December | 0.29 |

*Source:* Bomberger and Makinen (1980), citing United Nations Statistical Office (1947).

The shift to indexed deposits, if it did indeed accelerate inflation, did not do so immediately. On the contrary, as Bomberger and Makinen allow, a sharply increased demand for real balances in January 1946 was initially accompanied by a temporary slowdown in inflation, with prices rising substantially less quickly than notes and deposits. By the following month, however, the effect had become evident. The deposit/note ratio had doubled and inflation had septupled to a monthly rate of 503 per cent, soaring almost continuously thereafter until stabilisation. The deposit/note ratio, on the other hand, though it subsequently rose, did not do so dramatically until the single month of July. The force of the Bomberger–Makinen argument lies, therefore, not in any close correlation, lagged or other, between the monthly deposit/note ratio and the rate of inflation, but in: (a) the marked rise in the ratio after the indexation of deposits, and (b) the sharp difference between Hungarian experience in 1945–6 and that in the four hyperinflations of the 1920s with which Bomberger and Makinen compare it. The fact is that only in the case of Hungary in 1946, when deposits were indexed, has the deposit/note ratio ever even been suggested as a major cause of inflation; and the logic of the account presented is not only consistent with the figures but persuasive in itself. If, as seems all too likely, Bomberger's and Makinen's explanation is true, we have here an early case of iatrogenic illness - an economic ill dramatically worsened by the remedy, indexation (in this case, of the currency), which was intended to alleviate it.

## THE TAX PENGO AS A PARALLEL CURRENCY

The introduction of the tax pengo in January 1945 followed in the tradition of the sparkrone of 1924, the Polish zloty of 1919, and the Soviet chervonetz. Parallel currencies have at different times been variously intended to alleviate the effects of inflation and to help curb it. In this case the initial aim was to alleviate. The short-term effect was, as we have seen, to lower prices. In the longer run, given the absence of budgetary control, the reform, by cutting the inflation tax base and so compelling the government to accelerate the production of notes for budgetary purposes, seems likely actually to have speeded up inflation as measured in terms of the old currency. And in addition the real value of the tax pengo itself began to fall, for the reasons mentioned above.

External considerations may also have had some influence,

however small. The government could not guarantee the dollar value of the tax pengo except by supporting it on the exchanges and this it failed sufficiently to do until final stabilisation. The new currency therefore depreciated against the dollar at rates varying with market expectations. Most important of all, it depreciated in its later stages because it had by then replaced the regular pengo entirely, so that its value could no longer be maintained via its exchange rate with the latter. Nogaro, following a suggestion attributed by Keynes to a Mr S. Gessel, proposes a solution to the inflation problem through the indexation of a *single* currency − by, for example, making it possible for holders of the larger banknotes to claim, from specified government offices each month, interest which would in effect restore the notes' real value. In part, the intention would be to prevent accelerations in the velocity of circulation. Unfortunately, neither Nogaro nor any subsequent writer has succeeded in developing the proposal. Certainly, to the extent that its implementation made monetary growth follow inflation automatically, it could make stabilisation more difficult to achieve. An increase in the willingness to hold money balances might, however, have some offsetting effect. As far as Hungary is concerned, the lesson to be drawn from the 1940s seems clearly to be that the task of curbing inflation under a single-currency regime can prove even more difficult that that of stabilising one currency out of two.

## SUMMARY

In the Hungarian hyperinflation, supply reductions due to wartime devastation and disruption, state deficits and money creation played dominant roles. Over-indexation of some wages made matters worse. External factors, on the other hand, were of lesser importance. Much of the interest of the episode centres on the introduction of a parallel currency, an experiment which not only failed to check inflation but which, it can persuasively be argued, greatly worsened it. Stabilisation, when it came, was orthodox but for the addition of price and wage controls − a vital modification to the traditional remedy, of which more was to be seen in subsequent inflations.

# 9 Inflation in Centrally Planned Economies

## INTRODUCTION: THE CENTRAL PLANNING MECHANISM

The Hungarian inflation of 1945-6 took place before communist rule was established and may itself have assisted that change (Falush, 1976, p. 55). Similarly, the Soviet inflation of 1917–24, though it followed the Bolshevik revolution, preceded the establishment of the Stalinist economic system. It still remains, therefore, for us to consider how far the economies of Eastern Europe have suffered from inflation under central planning.

Before the evidence is surveyed, however, an outline of the system of central planning and economic agreement used may be helpful for readers unfamiliar with it. The task of presenting it is complicated by the fact that, starting from a position of substantial uniformity in the early postwar years, the Eastern European economies have since diverged considerably. Our account is therefore a general statement of the standard, basic system, unreformed in the direction of market socialism, as it operated generally during the decades before the early 1980s, with special reference to events in the Soviet Union under Stalin and in postwar Poland. The present tense is generally used because at the time of writing it is still generally appropriate; this may not long remain so.

In the standard Eastern European CPE much the greater part of output is produced in accordance with the central plan. The exception to this rule consists of a small amount of output, usually of agricultural produce surplus to the plan, which is sold on the free or collective farm market. Output is planned initially in physical terms and in considerable detail, figures being prepared of all the inputs needed to produce the target amounts of output. To this output plan the financial planners then add prices, wages and the amounts of money available for their payment. The prices have no role in allocating resources but are purely means of reconciling real aims with the monetary system, i.e. units of account. Prime importance is attached to the achievement of the planned levels of output, especially of investment goods, rather than to any financial target. The state bank, a 'monobank',[1] directly or through specialised intermediary banks, supplies enterprises with funds in the form of bank deposits for inter-enterprise transactions and of cash for wage payments. The bank lends little or no money to individuals or, if the plan is strictly followed, to enterprises; nor do its activities give rise to monetary growth via a 'bank credit multiplier', as can happen in market economies. The bank is, in fact, a fund for allocating money primarily in order to facilitate the fulfilment of the plan, and for keeping a check on that fulfilment, rather than a bank in the western sense. Individuals and enterprises can hold deposits in it; indeed, such deposits are, apart from cash and perhaps a limited number of state bonds, the only form in which they can hold liquid assets. There are no shares, bills or other financial instruments and the ownership of foreign currencies is discouraged. Nor can enterprises lend to each other, except informally by delaying or advancing payments for each other's products. The bank's main duty, therefore, is limited to scrutinising the use of funds it has allocated to enterprises in the light of the plan's aims.

## THE EXTENT OF INFLATION IN THE CPEs

Despite the central fixing of the overwhelming majority of prices, however, and despite official claims to the contrary, inflation has not been eliminated. Its extent has been the subject of debate throughout most of the postwar period and still remains shrouded in uncertainty. The official retail price indices (apart from those for Poland, Hungary and Yugoslavia – the last not a centrally planned economy, the first two attempting in widely differing degrees to diverge from the standard model) have for most of the postwar period shown only a trivial amount of inflation; but their reliability has been questionable. Even the widely held view that Soviet price indices are not freely invented has not altogether escaped challenge. Fyodor I. Kushnirsky (1984, p. 48) writes: ' . . . when I was participating in planning calculations, the aggregate index of the cost of living was set, *by normative considerations* [emphasis added], to equal 99 per cent of the base year level, i.e. its actual values were never computed.' He concludes (p. 50) that 'cosmetic manipulation of statistics on the cost of living makes the relevant official data practically worthless.'

Short of invention, East European price statistics are distorted by misleading compilation techniques. Thus, without any rise in the official price index the following events may occur: products whose ingredients have grown too costly and for which there is no cheap substitute may be, and often are, discontinued; the quality of products may be lowered; and new and more expensive products may totally or partially replace old ones (Kuchnirsky, 1985, p. 517). Free market prices have not generally been taken into account in compiling the price index, except in Hungary and the GDR (Portes, 1977, p. 112). Existing goods may be redesigned so that they count as 'new' and can be sold at higher prices, without any effect on the index. Furthermore, the 'basket' of goods used in constructing the index is often not made clear and may be subject to undisclosed changes as well as to changes in base year and in methods of calculation. Out-of-date Baskets are often used (Csikos Nagy, quoted in Portes, 1977, p. 112). Bornstein (1978, pp. 482–5) reports in addition widespread overcharging, inadequate discounts for low quality, misuse of procedures permitting a surcharge and the charging of high prices for 'special orders'. Bribes – a form of concealed price increase – are also quite widely reported.

On the other hand, it has been argued that widely accepted figures for rising nominal incomes would be inconsistent with observed improvements in the Soviet standard of living if prices had actually risen much more than the official indices suggest. A major difficulty here is to decide what figures for nominal incomes can be accepted in an economy where, in another view, 'unofficial earnings must fill the sizeable gap between visible living standards and the real wage earnings which would be equivalent to official earnings divided by shop prices' (Cambridge, 1981, pp. 354–5). Schroeder and Severin (Joint Economic Committee of Congress, 1976) have, however, in a well-known paper attempted to resolve the problem by estimating the gap between the official index and a more realistic one. Their conclusion is that in the first three postwar decades the official Soviet index seriously underestimated the extent of overt inflation – notably between 1970 and 1975, when the official index rose by 0.5 per cent compared with a rise of over 8 per cent in a preferred alternative index. They allow, moreover, that their alternative estimate may well be too conservative.

More widely debated has been the extent of suppressed inflation, the prevalence of which in Eastern Europe has been extensively claimed by commentators both casual and professional ever since World War II. Evidence cited for the claim includes: frequent queues and shortages; free and black market prices often two and three times as high as official prices; and secondhand prices nearly or actually as high as the prices of comparable new products. Attention is also drawn to the public's rapid accumulation of cash holdings, convertible state bonds and deposits in the savings bank, which are interpreted as being, in part, 'forced' savings i.e. those which are unspendable because desired goods and services are unavailable. Finally, those who diagnose suppressed inflation point to widespread apathy at work, which is in part attributed to the absence of any incentive to earn more unspendable cash.

This view has, however, been disputed. Portes and Winter (1977, 1978, 1980), relying on econometric estimates of demand in Poland, Czechoslovakia, the GDR and Hungary for time-periods before 1976, found excess demand evident in only 33 out of 78 annual observations. Portes (1981, p. 364) argues that 'For most of the period since the mid-1950s, repressed inflation cannot be verified', adding more recently (1983, p. 152) that 'Except in Poland, recent consumer price rises in Eastern Europe are not primarily due to aggregate excess demand or the effects of world inflation.'

Others have further pointed out that none of the alleged

evidence necessarily implies the existence of suppressed inflation. In Hartwig's view (1983), Soviet citizens' decisions to accumulate liquid assets are voluntary (perhaps influenced, others have argued, by the growing availability of better housing and consumer goods) while queues demonstrate a preference for buying goods cheaply but tardily, rather than quickly but expensively in the free market. Pryor (1976) argues that queues may result from lack of adequate numbers of shop assistants and suggests, more vaguely, that the smaller number of sales staff in centrally planned economies (CPEs) for any given volume of goods marketed per head arises from cultural or political, not economic, causes. J.R. Turcan (1977) likewise, in a study of Polish retailing, argues that defects in the sales system account for some of the alleged symptoms of suppressed inflation. A widely-made point is that shortages of some goods may be offset by surpluses of others so that the general price level, if freed from controls, might show no sustained overall increase.

On a definitional issue, some writers make the point that the fixing of prices below their market-clearing level does not in itself create suppressed inflation. Inflation being a *persistent* tendency for the general price level to rise, suppressed inflation would exist only if the price gap were to increase continuously. Joyce Pickersgill (1977), who makes this point, finds no evidence of large-scale suppressed inflation in the Soviet economy. Too little is, in her view, known of the labour supply function for the causes of workplace apathy to be clear. The growth of savings may likewise result from a variety of other factors; and the Soviet Union's average and marginal propensities to save out of personal income are not unduly high by international standards. Birman and Clarke (1985), on the other hand, counter this view with the argument that, since the savings required to finance investment are deducted from Soviet workers' wages before the latter are paid, the comparison of Soviet savings propensities with those in market economies, where private savings go far to finance investment, has little or no meaning. The only conclusive test of the Portes hypothesis would presumably be to decontrol all prices and to see whether a price index based on the selection of goods bought *after* decontrol rose or fell (one based on the selection bought *before* it would certainly rise). The test has yet to be made. At present, despite all the doubts and qualifications, a majority view continues to diagnose suppressed inflation as a serious problem in Eastern Europe generally.

## INFLATIONARY MECHANISMS AND POSSIBLE REMEDIES

How, then, can open inflation arise in an economy with planned prices, incomes and outputs? Of the numerous explanations suggested the following may be mentioned:

(a) 'Overtaut planning' or 'overambitious development and investment' may be responsible. On this view overoptimistic output planning creates demand for more resources than the economy can provide. Enterprises are unable to fulfil their quotas and so the supply of goods to the market is less than is necessary to satisfy demand at the planned prices. In order to eliminate the resulting shortages and queues – sources of public discontent – the planners eventually feel obliged to raise prices. One variant on this type of explanation concentrates on uncoordinated or misconceived investment (or, as in Poland during the later 1970s and early 1980s, falling labour productivity – see G. Blazyca, 1982) as a vital element in the underfulfilment of the plan.

(b) External shocks like the two oil shocks of 1973-4 and 1979-80 may create imported inflation. In the traditional STE the effect is indirect. When import prices expressed in foreign currency rise a state price-equalisation fund initially subsidises imports, thus preventing any automatic change in domestic currency prices. The fund thus incurs a loss, however, which must be met by increased taxation or reduced public expenditure if the state budget is not to move towards or into deficit, a move which most observers, at least until recently, have held to be unwelcome to most CPE governments. Should any extra taxes be passed on in higher prices, as has often happened in the case of turnover tax, then price increases will result. A steady continuance of this process would amount to inflation. Furthermore, trade with other STEs affords no immunity from imported inflation since the prices used in intra-bloc trade have traditionally followed world market prices, albeit after a time-lag.

(c) The explanation perhaps most commonly offered centres on wages and bank credit. In this account, 'overfull employment planning', by placing unrealistic demands upon the available workforce, creates a labour shortage. Enterprises therefore resort to a variety of devices to attract more labour, upgrading workers by fudging their qualifications, setting easy piecework norms, illegitimately increasing sick benefits and holiday pay or awarding bonuses for spurious task fulfilment (Blazcya, 1982, p. 122; Hadda, 1977, p. 48). The result is that wage payments exceed those planned. Even so, the bank supplies the additional finance for the payments, in the form of extra short-term credits (which may never be repaid), because it attaches greater importance to fulfilment of the output plan than to its financial accompaniments. Since, moreover, this year's wage payments are used as a basis for next year's planned allocation, excess wages may become built into future plans (Haddad, p. 49). Similarly, overfulfilment of the plan may, because of progressive systems of piecework payment, make the wage bill rise by more than productivity. The net result in either case is that wage costs and therefore personal incomes rise in relation to the planned value of output, producing excess aggregate demand in product markets. The resulting queues and shortages may again in time induce the authorities to raise prices. If, moreover, production costs rise above the planned value of output, subsidies will be needed to maintain price stability and prevent bankruptcy, which would lead, unacceptably, to unemployment. In so far as the authorities may be reluctant to use tax increases or cuts in 'non-consumption expenditures' (a broad category of public spending including that on administration, education and health) as means of preventing budgetary imbalance, they may seek to eliminate the subsidies by raising prices.

(d) A further major possibility has recently emerged. Over a long period there was general agreement among western scholars that CPE governments aimed at, and usually achieved, balance or surplus in the state budget (e.g. Portes, 1977(I), p. 78; Millar 1981, p. 171). In this aim they succeeded to the extent that no fiscal deficit had been recorded in the Soviet Union, for instance, since 1943. Recently, however, doubt has been expressed on the issue. Igor Birman (1980; and with Roger Clarke, 1985), argues that the Soviet budget has been kept in deficit for many years in an attempt to maintain, in combination, an acceptable rate of growth, a rising standard of living and a massive armaments programme. The result, Birman claims, has been constant growth of the sum of bank credits, long-term and short-term, and an excessive money supply which (1980, p. 98) 'is undermining the basis of the planned administration of the economy' by leading to uncompleted projects (for lack of real resources), the holding of unnecessary stocks (against risk of shortages) and suppressed inflation. The claim, as we have seen, has not gone unchallenged, with dissentients including Karl-Hans Hartwig (1983) and Joyce Pickersgill (1977). Nuti (1982, pp. 23–5), however, finds a similar situation applying in Poland.

If there is indeed a huge 'overhang' of liquid assets in private Soviet hands, amounting to ten times the amount needed for normal transactions and threatening, if spent, to create overt or suppressed inflation on a gigantic scale, the question of remedial action arises. Keith Bush (1973), writing before the perceived problem became acute, followed Preobrazhensky and Stalin (A.H. Smith, 1983, p. 102) in suggesting that large imports of 'luxury' goods – tropical fruit, coffee, shoes or foreign cars – might be sold at high prices, the profit or turnover tax being used as a syphon for reducing the money supply – an interesting case of exchanging a (potential) inflation for a balance of payments burden. Sales of cooperative housing might achieve a similar effect, but ideology argues for distribution of housing according to need rather than ability to pay. Alternatively, the general level of prices might be raised dramatically, at the risk of the type of unrest which the meat price rise of 1962 provoked. Other countermeasures – a shift to market socialism, agricultural price reforms, cuts in defence or the encouragement of private enterprise, Bush regarded as being politically unacceptable; Soviet governments had thus in his view chosen inflation as the least of available evils. Alternatively, some argue, a prolonged period of budget surpluses could slowly erode the 'overhang'. More dramatically, a 1947-style monetary confiscation remains a possibility.

As for the more general problem of inflation, short of a basic reorientation towards market forces the government of a Soviet-type economy (STE) disposes of much the same general remedies as any other government:

(i) It can increase the supply of domestically produced goods and services through the central plan. In principle, this could come about either through 'extensive' growth (bringing new factors of production into use) or through 'intensive' growth (increasing the productivity of factors already in use). In a widespread view the era of extensive growth in Eastern Europe and the Soviet Union is over, unless an agreed disarmament programme makes its renewal in the civilian sector possible for a time. In the case of Poland, George Blazcya (1985) has argued that in the short to medium run improvements in efficiency could bring about faster growth. Z. Fallenbuchl (1984, p. 513), on the other hand, joins many others in regarding reform of the economic mechanism as essential for any substantial improvement in that country.

(ii) The government could freeze real wages over a period of rising labour productivity, thus allowing the supply of goods and services to increase faster than household incomes and aggregate demand. The strategy would resemble that which Garvy (1977, p. 8) and Adirim (1983, p. 1) report to have been used with success in the Soviet Union during the early postwar years.

(iii) The government could cut real wages, either by cutting money wages, or by freezing money wages while prices were increased. Neither course would be popular in STEs, where public sensitivity to real wage cuts is often intense. Even so, in an era of slowing growth the view that such policies are non-starters (Portes, 1977, p. 4; Haddad, 1977, p. 48; and for Hungary, Csikos Nagy, 1983, p. 3; and Huszti, 1977, p. 74) may yet need revision.

(iv) The government could restrict credit to enterprises, thus preventing wage drift and the acquisition of excess liquidity by firms. The risk would be that enterprises short of finance might fail to fulfil output plans which were otherwise physically achievable, for lack of the necessary finance.

(v) The government could cut 'non-consumption expenditures'.

(vi) It could scale down its plans for output and investment, reducing the desired level of aggregate demand.

(vii) It could raise income tax or profits tax, prohibiting any possible (but in any case very unlikely) shifting forward of the extra tax in the form of higher prices or wages, and add the additional revenue to the receipts of the state budget. In the Soviet Union at least, where income tax revenue has been continuously at a low level, there seem to be no signs of this method having been adopted.

(viii) It could raise turnover tax. Since this tax is shifted forward there is no presumption that this, the response most widely reported to be adopted in practice in the Soviet Union, would serve to prevent inflation.

## SOVIET INFLATION UNDER STALIN

Of the periods during which open or suppressed inflation, or both, did by general consent occur in the STEs, we pick two for brief narration. The most marked example of open inflation in the Soviet Union after the stabilisation of 1924 arose between 1928 and 1947. There is little doubt that the beginning of the inflation arose from the introduction of Stalin's first Five Year Plan and the overambitious non-consumption and wage expenditures which accompanied it (see, e.g. Holzman, 1960). Thus, not only did investment, in the planning of which costs were underestimated, rise sharply. In addition, estimates for wages, fuel needs and overheads were exceeded and raw materials were reported to have been wasted (see e.g. Hubbard, 1936). The demand for labour was high and the system of monetary control proved inadequate (Garvy, 1977, p. 28), notably in restraining the growth of wage payments. Numbers in employment rose fast and average wages over the economy as a whole soared, with household incomes far above those planned, while errors in management led to concurrent supply shortfalls. Events, in short, resembled the models outlined in both (a) and (c) above.

Rationing, introduced in the winter of 1928–9, partially

substituted suppressed for overt inflation. Scarcities of basic goods became widespread; the black market flourished; and free market prices rose far above the prices of similar rationed goods. Figures quoted by Holzman (1960, p. 168) record a thirtyfold maximum rise in collective farm market prices between 1928 and 1932, but a mere doubling of comparable prices in state stores.

The years up to 1932 – years of extreme hardship and turmoil accompanying farm collectivism – saw the gravest inflation, after which for some years free market prices declined again. State retail prices, however, continued their upward trend. In the late 1930s a period of temporarily slower inflation followed the imposition of controls on labour mobility designed to cut wage drift and of tighter curbs on enterprises' expenditure, the latter introduced in 1939. Holzman is, however, reluctant to cite the 1939 measure as a cause of slower inflation, pointing to the continuation of monetary laxity even after it. Despite severe tax increases inflation continued through the war and early postwar years, reinforced first by further ambitious plans insufficiently tightly financed and subsequently by the immense strains of the war effort. Holzman gives estimates showing consumer goods prices in state and cooperative stores as having risen by a factor of about 39 between 1928 and the fourth quarter of 1947; for the collective farm market his corresponding figure is 115. Clarke and Matko (1983 (1972), pp. 216–17, drawing on Garvy (1974, pp. 316–17) and Moorsteen and Powell (1966, p. 565)), cite figures broadly supporting an inflation of this order of magnitude. Currency reform was decreed on 14 December 1947. By then, according to official data, the volume of banknotes in circulation had quadrupled during the war alone. The reform resembled not only the monetary confiscation which accompanied the end of rationing in 1935–6 but also, in outline, the reforms introduced in Central Europe in the 1920s. Privately held cash was compulsorily exchanged at a rate of ten old roubles for one new one, deposits of less than 3000 roubles in savings banks at a rate of one for one, but bigger holdings at less favourable rates. In effect, a progressive tax was levied on savings deposits. State bonds were exchanged at a rate of one for three. The rates chosen thus discriminated strongly against the peasants, whose assets were more likely to be held in cash than were those of town-dwellers. A simultaneous restructuring of prices as rationing ended reduced the overall level of state retail prices by some 17 per cent and in addition, the government continued its policy of requiring virtually compulsory purchases of state bonds. In these ways price stability was achieved, though at the cost of some hardship to those on low incomes whom rationing at low prices had previously protected.

With output of consumers' goods increasing over the following years the government chose to reduce prices in the years 1949–53. How far these reductions accompanied a genuine and well-sustained end to underlying inflationary pressures generally, or how far administered price cuts were made 'in reckless defiance of economic laws', remains a matter of some debate (Bush, 1973, p. 99; Bornstein, 1962, p. 92; Holzman, 1960 and 1962, Chapter II; Adirim, 1983, p. 70), though majority opinion favours the first explanation. Stabilisation was in any event achieved in a manner somewhat similar to the 'League of Nations' method. True, no new currency or currency unit was introduced and no external loan or guarantee involved; like the Hungarian reform of 1946 the reform was carried out purely through the country's own efforts. It involved, however, traditional elements. The money stock was reduced; this, together with the readjustment of prices (by plan rather than market forces on this occasion), produced a closer matching of aggregate supply and demand; and strict measures designed to avert excess demand in the future were taken. The state trading system similarly continued to guard against inflation. Measures to reform the central bank, normally at the core of interwar capitalist stabilisations, were not, however, taken in a country where there could be no suggestion of the bank's becoming independent of government, and where the minor role allotted to foreign trade greatly weakened any case for relating the money stock to the gold and foreign exchange reserves.

The Soviet stabilisation does not, however, seem to have brought about recession. Official statistics for the period are exceedingly few and the figures for grain production are known to be greatly exaggerated, but Alec Nove (1969, p. 291) reports general agreement that during the period 1946–50 industrial output rose very quickly, with the investment plan reported as substantially exceeded and a widespread dramatic expansion in output and employment. The episode seems to contrast sharply with stabilisations in market economies, both before and since, among which we have found no unambiguous example of one which was costless in the long run in terms of output foregone.

A familiar argument may explain the contrast. In market economies recession follows stabilisation chiefly for two reasons. First, during the inflation labour and other resources are drawn into speculative activities in which, when inflation halts, they are no longer needed. Until they can be redeployed a period of lower output and employment ensues. Second, recession results from a fall in the velocity with which money circulates. As people cease to expect money to depreciate, their demand for cash holdings rises and the level of demand for goods and services correspondingly falls. Third, recently-incurred debts can no longer be repaid in depreciated currency and insolvencies result.

In CPEs these effects are far smaller. With wages, prices and the pattern of output and employment planned, the scope for speculative activities, even including illegal ones, is generally much less. Furthermore, under the CPEs' monetary system the authorities aim to keep the public's holdings of cash to a minimum (see e.g. Garvy, 1966, p. 47), thus limiting the scope for variations in velocity, while payments between government and enterprises are non-cash book transfers made only in accordance with the plan. Both these features strictly limit variations in the level of demand.

The argument is generally accepted, even though planning errors occur. Errors of 'underplanning' (setting output targets below the maximum physically possible) will tend to lead to overfulfilment of the plan (which is regarded as a desirable goal), not to unemployment. Errors of 'overplanning', such as were in fact made in the Soviet Union, obviously do not create recession. Rather did they, after the 1947 reform, place a renewed strain on resources such that by the early 1950s the gap between official and free market prices was again widening. A tentative conclusion on the Soviet evidence would therefore be that the 1947 stabilisation within a planned economy did avoid the usual costs in the form of recession. It seems, however, to have been only at best temporarily successful in removing inflationary pressures, and then at some considerable cost in the form of microeconomic inefficiencies.

## POSTWAR POLAND

The postwar Polish economy deserves note as one of the least successful of the European CPEs in curbing inflation. For the year 1955–75 the annual rise in its consumer price index averaged about 1.5 per cent, higher than in any Eastern European country except Yugoslavia. The later 1970s saw, moreover, the beginnings of a marked acceleration of the trend, as Table 9.1 shows.

*Table 9.1: Recorded Open Inflation in Poland, 1971–82*
*(% change)*

|      | Prices of consumer goods and services | Cost of living |
| --- | --- | --- |
| 1971 | − 0.1 | − 0.2 |
| 1972 | − 0.1 | − 0.2 |
| 1973 | + 0.5 | + 0.3 |
| 1974 | + 6.4 | + 4.7 |
| 1975 | + 6.2 | + 7.5 |
| 1976 | + 4.4 | + 4.7 |
| 1977 | + 5.1 | + 4.8 |
| 1978 | + 8.1 | + 8.7 |
| 1979 | + 7.0 | + 6.8 |
| 1980 | + 13.5 | + 13.0 |
| 1981 | + 33.3 | + 38.2 |
| 1982 | + 100.8 | + 101.5 |

*Source:* P.T. Wanless (1985), p. 405.

Up to a point the Polish experience resembles quite closely that in other CPEs. After a more than 100-fold rise in retail prices between 1938 and early 1945, the Three Year Plan of 1947–49, later admitted to have been overambitious, was accompanied by a rise of over 400 per cent in investment costs (mainly wages) and by inevitable price increases. With the launching of the Six Year Plan for 1950–5 and an expansion of defence expenditure in the wake of the Korean War, excess demand created by above-plan wage payments made counterinflationary measures urgent. In the autumn of 1950 a monetary reform converted all prices, wages and savings accounts at the rate of 100 old zlotys for three new ones and all cash holdings at 100 for 1, the effect being to confiscate two-thirds of the population's real cash holdings. The reform did not, however, halt inflation and between September 1951 and January 1953 rationing of basic foods and meat was reintroduced in towns. Periodic further reintroductions were to continue into the 1980s.

By general consent one underlying mechanism at work throughout our period was the same combination of models (a) and (c) above as was observed in the Soviet Union. Throughout the 1950s attempts to fulfil ambitious output targets, accompanied by lax control over enterprises' expenditures, produced rapid wage increases. 'Overplan' wages were, moreover, automatically provided to finance overplan output falling within wide categories. Between 1949 and 1956 the wage bill for all non-agricultural workers (excluding those in handicrafts) rose more than fourfold, with only one quarter of the increase reflecting the growth of the labour force. Montias (1962, pp. 71–2) detects continuing inflationary pressures in 1953–6 and relates the substantial wage increases of the next two years to the sharp rises in overt inflation. Ehrlich (1959), too, reports capacity shortages and excess demand.

That the Polish government itself attributed an important part of the inflation of the 1950s to insufficiently tight control of wages is evident from the policy changes it introduced. In 1957 a new principle of wage control became law, under which 'unjustified' expenditures could subsequently be recouped by the central authorities and any overfulfilment of an enterprise's output plan would entitle it to a less than proportional increase in its wage plan. Again, in 1964 further changes provided that wage plans should not be automatically adjustable because of output overfulfilment or past wage expenditures. Central control over the wage bill was thus tightened.

Writing of the 1950s, Montias (op. cit., p. 139) sees the foregoing process as part of an inflationary spiral. In his account, when wage rises forced the government to raise prices in order to curb industrial subsidies, the resulting rise in the cost of enterprises' inventories necessitated the extension to them of further credits. The excess liquidity thus created led to unplanned purchases of inputs, including labour at wages bid up still further by high demand, and the inflationary spiral then began a new turn.

That the same combination of overoptimistic planning and excessive wage growth prevailed in and after the 1970s is common ground among commentators, with excessive investment plans and the absence of any effective incomes policy during Gierek's 'dash for growth' producing at once wage–push and demand–pull. The process received fresh momentum in August 1980 when the Gdansk Agreement raised workers' incomes by as much as one third (Nuti, 1982, p. 60). The problem remains one deeply embedded not merely in planners' hopes but also in the psychology of ordinary citizens. It is, in Alex Pravda's words, 'a textbook illustration of how discontinuous and unbalanced economic development can foster a gap between expectations and performance'; to which Nuti (1982, p. 48) adds that 'The majority of the population does not seem to understand the connection between the country's economic situation and their own individual consumption', preserving instead the illusion that protests can always reverse price rises.

Other strands also appeared in the Polish inflationary process. One, obviously, stemmed from imported inflation following the deterioration in Poland's terms of trade which resulted, after time lags, from the oil shocks and upsurges in other raw material prices on world markets in 1973–4 and 1979–80. The impact of these was amplified for Poland by the very high degree of energy-intensiveness of the economy. Furthermore, the effects were felt more quickly when, after the reforms made in 1973, the price equalisation system was (temporarily) abandoned. A reduction, in 1975, in the time-lag by which the trading prices of the CMEA followed behind world prices had a similar effect. Hare and Wanless (e.g. 1981, p. 513) suggest, in addition, that as world inflation brought about sudden increases in the value of Polish enterprises' sales abroad the effect was to raise profits and value added and thence, because of links between output and the wage plan, overall wage bills.

A second inflationary strand lay in the authorities' attempts, first in 1973–4 and again in 1981–2, to devolve to individual enterprises both some price-fixing powers (in 1973, for new products) and also a degree of self-management. Nuti (op. cit., p. 23), Hare and Wanless (for 1973–4, 1981, p. 502), and Gomulka and Rostowski (for 1981–2, 1984, p. 399) agree in attributing to these moves, at times of excess demand and in a country where monopolistic markets are common, a part of the blame for price increases. Considering the 1981–2 reforms, which aimed to devolve certain managerial powers even as far as to the workforce and which were accompanied by the establishment of self-managed organisations on a large scale (Nuti, 1982, p. 39), Gomulka and Rostowski conclude that enterprises' main aim thereafter was the maximisation of after-tax wages and bonuses, including retained profits, per employee. This part of the story thus importantly resembles that which, for example, Prout (1985, p. 21), Sirc (1979, p. 93), Duncan Wilson (1979, p. 108) and Saul Estrin (1982) tell for Yugoslavia under self-management. The moral drawn is also similar: 'the economy . . . appears increasingly strongly to be drifting under the influence of anarchic processes, controlled neither by market nor plan' (quoted by Blazyca, op. cit., p. 117, from W. Brus, 1979). Self-management, with workers running state-owned enterprises under conditions of market competition, may still prove to be workable. There are, however, no signs that it has yet been given a fair trial in Eastern Europe.

More clearly, perhaps, than in any of our inflationary episodes, the course of Polish inflation during our period was marked by a visible struggle over the distribution of available output. This broadly followed a distinct pattern, peaking in 1956, 1970, 1976 and 1980. On each occasion an attempted price rise was followed by popular protest taking the form of strikes and demonstrations, and, after violent and often bloody suppression, at least a partial or temporary government climbdown. Mieczkowski (1978), among others, was quick to detect a cyclical mechanism at work, with governmental strength leading to cuts in real consumption, then protests weakening the Party's hold and forcing the government to adopt, for a time, a more lenient policy towards the consumer.

If there was indeed a cycle, at least a temporary break in it seems to have occurred after the 1970s, though less in 1980, when wage increases were granted in preference to a reversal of price increases, than in 1982, when under martial law meat prices, an unusually sensitive variable, were raised without open opposition. The inflationary struggle has, moreover, been about more than the allocation of shares in income. As Brus (1973, p. 109) points out, the slogan used in a student demonstration brutally suppressed in March 1968 — 'There is no bread without liberty' — unmistakeably linked economic with political claims in a way which revived memories of workers' protests in June 1956. Growing wage–push was supplemented by growing vote push. This openness of political and sectional conflict, evident in the literature's continual references to 'scissor-type' redistributions between town and country, as well as to the consumption-investment conflict, lends support to a 'power struggle' theory of the inflation and may help to explain why inflation in the three decades after 1950 was worse in Poland than in any other communist country except Yugoslavia (where, again, central government failed to impose a solution upon warring economic, regional and bureaucratic groups).

Perhaps the most distinctive feature of all, however, has been the continual failure of domestic supply in Poland. As early as 1969 substantial underfulfilment of the planned output of consumer goods prompted the real and nominal wage cuts which led to the 1970 crisis. More recently accounts of the falling productivity and structural imbalance of the Gierek years have begun to read, on paper at least, strikingly like those of countries traditionally described as 'underdeveloped'. Huge foreign borrowing; consequent high dependency on western countries for current as well as capital imports; investment drives aimed at long-run import-substituting industrialisation; an obsession with large scale projects; bottlenecks in the form of stagnant agricultural output; uncontrolled public spending; a weak balance of payments; the deliberate choice of inflation as a way of veiling inter-group conflict — all the familiar symptoms have been reported. As in Latin America, unbalanced growth is widely attributed to bureaucratic incompetence and corruption; but in Poland low labour morale has also frequently been cited. The overall outcome, at all events, has been to contribute towards an inflation which has at times owed more to supply-side deficiencies than any other purely peacetime inflation considered here.


## PROBLEMS OF CURING INFLATION

Apart from slowing the planned rate of growth and attempting to effect the transfer of technology from abroad, governments in Soviet-type economies (STEs) have used other policies, more familiar to Western governments, against inflation. Two in particular deserve mention.

First, a policy has often been adopted of subsidising, and so stabilising, the price of basic wage goods, even when the cost of producing those goods has been rising. This can be regarded as an indirect form of wage indexation, the aim being to safeguard to some extent workers' real wages. The Polish experience exemplifies with great clarity the dilemma such a policy poses. On the one hand, the ever-growing subsidies to which the policy can give rise may themselves push the budget into inflationary deficits. On the other, attempts to phase out the subsidies may lead to violent protest and possible wage explosion. The Polish authorities, treading a precarious path between the two dangers, fell into one or other pitfall more often than they succeeded in neutralising the inflation peacefully. Their task may, however, have been an impossible one, given the fundamental nature of the economy and the unpopularity of the regime. No general lesson seems, therefore, to present itself. As in connection with systems of indexation more generally, the right extent and timing of such a policy is a matter of nice judgement, varying according to a thousand particular circumstances.

Second, Poland, among other CPEs, sought during our period to strengthen its external position against the depredations of internal and external inflation by what are termed 'internal exports' – the sale of goods in state stores for foreign currency (Nuti, op. cit., p. 21). The noteworthy thing here is that the incentive to citizens to disburse their hard currency in this case was not that which brought gold and dollars flooding back to the reserves after stabilisations in the 1920s – not, in short, a restoration of confidence in the domestic currency. What made people part with hard currency this time was a (perhaps momentary) restoration of the chance to use currency for high quality purchases. The more fundamental problem of inducing citizens to want to hold domestic currency or to spend it on domestic products remained to be solved.

## DO STE GOVERNMENTS SHUN INFLATION?

The view has long been widespread that STE governments neither need nor want inflation and are consequently willing to adopt strict 'monetarist' measures to curb it. The argument can be couched in terms of the 'equation of exchange', $MV = PT$, though in a rather unorthodox manner. The traditional presentation of the equation postulates that the volume of transactions, $T$, and the velocity of circulation, $V$, are reasonably constant, so that the price level, $P$, changes in fixed proportion with the money stock, $M$. The interpretation of the equation suggested in connection with STEs, however, takes $V$ and $P$ to be held constant and sees the government as consciously adjusting the money stock to accommodate changes in the volume of transactions. Portes (1977, pp. 76–8) argues that one reason why STEs avoid inflation is that central planning and control render it unnecessary as a means of achieving full employment or of bringing about a desired distribution of real income. In this view, STEs do not rely on money illusion – the mistaking of money income for real income which can arise when people neglect changes in the price level – to soften or conceal the impact of unpopular policies. Changes in prices are also unwelcome because they involve huge administrative costs. The experience of the interwar hyperinflations, moreover, still exerts strong influence on Eastern European governments. Even suppressed inflation and its accompanying queues, shortages and involuntary savings are wherever possible avoided as focuses of discontent and sources of potential instability. Bergson, likewise (1964, e.g. pp. 65–6), has emphasised the great merits of price stability in Soviet eyes.

In recent years the limitations of this view have been increasingly discussed. Keith Bush (1973, p. 104) argues that the Soviet Union has deliberately chosen inflation as a lesser evil than alternatives such as a partial retreat from central planning or cuts in defence and heavy industry. In Poland and Hungary inflation has indeed been built into the plan in recent years. Possibly (Wanless, 1985, p. 414) its purpose is to 'mop up' excess demand. More radically, Igor Birman has, as we have seen, claimed that the Soviet Union, far from being 'monetarist', has for long been building up a cumulative budget deficit amounting at the end of 1977 to about 254 billion roubles. Such huge public holdings of liquid assets constitute a potential source of future inflation not only in the Soviet Union (Zwass, 1979, p. 74; Kaser, 1982, p. 192) but also in Poland (Nuti, 1982, p. 60). Other writers remind us that the so-called 'Mikoyan Doctrine' (that aggregate demand should be planned so as to exceed supply in order to ensure maximum employment and growth) represents another inflationary strand in official Soviet thinking.

Even the absence of strategies involving money illusion (defined above) in CPEs has been questioned. Holzman attributes the extensive use of turnover tax in the Soviet Union to the need for such an illusion to conceal the high tax burden, while Adirim (1983, p. 84) reports that 'inflation is useful as a means to gloss over economic inconsistencies. It is a means to "camouflage" unfulfilled plans . . ... Inflationary prices serve a redistributive function; an indispensable tool in the hands of planners . . .' For Poland, Z. Fallenbuchl (1984, p. 520) claims deliberate use of money illusion in the early 1980s, to soften the perceived scale of economic problems. Views on the 'usefulness' of inflation to STE governments thus by now cover a wide range. At one end of the range we have the view that STEs shun inflation. At the other we have Kushnirsky's (1984, p. 53) unorthodox, claim that 'fighting inflation is not a priority for Soviet authorities'. Close to this, too, is Haddad's outlying view (1977) that in CPEs both the evils of inflation and also the costs of curbing it are small. Thus inflation itself has, in this view, no effect on unemployment, the balance of payments or the distribution of income, and no tendency to produce such phenomena as wage push and wage leapfrogging. Equally, attempts to end it have a low cost in that they do not curb growth. Haddad's conclusion is that 'Soviet-type inflation cannot be regarded as an evil; it is merely an inconvenience to consumers' (p. 51).

## CONCLUSIONS: CPEs AND INFLATION

Are CPEs better able to prevent or cure inflation than market economies. Have western countries anything to learn from their experience?

Naive claims such as that made by the eminent Soviet economist, Ia.A. Kronrod, that 'inflation in a socialist society has been eliminated' (cited Bush, 1973, p. 97) clearly cannot be sustained. Nor, any longer, can the claim that the CPEs of Eastern Europe have since the mid-1950s been substantially free from inflationary symptoms. This is especially true where trade deficits and growing foreign debt can be interpreted as a partial substitute for (or 'exporting' of) inflation.

Even where overt inflation has been small the claim that the commonly encountered substitute − suppressed inflation − does not produce comparable ill-effects requires major qualification. The effects in question are normally, in market economies, taken to include: self-aggravating tendencies which if unchecked lead to the anarchy of hyperinflation; payments deficits leading to successive devaluations with their supporting deflationary policies; greater uncertainty about future prices, making investment decisions harder; and distortions in the pattern of income distribution, production, investment and employment. As our discussion has made clear, central planning possesses weapons designed to avoid uncontrolled trends of any kind, insulate external payments from internal prices, remove uncertainty, and insist on a desired pattern of output, employment and investment. The trouble is that in practice, given a large measure of freedom of employment for citizens and the right to buy according to taste, suppressed inflation in its turn produces major problems. Real welfare is redistributed through the extra advantages conferred on those who have time for queuing, money to spend on the free market or for bribery, and the privileges of office and status. The accumulation of cash balances which cannot purchase any desired goods lessens the will to work and diverts efforts into legal or illegal secondary activities – a covert distortion of the pattern of employment. If, moreover, as most western writers suggest, central planning is inseparable in practice from otherwise avoidable micro-efficiencies, supply deficiencies may themselves tend to worsen inflationary pressures.

The advantages in combating inflation are therefore by no means all on the side of central planning. Of Soviet-type economies generally Roger Clarke (1983, p. 530) has written: 'there is a broad consensus that the prospects . . . are now gloomy. With the exception of Hungary, they are seen as clinging on to a system which is at best outdated and increasingly unsuited to its current circumstances and tasks.' The aspects of central planning most relevant to the avoidance and cure of inflation form no exception to this judgement. Possibly, what Western countries can learn from the CPEs, in this as in other respects, may in part depend on precisely which elements of central planning, if any, can be divorced from the overall system and introduced on an eclectic basis in a market-socialist economy. Until this is known, however, the case for central planning as a guard against inflation remains unproven.

## NOTE

1. Hungary's banking system affords a recent marked exception to this account.

# 10 The Upsurge in World Inflation After 1965

Little doubt is expressed, even by those writers who add certain reservations, that the great world inflation of the seventeen years following 1965 had its origins in the United States and in the increase in defence expenditure which accompanied intensification of the war in Vietnam. During the late 1960s other countries certainly added momentum to the trend. In the United Kingdom wages rose ahead of prices in 1968–9 as trade unions competed, first to regain ground lost during the preceding period of more strictly enforced incomes policy, then to take full advantage of the easing of restraints which they rightly expected would precede a general election. In France the disturbances of May–June 1968 were followed by a settlement leading to a 12–14 per cent general rise in wages, a shortening of working hours and increases in fringe benefits, all of them strengthening inflationary pressures. The following year Italy saw similar disturbances. None of these, however, could impart anything like the momentum of the American boom to world inflation.

Excess demand in the United States was becoming evident in 1968. It transmitted its effects abroad chiefly in three ways: by raising the prices of American exports; by stimulating American demand for imports of foreign goods; and by increasing, via a worsening deficit in external payments, foreign holdings of dollars and other US liabilities and thereby permitting, and perhaps encouraging, expansionary policies abroad.

The first of these channels was not at first important since

American prices were rising no faster than those in many other countries. The second likewise added only a small amount to other inflationary pressures. Over the entire period of the first inflationary episode, 1965–75, the third channel was much the most important. It therefore deserves special mention.

Throughout the postwar period the dollar had been the world's main reserve currency, tied to gold at a price of $35 to the fine ounce and maintained at that level, whenever necessary, by sales from the United States' gold reserve. By the mid-1960s a system of this kind was beginning to look unsustainable. The growing weakness of the United States' currency account can be traced back as far as 1949, when many other countries followed the British example by devaluing their currencies. To this were added the effects of postwar recovery in Europe and Japan, the foreign exchange costs of the Korean War and the burden of extensive foreign aid and military expenditure. With the non-communist world's gold production stagnant in the mid-1960s and with Soviet sales drying up, a world shortage of reserves was widely predicted and there took place a marked rise in speculative and savings demand for gold. In the early 1960s the chief banking countries set up a gold pool which would enable them collectively to intervene in the market in order to maintain the gold price. The underlying assumption was that the gold pool as a whole would on balance be in surplus and thus able to play this role; but as the perceived threat of scarcity grew the gold pool countries became less and less sure of their ability to maintain the surplus of reserves on which the system rested. The United States, one of the most vulnerable of them and the central support of the system, brought pressure to bear on other industrial countries to hold their reserves in the form of dollars rather than gold; but the French decision in June 1967 to stop participating in the pool's gold sales was merely one of many symptoms of the impending collapse of the Bretton Woods system, which was to accompany and perhaps exacerbate the inflation of the early 1970s.

The detailed developments of the period need not concern us here. It is sufficient to note that in March 1968, in response to a renewed bout of speculative turmoil in the exchange markets, a new two-tier gold system was introduced. Under this the price of monetary gold used in the settlement of deficits between central

banks was to be held at $35 but central banks undertook neither
to sell nor buy gold in the market, where supply and demand
would be free to determine the price. The new system can
scarcely be said to have tackled the underlying problem
satisfactorily. The continuing dramatic growth in world trade –
combined, some would add, with the maldistribution of world
reserves – necessitated additions to the volume of those
reserves; and any such additions usually had to take the form of
foreign exchange, notably dollars. Yet loans of foreign
exchange, including dollars, to deficit countries were in practice
made only through *ad hoc* arrangements in times of crisis.
Continual crisis was thus a precondition of the adequate growth
of world reserves. Still worse, the American payments deficits,[1]
which permitted world reserves to rise, themselves created a
major threat of crisis by undermining confidence in the dollar's
future value.

In 1970 matters began to take a further substantial turn for the
worse. Foreign private holders of US liabilities began on a large
scale to shift out of dollars, which were then taken up by official
monetary authorities. Mainly for this reason, but also because
of a marked deterioration in the American external deficit, the
world's official dollar reserves trebled in the course of 1970–1.
Such a growth not only weakened any external constraints
which foreign governments may have felt in contemplating the
creation of domestic booms; it also stimulated speculation by
creating expectations that the massive dollar overhang would
before long inevitably lead to the revaluation of gold.


## THE BOOM OF THE EARLY 1970s

Through the recession of 1970 world inflation abated little, with
wages in many countries still buoyant in accordance with what
the Bank for International Settlements (1967, p. 7) had long
before termed 'a familiar refrain: the boom has ended, but the
wage–push lingers on.' A number of factors prompted the
upsurge of inflation which was to follow in the early 1970s. First,
a simultaneous boom in many industrial countries, often
assisted by governments' fiscal and monetary policies, helped to
boost aggregate demand worldwide to high levels. A number of

possible explanations of the boom have been suggested. One is that governments outside the United States, embarrassed by the accumulation of dollar reserves which could only be invested at interest rates lower than the value of the real resources foregone by continuing to hold them, chose to 'inflate away' their surpluses by stimulating booms. According to this explanation the creation of inflation was voluntary, even 'optimal', for the spenders.

Another 'voluntary' explanation is that the boom resulted principally from the coincidence, in the second half of 1972 and the first half of 1973, of major elections in the United States, Canada, Germany, Italy, France and Japan. This view assumes that the industrial countries generally displayed the well-documented tendency of British and American governments to stimulate pre-election booms (Tufte, 1975, pp. 65–70; Dow, 1964, pp. 78–9; Hutchison, 1968, p. 123). In the case of the United States, Stein (1984) and Tufte present strong testimony to President Nixon's belief that economic stagnation was a major cause of electoral defeat for governments; while Blinder (1979) and Gordon (1981, p. 389) report widespread attribution of the boom, at least in substantial part, to electoral calculation.

A widespread view, then, would be that high American spending, via a payments deficit, stimulated expansion elsewhere. Another view, however, claims that during the 1971–4 boom most countries aimed at some growth of reserves rather than at 'spending reserves away', and thus *imposed* a deficit upon the dollar. On this line of reasoning the worldwide boom, whether stimulated in order to win elections or to cut unemployment, overshot and produced inflation as an unintended and unforeseen outcome, with the American external deficit a necessary means to achieving the boom rather than an active cause of it. The extent to which official forecasts in many countries underpredicted inflation may be cited as a reason why European and other governments allowed their booms to overshoot so dramatically. It must, however, be borne in mind that the overflow of dollars from the United States long preceded the 1972–3 boom, while the economic climate in other industrial countries at that time was much more favourable to expansion than to reserve accumulation. On the whole the claim that the US deficit was incurred under duress seems less than convincing.

How far the Nixon administration was influenced in its policies by the United States' ability, as the issuer of a reserve currency, to run a payments deficit in excess of what would be possible for a non-reserve currency is another debated issue. Whatever the psychological causation, reserve currency status certainly freed the United States from balance of payments constraints which would otherwise have compelled it to curb inflation earlier. When inflation helped to produce a payments deficit other countries were willing to absorb the resulting outflow of dollars and to hold dollar assets yielding rates of interest slightly comparable rates elsewhere. The system did not make US borrowing costless or remove the risk of loss of confidence in the dollar's value; on the contrary, the signs of such a loss became increasingly evident as the 1960s and early 1970s progressed. None the less, the dollar's role as a reserve currency under fixed exchange rates certainly freed the United States from what would otherwise have been strong incentives for avoiding inflation.

Throughout the whole of our period the United States' basic balance of payments, comprising the current account plus the long-term capital account, showed a deficit which was both large and, on trend, increasing. Initially it was financed by an inflow of short-term capital but by 1970, when that year's deficit coincided with repayment of short-term funds borrowed to finance the previous year's deficit, the underlying trend became startlingly evident. Differences in national monetary policies and rates of interest joined with speculative movements of funds arising from uncertainty about the dollar's future value to produce huge worldwide capital movements, notably out of the United States, and during the three years beginning 1970 global reserves approximately doubled. This was followed by a further sharp rise in 1973, of which roughly one third was attributable to valuation changes, notably in the prices of gold and the dollar, as a result of floating. The growth was, statistically, still further swollen by the fact that when official dollar holdings abroad were placed in the Eurocurrency markets and on-lent to foreign residents who exchanged them for local currency the funds appeared twice in measures of world foreign exchange reserves.

Even this staggering growth did not of itself, however, assure world inflation. If governments generally had been more aware of the precarious and ephemeral nature of reserve gains, if there had been no synchronised boom, if forecasts worldwide had not so regularly underestimated the effects on prices, or if a shortage of new monetary gold had not changed the proportions in which reserves of gold and dollars were held in such a way as to threaten dollar convertibility, the inflation might not have occurred. But in retrospect at least, to envisage such a situation seems like indulging in fantasy. The actual outcome emerged in August 1971 when President Nixon, simultaneously with his announcement of the New Economic Policy of wage and price controls, allowed the dollar to float and thus inaugurated (except during one short period of reversion to fixed rates after the Smithsonian conference of December 1971) the era of generalised floating.

The relationship of inflation to floating proved to be complex. There is, on the one hand, widespread agreement that by 1971 the divergence of national rates of inflation made some degree of exchange rate flexibility inevitable. How far floating itself made world inflation worse than it would otherwise have been has been the subject of more debate. As Corden (1977) points out, theoretical analysis presents no unambiguous presumption either way. Under fixed rates a country's tendency to inflate is restrained by fear of payments deficits. Increases in its export prices, however, are transmitted automatically and without modification to trading partners. Under floating rates, by contrast, a country is, according to usual doctrine, freer to choose its desired individual rate of inflation. If it chooses a high one the continual depreciation of its exchange rate will tend, it is argued, to restore balance to its international trade, preventing a rise in the foreign currency price of its exports. The likelihood of its trading partners' importing inflation from it is thus reduced. In the case of perfectly adjusting markets for goods and money and in the absence of disturbing flows of capital, imported inflation may indeed even be eliminated. True, the increase in each country's freedom to choose its own rate of inflation may still be claimed as a likely source of accelerated world inflation. On the other hand, although some countries may choose to have more inflation than they would under fixed rates, others may choose less. No overall outcome for the whole world is therefore to be presumed.

To this claim a counter-argument may be presented. Under floating rates, it may be argued, some countries will choose to inflate more than they would have done under fixed rates; while those who would ideally prefer to inflate less will be unable to do so because of the impossibility of cutting money wages. The overall effect of floating, worldwide, will therefore be to worsen inflation. In times of high general inflation, however, such a counterargument based on asymmetry is no longer valid. The objection to it is that, in a time of general severe inflation, an absolute fall in money wages and prices in inflation-avoiding countries is not needed for floating to produce the full symmetrical effect of raising inflation in some countries and lowering it in others. All that is needed is a cut in the *rate of increase* in prices and wages in the inflation-avoiding country; and the rigidity of money wages does not prevent this. If such a fall in the inflation rate does take place in some countries, it will offset the rise which may take place in others. The process need not, therefore, be asymmetrical.

In the circumstances, the question whether general floating worsened world inflation seems strangely unreal. Too many exogenous shocks affected the world economy in the 1970s for fixed rates to have survived generally; and a comparison between floating rates and rates notionally fixed but in fact continually subject to adjustment in unspecifiable ways is too vague for consideration. During the final years of fixed rates, however, a number of asymmetries seem to have worked in favour of higher worldwide inflation. Surplus countries chose to inflate away part of their growing reserves rather than revalue at the risk of increased unemployment, while deficit countries allowed their exchange rate to depreciate, raising the domestic prices of tradeable goods. Similarly, when exchange rate flexibility became increasingly widespread, the downward adjustment of internal prices resulting from currency appreciation seems to have been weaker than the upward adjustments following currency depreciations.

In addition, the startling growth of the world money supply and of reserves, in company with the world boom, brought many parts of the industrial countries' economies to capacity working. From 1972 an accelerating rise in the prices of many commodities, notably foodstuffs and other agricultural products, became increasingly evident. In the twelve months to December 1973, at the peak of the price boom, Moody's index of dollar commodity prices rose 46 per cent, Reuter's index of sterling commodity prices by 80 per cent and *The Economist*'s wider sterling index by 65 per cent. Over the three years 1971–4 the last of these rose, unprecedentedly, by 159 per cent. The boom culminated in the last quarter of 1973 when, after earlier small increases, the OPEC countries, intervening to exert economic pressure upon western countries in the course of the Arab–Israeli war, cut back production and announced, in two stages, a quadrupling of the price of their crude oil.

That the rise in primary commodity prices was an important cause of world inflation in this period is scarcely to be doubted. For the United States, Popkin (1977, p. 256) has attributed 45 per cent of the rise in consumer prices between 1973 and 1974 to above-trend increases in commodity prices, while Nordhaus and Shoven (1977, p. 35) attribute over half of the rise in the wholesale price index over the two years to July 1974 to primary product and import prices. For the industrial countries as a whole a 1975 UNCTAD study, using a single reduced-form equation to relate current inflation to the three variables: (i) previous year's inflation, (ii) changes in the pressure of demand, and (iii) changes in primary commodity prices, finds the last two factors adequate to account for the acceleration of inflation over 1970–5. According to this model, moreover, the rise in commodity prices relative to the general price level between 1970/1 and 1974 accounted for 80 per cent of the acceleration in general inflation. Bosworth and Lawrence (1982), applying a similar equation to individual industrial countries in the 1970s, found a varying picture reflecting different purchasing patterns and exchange rate adjustments. The direct effect of higher raw material prices on their estimates, however, represented nearly one third of the rise in final demand prices in the United States both in 1972–4 and in 1979, and about 20 per cent in Germany and Japan during 19721–5. Raw materials other than food and energy constituted, for these three biggest economies, only a fairly minor cause of inflation.

## CAUSES OF COMMODITY PRICE INFLATION

A great deal therefore hinges on identifying the causes of the inflation of energy and food prices in the early 1970s. Evidence analysed by Bosworth and Lawrence (1982) suggests that conditions in both markets were the result of special factors. In the case of cereals, the world market had, in 1970–4, been destabilised by the breakdown in 1968 of the International Wheat Agreement of 1948. Under the Agreement, governments – notably those of the two main exporters, the United States and Canada – had cooperated to limit fluctuations in grain prices by buying when an agreed floor was reached and by maintaining stocks sufficient to enable them to maintain an agreed ceiling. When the Agreement broke down exporting countries sought to reduce their stocks by restricting production; the world acreage devoted to wheat fell by 8 per cent between the marketing years 1968–9 and 1970–1, while stocks fell by 35 per cent, effectively ending suppliers' ability to prevent an explosive rise in prices. Sluggishness in production was not itself a major factor, with a fall of only 3–4 per cent below trend taking place in world cereals (grains and rice) production in 1972/3. Nor, in the view of Bosworth and Lawrence, were rising world incomes. Of much greater importance was the Soviet Union's decision in 1972–3 to increase grain imports substantially in preference to reducing current consumption or stockholding, as had usually been done in the past. The new policy accompanied an apparent slowing of the growth of Soviet grain ouput and was to continue throughout the decade. Its initial effect in sharply raising world market prices was quickly visible. The role of other individual countries in the inflation varied widely according to the agricultural policies in force there. The policies of Japan and the EEC, however, certainly worsened the inflation in world markets since by insulating their own markets from the influence of world price trends they removed any domestic incentive to cut consumption.

The rise in cereals prices may therefore broadly be put down to the breakdown of the power to control a managed market. The rise in petroleum prices, for its part, resulted from a fundamental shift of power within the world market. Throughout the 1950s and 1960s a group of seven large oil companies had exerted a dominant influence over almost every aspect of oil production, thus effectively controlling world market prices. A gradual erosion of their power during the 1960s accelerated sharply in 1970, however, when Libya took advantage of a period of temporary curtailment in Middle Eastern oil supplies to Western Europe to cut its production and raise prices. From then on the power of the OPEC countries acting together to enforce price increases became increasingly evident. It was this shift of power, combined with the worldwide boom, rather than any long-term pressure of demand in world markets, which, in the view of Bosworth and Lawrence, accounted for the part played by oil in the inflation of the period. Perhaps, none the less, the last three words of this claim should be emphasised. In the longer run, with growing awareness of the limitations on world oil reserves, energy prices seem bound to have risen in any event. Nor was it to be expected that the OPEC cartel would go on indefinitely selling at a price where demand was to all appearances highly inelastic – that is, at a price well below the profit-maximising level.

Shifts in political and economic power thus provided a large part of the immediate inflationary impulse of the 1970s, additional to that arising from ordinary market forces. These latter, for their part, moved in response to a boom fuelled by international money supplies, which drove consumer price inflation in most industrial countries to a year-on-year level of over 15 per cent by the end of 1973. What sustained the inflation long after the boom had given way to recession was the continuing rise in wages. By the end of the 1973 governments in the United States, Germany and Japan had adopted anti-inflationary policies and world industrial production had passed its peak. Wage increases, on the other hand, accelerated in the spring of 1974 in all the main industrial countries and thereafter remained high, admittedly undergoing temporary real falls in a number of countries but in all cases recouping them. In one such country, the United States, 'wage inertia' had often been noted as especially strong but it was in another, the United Kingdom, that one of the most powerful wage explosions took place. Here, trade union pressure, strengthened by an unfortunate system of wage indexation, by the demise of one government's incomes policy and by political divisions which prevented the successor government instituting a new incomes policy until after long delay, led to a rise in average earnings totalling 25.4 per cent in the four quarters to 1974:4 and 21.6 per cent in the following four quarters. As a consequence of wage-push in many countries world consumer prices generally went on rising at double-digit rates right through the years 1975–7 despite the recession. Understandably, fears were kindled afresh that any general relationship between wages and the level of demand had now vanished, with both unemployment and inflation rising in tandem.

## THE SECOND BOUT

From a trough in the first half of 1975 output began to recover slowly, and with it commodity prices. The recovery period was accompanied by continued turbulence in currency markets arising from fluctuating exchange rates and widespread imbalances in international payments, most notably the continued and, by 1976, growing weakness of the US external account. With the major currencies now floating, it was essential to the stability of the international monetary system, if such it could be called, that confidence in the main reserve currency, the dollar, should be maintained. This the expansionary US policies of the period, unaccompanied by any effective restraints on inflation, signally failed to achieve. Certainly, measures aiming at monetary control were implemented. In November 1978 US monetary policy was tightened at the same time as a voluntary programme of wage and price restraints was introduced. The result was disappointing, with inflation continuing to rise. The experiment is, however, of interest as one of the very few in which monetary restraint was combined with broadly expansionary fiscal policy. Even though the monetary targets were exceeded monetary growth was, by the standards of the decade, widely judged to be fairly moderate; yet there was no sign that monetary policy was by itself adequate to curb inflationary impulses stemming from elsewhere.

An omen of things to come was present in a third measure of the same November. The US monetary authorities, in what may be seen as a first step towards a multiple-reserve system of international payments, began to acquire deutschmarks and Swiss francs by borrowing abroad. For the moment, however, the emergence of such a system was not regarded as inevitable. Nor was the second inflationary bout of 1979–81, for it remained possible to argue that the fast and accelerating growth of world reserves in the late 1970s presented no threat of inflation because the growth of reserves held by some countries was offset by indebtedness on the part of many other (non-US) countries.

Any such argument was quickly to be rebutted by events. Anti-inflationary policies both in the United States and abroad proved largely ineffective. In 1979 and 1980 world food and other agricultural prices soared; and protracted political crisis in Iran, leading first to cutbacks in exports, then for two months to total cessation, both created temporary shortages and stimulated precautionary buying on a large scale. As a result the spot price of crude oil rose by a total of over 130 per cent.

The general course of events showed a marked resemblances to that observed earlier in the decade. The rise in food prices led the commodity markets on both occasions and in each case the rise in oil prices followed. On the first occasion, the outbreak of the Yom Kippur War provided the occasion for OPEC to enforce its price increases, with overtly military and political intentions which became particularly plain when an attempt was made to curtail oil supplies to countries supporting Israel. On the second occasion, the Iranian revolution of 1979, which brought the fundamentalist Ayatollah Khomeini to power, and the subsequent cutbacks in oil sales, provided the trigger for widespread precautionary and speculative buying. Both inflationary bouts were preceded and accompanied, though to different extents (BIS, 1980, 1981) and with differing time lags, by fast monetary growth. In both cases inaccurate forecasts tended to mislead policymakers. In 1979–81 the increase in the Bank for International Settlements' consumer price index for a weighted average of the Group of Ten (G10) industrial countries plus Switzerland soared not far short of the levels reached in 1975; for the world as a whole the corresponding BIS figures were 20.4 and 24 per cent – the increases for 1975 and 1979 respectively, On the face of things, economic history was repeating itself with some precision.

Despite the generic similarity, however, the two inflationary episodes were importantly different. In 1971 American recovery led the world out of recession into the early stages of boom, but inflation rose simultaneously in the industrial countries as a whole; whereas in the early stages of the second episode American inflation accelerated ahead of that in the other main industrial countries. The oil shocks of 1979–80 were more staggered and so had a rather less alarming impact than did that of late 1973, though they were passed on more rapidly in consumer prices. The first shock tended to be more inflationary in percentage terms; the second represented a greater financial and real loss to oil importers. By far the most striking difference between the two episodes, however, apart from the level of underlying inflation from which they began, lay in their effects on two variables: wages and government policy. At its peak in the twelve months to December 1980 the BIS's (1982, p. 44) weighted average of nominal wages for the G10 countries plus Switzerland rose by only 10.0 per cent, compared with 14.3 per cent in the twelve months to December 1974. The jump in unit labour costs was also much smaller on the second occasion. This difference may, in turn, have resulted from the markedly tougher attitude taken by MDC governments in 1979–80. With a rare display of near-unanimity these concentrated their main attention neither on the incomes policies which had been popular in the earlier 1970s nor, as a direct instrument of control, on measures of fiscal restraint. Instead they chose monetary policy. The chief objective, exemplified in the anti-inflationary policies announced in October 1979 in the United States and by the policies of Mrs Thatcher's government in Britain, was no longer to influence prices by direct controls, by fiscal deflation or even by means of a controlled rise in interest rates. It was rather to control certain monetary target aggregates such as the money supply and public borrowing, especially borrowing from the banking system, which were believed to be the underlying active causes of inflation, and to maintain control whatever the resulting rise in interest rates. The resulting monetary stringency, backed by fiscal retrenchement, brought with it an upsurge of company failures and major recession – the second within a decade. In the G10 countries plus

Switzerland unemployment rose to 7.5 per cent by March 1982 compared with only 5.2 per cent in 1976. By 1980 interest rates in almost all the industrial countries were in double digits and displayed a volatility which, along with large-scale capital movements, contributed to extreme exchange rate instability. The high levels were, moreover, to prove long-lasting. The result was that as inflation subsided in the early 1980s, real rates in several countries lingered at exceptionally high levels, impeding recovery.

In curbing inflation in the main industrial countries the new mix of policies was certainly *attended* by success. Inflation fell sharply, halving in Britain and the US in the course of 1982 and falling, though more gently, in the other five main industrial countries. Whatever caused the fall, however, it was not governments' success in achieving their monetary targets. On the contrary, such success was in general rather limited (OECD, 1983, pp. 35–9). In the disinflationary process one of the main factors at work was the fall in the dollar prices of commodities, including that of petroleum, which faltered for several years despite OPEC's best efforts to sustain it, before at last collapsing early in 1986. That this resulted from the MDCs' collective effort towards disinflation is scarcely questionable. From a 1980 annual peak of 100 the IMF all-commodity dollar index fell sharply by 24.7 per cent by 1982, and then, after a moderate rise in the next two years, fell again still lower in 1985.

For most industrial countries with the suggested exception of Italy (OECD, June 1985, p. 68), the moderation of wage increases was also a major influence. For the OECD countries as a whole the rate of increase in hourly earnings in manufacturing (OECD, 1984) fell from an annual average of 11.4 per cent in 1972–81 to 8.4 per cent in 1982 and 6 per cent in 1983. Evidence of a structural change in the process of wage determination was inconclusive (OECD, 1984 p. 53; for USA see Perry, 1983; Cagan and Fellner, 1983) but with OECD unemployment in 1982–4 roughly steady at the high level of 8–9 per cent it seems certain that the check to wage growth, like the fall in commodity prices, was, except perhaps in Britain (Beckerman, 1985; with Jenkinson, 1986) primarily the result of the prolonged and deep recession. In bringing about this recession monetary policy with its soaring interest rates, unavailability of credit, and record unemployment and bankruptcy rates, did, despite often failing of its intermediate targets, play an important role. This is not to deny that the earlier commodity price boom may itself have contributed to eventual disinflation by reducing real cash balances and so leading, at the first slackening of inflation, to a fall in expenditure on the part of citizens wishing to restore them. Equally, there is evidence that once inflation did slacken, the reduced opportunity cost of holding money led to a fresh rise in the demand to hold it. What is hard to believe, however, is that any fundamental change in the institutions of most countries' labour markets (including those of Britain as of 1987) had taken place which made it likely that the new lower rate of wage inflation would be maintained when full employment returned.

## SUMMARY; IMPACT ON OPINION ABOUT MONETARY POLICY

In outline, the two bouts of world inflation in our period resulted proximately from an upsurge of American spending to finance the Vietnam War and from a coincidence of booms in the industrial countries generally, the finance of which was facilitated by a massive outflow of dollars from the United States. Perhaps more fundamentally, however, the inflation arose when it did because of longer-term shifts in power in two vital markets, those for energy and food. Once inflation began, rigid wages in the MDCs guaranteed that it would be slow to abate until, with the slump of 1980–2, primary product prices plunged, long-term unemployment soared and union attitudes softened substantially.

In intellectual terms, however, the later part of the period was chiefly noteworthy for its reversal of dominant opinion on a question which many had thought settled less than a decade earlier. The first inflationary bout had been preceded by a surge of growth in many countries' money supplies, which seemed to confirm the monetarist claim that monetary growth in excess of the growth of output unfailingly produces, within two years, inflationary consequences. In 1976–8, the years immediately preceding the second bout, rates of monetary expansion outside the United States were lower than in 1971–3 (see BIS, 1980, p. 59); while in the United States the rates on the two occasions were broadly similar. For the world as a whole, because of the difficulties of defining and measuring the money supply on the second occasion, when exchange rates generally were floating and highly volatile, the statistical issue remains clouded. The time profiles of inflation and monetary growth in individual countries were this time substantially different and the correlations weaker than in the earlier bout, but a version of the monetarist thesis could still be defended. That governments and academics alike adopted no such version was, however, evident. Once confronted with the experience of the late 1970s and early 1980s, all concerned shifted their attention away from monetarist hypotheses, casting a discreet veil over theories so recently and enthusiastically propounded.

The reasons for this were in essence simple. Monetary aggregates as targets had proved too hard to hit. The statistical correlations underlying the policy were seen to be unreliable. In so far as the policy worked it did so via deflation which could be engineered in more controlled and less damaging ways. Even as monetary restraints, interest rates seemed better instruments than money aggregates. The monetarist grand strategy, like its predecessor, the Keynesian, seemed to have failed. Was there, it was even asked, enough understanding of the macroeconomy to justify faith in any grand macroeconomic strategy? Would not a step-by-step explorative approach be preferable?

Yet, at least until 1987, it remained possible to argue that the retreat from monetarism had been taken too far. In the first half of the 1980s monetary growth proceeded apace and, for many industrial countries, at a rate well into double figures despite governmental attempts to check it. What was bringing about the new money explosion? And did it pose a threat of renewed eventual inflation?

If any government had ceased altogether to believe in the macroeconomic importance of money, it did not publicise the fact. In practice, what seemed to happen was that governments, where they chose to tolerate fast monetary growth, did so for one or more of three main reasons. Either they were unwilling to risk any further deepening of their industrial recessions by enforcing tighter monetary conditions; or they feared precipitating default by debtor countries, as almost happened in the Mexican debt crisis of 1982; or - the reason officially presented – they believed that there was taking place in many countries, in addition to a once-for-all rise in money holdings resulting from the decline of inflationary expectations, a secular decline in the velocity of circulation of money. This was reported to be occurring as financial innovations such as interest-bearing current bank accounts in Britain or the American NOW (negotiated order of withdrawal) and super-NOW accounts increased the demand for money balances and as companies' money holdings, for analogous reasons, registered a permanent growth. In particular, those undisturbed by the monetary growth pointed to the growth of the proportion of the non-transactions part of M2 which bore market-determined yields, which, because they adjusted to market rates, rendered the demand for broad money less sensitive to interest rate changes (Clark, 1985). Further, in so far as broad money was owned by corporations, an increase in aggressive borrowing on the part of banks was cited as a probably lasting reason why money holdings were higher.

Those critical of rapid monetary growth, on the other hand, argued that much of the reason why the demand for money was high lay in the fact that real interest rates were also at high, and even record, levels. On this view, the danger was only too clear. Any rise in inflation, any fall in nominal interest rates, or even some institutional changes such as a country's decision to peg its exchange rate in relation to that of a major trading partner or bloc, could all too easily lower the real interest rate past some critical level, producing, directly or indirectly, a disgorging of money on to the markets for assets or goods, domestic or foreign. In one view at least, therefore, there still existed a grave danger that in the early and mid-1980s fuel was being accumulated for a further, long-delayed but potentially great, inflationary upsurge.

# 11 The United Kingdom from Wilson to Thatcher

## THE ACCELERATION OF 1967

Between 1948 and 1967, despite a brief period of high inflation accompanying the Korean War, the British retail price index did no more than double itself. By 1975, however, it had more than doubled again and by 1982 the index stood a further 138 per cent higher, at about five times the 1967 level. Such a dramatic worsening, the most sustained of the century, demands an explanation. How far was it merely a reflection of broader world conditions, how far home grown? And how far did the course, effects and policy responses of this still fairly moderate inflation reinforce, how far modify, the lessons the world had drawn from the experiences of the previous half-century?

The inflation began from apparent stability. During 1966 the persistent spiral seems to have weakened, with the retail price index rising, between 1966:4 and 1967:4, by only 2.1 per cent. Under the impact, first, of the statutory incomes policy of late 1966 and then of an ensuing period of 'severe restraint', the rise in wage costs per unit of output slowed. The cost of imported raw materials remained stable through most of 1967, and an easing of demand followed the restrictive measures of July 1966. In the later part of that year and the first half of 1967, therefore, the economy seems *prima facie* to have come sufficiently close to equilibrium to be useful as a yardstick for identifying the main active causes of the deterioration which followed.

The acceleration of price and wage increases began late in 1967 and continued with few and brief intervals for nearly eight years. In November 1967 sterling was devalued by 14.3 per cent, a measure accompanied by an immediate rise in the price of imports amounting to 9 per cent between October 1967 and February 1968. The most obvious active cause of the growing inflation was therefore the devaluation.

To say this, however, is to prompt a further question: what brought about the devaluation? Here the cause was almost certainly Britain's persistent tendency throughout the postwar years to move into ever deeper deficit on visible trade; and as Paish (1966, pp. 163–78) persuasively argues, this in turn substantially resulted from the maintenance of too high a level of demand (along with slow growth of productivity) in the domestic market. An important role in the process was played (Hutchison, 1968, p. 123 n.) by the protracted boom which preceded the general elections of 1964 and 1966.

In addition, but perhaps less compellingly, the inflationary role of wages must be acknowledged. With the ending in July 1967 of the period of severe restraint the rise in average weekly earnings accelerated and by April 1968 these were 9 per cent higher than a year earlier; basic hourly wage rates showed a similar rise. Although an incomes policy was still officially in operation it seems likely that at least part of the wage upsurge was due to 'catching up' after the most rigorous phase of the policy ended. A further part is also widely accepted as having been due to 'real wage resistance', the refusal of trade unions willingly to accept any reduction in real wages. In this case, such resistance may have arisen not only from import price increases but also because, as nominal earnings rose, workers had to pay a rising proportion of their earnings in tax and social security contributions – the phenomenon known as 'fiscal drag'. On any of these views, the pause in inflation during the early part of 1967 did not arise because the economy was in equilibrium. Rather, a fixed exchange rate and an incomes policy had suppressed inflation, and when these temporary measures came to end, the spiral resumed its ascent.

It remains possible, however, that in addition to real wage resistance and post-controls 'catch-up' other, independent pressures on wage levels were at work. What these causes were has been a question provoking considerable perplexity. Several writers, including Sir John Hicks (1975) and Sir Roy Harrod (1972, p. 44), have described their causation in sociological terms, linking them with the outbreak and spread of protests among students which marked the end of the decade. Thus, the rapid growth of student numbers in the mid 1960s is thought to have led, across the globe, to claims for greater influence, which the universities, primarily adapted to the needs of academics, were ill-organised to satisfy. Local and occupational dissatisfactions of this kind easily merged, it is argued, with the political discontents traditional among students in evoking protest. Yet even if this is true, the question remains whether increased agitation among students had any link with increased wage pressure from trade unions, and if so what it was. One possible common factor could be the lagged effect of growing confidence in the permanence of full employment. Thus, Phelps Brown (1983, pp. 147–67) argues that by the late 1960s western trade unions had come to be dominated by members with no recollection of the unemployment of the 1930s. The result, in his view, was that more militant policies were adopted. The claim is a hypothesis only; but until the sociology of such processes is better understood the explanation seems to be the best on offer.

Throughout 1968 and 1969 inflation continued to accelerate, the upward trend being led by import prices and by increases in indirect taxes introduced in belated reinforcement of the devaluation. One factor to which the acceleration cannot be attributed was demand; both the level of unemployment and the percentage of vacancies unfilled remained constant or, if anything, tended to show an easing of pressure. It was not, however, until the later part of 1969 that the divergence between wage changes and the level of demand became most marked. In the last quarter, despite a flattening out in demand consequent upon a severe Budget, there was a further acceleration in the rate of pay increases, which resulted in wages and salaries per head rising by 12.5 per cent between 1969 and 1970, and hourly wage rates by 10.3 per cent, both figures approximately double their level of a year earlier. The rise could not be attributed to import prices, which tailed far behind. It was here, therefore, more perhaps than at any other point in the 1960s, that the plausibility of a purely demand-based explanation of British inflation began most visibly to wane.

To point to wages as the main motor of inflation at this point is, however, to tell only half the story. Why did their rise accelerate in the autumn of 1969? To journalists and to the general informed public of the day there was little doubt about the answer. By September of that year three and a half years of the government's term of office had elapsed and since few parliaments run their full five years there was every reason to think that the last full session of the current one had begun. With unemployment at what was then regarded as the unacceptably high level of 2.5 per cent, it was to be expected that early steps would be taken either to boost demand or to allow wage increases to have that effect. The behaviour both of unions and of employers consequently adapted itself in the direction of higher pay settlements. By early 1970, moreover, the likelihood of an even earlier election date had begun to be widely realised as the visible trading account of the balance of payments began a continuous deterioration which took it from a seasonally adjusted surplus of £27 million in 1969:3 to a deficit of £86 million in 1970:2.

The general expectation was not disappointed. In June the election was held and a new government took office. It did so in conditions of stagflation which by mid-1972 had brought about the unprecedented postwar combination of 3.8 per cent unemployment and 6.2 per cent inflation.

## INFLATIONARY FACTORS, 1971-3

The simultaneous growth of unemployment and inflation presented problems, to be discussed later, for the many observers who had become accustomed to regard those evils as substitutes one for the other. Edward Heath's government, however, seems to have had no doubt not only that it could reduce unemployment by reflationary measures but also that any likely cost in terms of increased inflation would be acceptable. From mid-1971 onwards the new Chancellor, Mr Barber, directed his policies towards rapid expansion of output and employment with what proved to be all too little regard for the consequences.

In July 1971 all hire purchase restrictions on the sale of motor vehicles were abolished and in the following year's Budget taxation was cut by £1200 million. Still more striking, interest on loans was declared deductible from income subject to tax, so that the cost of borrowing was reduced by as much as 95 per cent for those with high incomes. A correspondingly easy monetary policy was initiated, which was followed by a marked acceleration in the growth of the money supply.

In September the system of Competition and Credit Control (CCC) was formally inaugurated which, as the name implies, aimed both to encourage inter-bank competition and to strengthen the authorities' hand in controlling, by means of changes in interest rates, the growth of credit in the economy. The CCC system replaced the banks' former (28 per cent) liquid assets ratio and its accompanying cash ratio by a single new (12½ per cent) ratio, which was to relate a newly defined category of reserve assets to eligible (deposit) liabilities. Not unnaturally, many commentators interpreted the new system as one of monetary base control (see Glossary) of the kind often described in textbooks, under which the authorities could, by controlling the stock of assets used as bank reserves, also control the total money supply. On this view, CCC greatly relaxed the restraints on bank lending and was held responsible for much of the monetary explosion of the following period.

Any such claim was, however, officially denied. Monetary base control had, it was said, never been used in Britain, and the growth of bank lending and of the money supply after 1971 could not, therefore, be attributed to its relaxation. Richard Coghlan (1981, pp. 73–4), supporting this view, is prepared to allow that the post-CCC increase in banks' reserve assets made the banks lend more aggressively, but cites the lifting of bank lending restrictions in 1971 as the probable main cause of the subsequent explosion of credit. Whatever the true explanation, between 1971:4 and 1973:4 the broadly defined measure of the money supply, M3, increased by over 60 per cent.

By June 1972 the first adverse effect of the boom became evident in the form of a balance of payments crisis prompted by a deterioration in the balance of visible trade and, more immediately, by a large outflow of capital. The government's response, rather than to resort to fiscal retrenchment, was to float sterling; but from then on a growing number of measures of restraint was introduced. Interest rates were allowed or circuitously encouraged to rise; fresh calls were made for special deposits (see Glossary); and requests were sent to banks urging caution in extending credit. The money supply continued to soar, however, and with it prices and the deficit on current external account. In July 1973 another sterling crisis forced the pound down by about 10 per cent within four weeks and this time the central bank's minimum lending rate was allowed to rise to 11.5 per cent in the third quarter and 13 per cent in the fourth. This, however, even when combined with further calls for restraint in bank lending, was unavailing. With intense speculation gripping the commodity markets and with bank lending rising at unprecedented rates, OPEC's oil price rises in October and their extension into a fourfold increase before the year's end only added fuel to an inflationary bonfire already well out of control. The final quarter of the year thus saw Britain and the industrial world enter upon a long period of stagflation from which it was only to start to emerge, fitfully and uncertainly, a decade later.

Throughout the period 1967–72 the rise in import prices, after its temporary high level of 12.3 per cent in 1968, lagged behind the rate of general price inflation. The leading variable, after the money stock, was wages: the rise in manual workers' weekly wage rates approached double figures in 1970 and by 1972 was running at 13.8 per cent. Average earnings between the fourth quarters of the two years rose even faster, at 26.9 per cent. In an attempt to check this trend the government in November 1972 moved away from its informal attempts to bring wage settlements in each year down by 1 per cent from the previous year's level (the 'n-1' policy) and instead resorted to a statutory pay standstill. This gave place the following spring to Stage II of the policy, which aimed to enforce, in its first year of operation, pay increases of £1 per week plus 4 per cent of the employer's total wage bill, and to ensure that successive pay settlements were separated by at least a twelve-month gap.

A fair summary of specialist opinion on the 1972–4 incomes policy, and indeed of British incomes policies generally (cf. Cohen, 1969, pp. 235–62) would be that after showing some initial success it quickly lost its efficacy and that most, if not all, of the slowdown in pay increases which it brought about was lost in the subsequent period of 'catching up'. The Heath government's policy was introduced at a time of great economic disruption, making both personal judgement and regression analysis highly uncertain guides. The salient fact remains that no one claims more than modest success for the policy. Its most unfortunate aspect became evident only in the light of the oil shock of October 1973 for it was in the following month that a new and, as it proved, final stage of the policy was formally introduced. This made provision that pay rises should be subject to a statutory norm of 7 per cent or £2.25, whichever was the higher. More pertinently, however, it permitted, in addition to the approved norm, flat-rate wage increases of 40 pence per week payable once the retail price index had risen more than 7 per cent during Stage III's operation. To this extent it represented widespread and almost instantaneous wage indexation, and, largely because of the time of its introduction, almost certainly became a major source of faster wage inflation in the course of 1974, adding substantially (indeed; according to many estimates, by a double-digit figure) to average wage increases.

## THE BOOM OF 1971–4 AND THE FIRST OIL SHOCK

In retrospect the 'Barber boom' with its accompanying and ensuing inflation has become a major, almost legendary episode in British economic history. What brought it about and what allowed it to continue once its consequences for prices and the balance of payments had become evident?

In the early stages, a desire to reduce unemployment and indeed to reduce taxation as an independent goal certainly played an important and avowed role. The Conservative dislike of controls seems also to have influenced the Chancellor in his abolition of hire purchase restrictions on the purchase of motor vehicles in July 1971, a measure introduced with singularly poor timing at a moment when the domestic car industry was already operating at a high level of capacity, with predictable consequences for car imports. More surprisingly, David Gowland (1982, p. 108) reports that the goverment was still seeking to make a 'dash for growth', a type of strategy popularised, from academic origins, by Andrew Shonfield in the early 1960s and adopted with little success by Reginald

Maudling during his Chancellorship in 1962–4. The policy promised faster growth resulting from boom-induced investment once an initial balance of payments deficit, occasioned by a temporary influx of imported raw materials, had been surmounted. What was not clear – and the point was important if such a policy was indeed intended in the early 1970s – was the extent of the external depreciation which the government should, in accordance with at least one version of the theory, have been prepared to accept as a remedy for any balance of payments deficits which the new policy might temporarily bring about. Nor was the danger of inflation arising from compensating wage settlements much discussed.

Failure to realise the full extent of the inflationary effects of the boom also seems to have played a part in its continuance. Mr Barber was, with hindsight, blamed for his expansionary budget of 1972, designed to curb the ever-rising level of unemployment, in which he cut taxation by some £1200 million. What is less often remembered is that he was at the time subject to urgings from many quarters to take still stronger expansionary action. Thus the NIESR (February, 1972, pp. 31–2) spoke of the need for reflation involving either tax cuts of £2.5 million or extra investment of £1.5 billion.

External factors also exerted inflationary pressures. The floating of the pound and consequent exchange rate depreciation helped substantially to bring about a sharp rise in import prices – by 35 per cent between 1972:2 and 1973:3, *before* the OPEC oil price rise. Overseas price trends, giving rise to further sterling depreciations, notably in July 1973, were also important motors of inflation, even after correction for the effects of sterling's downward float. They were, moreover, almost entirely outside the control of the British government.

Perhaps the most fundamental and persistent question, however, to arise from this uncanny concomitance of naive policy, mistaken forecasts and external shocks concerns the role of wages and salaries. That pay increases prolonged and worsened the inflationary bout can scarcely be doubted. Between 1967:3 and 1973:3 the index of wages and salaries per unit of output rose by 49 per cent, in the following year by another 22 per cent, and in 1975 by a further 31 per cent. The 1967–73 rise in the retail price index was 46 per cent, a figure which compares with a rise of 80 per cent in the average earnings of all employees. It must be remembered, however, that the price stability of 1966–7 hid pre-existing inflationary pressures, suppressed by a temporarily fixed exchange rate and an equally temporary incomes policy. Some part of the resurgence of wages in the late 1960s was therefore not an autonomous initial cause of accelerated inflation, but a defensive delayed reaction to earlier price increases. All the same, it is difficult, in the light of the huge and growing divergence between wages and prices over 1967–73 as a whole, not to conclude that any initial defensive reaction overshot, borne foward by competition and comparison between different wage-groups. Most important of all, the Heath government's system of wage indexation, as noted above, added powerfully to the immediate wage upsurge resulting from other inflationary shocks, preventing adjustments in real wages which would otherwise almost certainly have moderated or at least delayed the effects on both output and prices.

The oil shock, when it came, did no more than provide the climax of a worldwide inflation already in full spate. Indeed, but for the pre-existing inflation OPEC might not have chosen to exercise at the time the monopolistic power it had possessed for several years. According to NIESR estimates (February 1974, p. 9) the effect of the price increases of late 1973, reinforced as they were by reductions in oil supplies, was to cut British energy supplies by an estimated 3.5 per cent, to reduce GDP by roughly 1.75 per cent and to increase very substantially the balance of payments deficit on current account. Directly, the retail price index was raised by some 2.25 per cent, as much again being added by the non-oil commodity price boom (NIESR, May 1974, p. 9).

The less direct consequences are scarcely calculable. Not only was the wage–price spiral powerfully reinforced. An atmosphere of crisis was created, which was reflected in an increase in the velocity of circulation of money, by 29.5 per cent between 1973:3 and 1977:2. The addition to the oil import bill worsened the balance of trade, assisting the slide in sterling's exchange rate. Of still greater immediate consequence was the decision of the National Union of Mineworkers to strike in February 1974 (after a three-month overtime ban) in support of a pay claim above the approved limits, a decision which can scarcely have been taken independently of the fuel shortage and the attendant restrictions upon the use of oil. Faced with the miners' action, the Prime Minister, Edward Heath, decided to call an election, launching his campaign with the slogan 'Who Governs?' (the government or the trade unions). The slogan was soon dropped. Nor was it easy to feel that any clear answer had been given when, after the election of February 1974, a Labour government assumed power without gaining as many votes as the Conservatives and without an overall majority in Parliament.

The new government was from the first known to be transitional. As in 1950–1 and 1964–6, two general elections were to be needed to complete a change of governing party. What was not at first so evident was that after the second general election (held, as it happened, in October) divisions within the ruling party would prove so great that they would crystallise over the issue of continued membership of the EEC and induce the government to resolve its conflicts by means of the European Community referendum of June 1975. In effect, an open primary election was held after, rather than before, the main election.

These various elections delayed the introduction of firm economic policies and though the outgoing government's machinery for securing wage restraint was provisionally maintained, inflation meanwhile continued to accelerate to a peak of 27 per cent in July 1975. Wage rates and average earnings, year on year, each rose by over a quarter. It would be possible to argue that the monetary growth of two years earlier constituted the main real (though delayed) cause of the continuing inflation, but if so some additional thesis is needed to account for the rise which had taken place in the 'natural' rate of unemployment, i.e. the minimum level consistent with price stability. For, so far as could be judged, the amount of inflation accompanying any given level of unemployment was edging steadily upwards. An explanation widely advanced was that prevailing notions of fairness required the maintenance of comparability links between wages in industries where labour was scarce and those in industries where it was oversupplied. Certainly, some such account was necessary. With 5.2 per cent of the labour force unemployed by 1975:4, the labour market provided little evidence of general excess demand.

The period between the first general election and the EEC referendum saw, along with a growing concern with monetary policy, the partial retention or reintroduction of measures of the type familiar in the 1960s. These included hire purchase restrictions and supplementary special deposits, a form of graduated penalty payable by banks which increased their interest-bearing eligible liabilities (i.e. *deposits*, not, this time, loans) by more than stated percentages. Meanwhile, the current account of the balance of payments ran a deficit of over £3 billion, while the growth of output, at times almost to zero.

In July 1975, however, with the EEC referendum complete and the more centrist section of the Labour Party victorious, a seemingly radical change of policy was by stages introduced. Its principal components may be summarised as:

(i)   a greater, indeed theoretically a primary, concern with control of monetary aggregates, namely £M3 and the PSBR;

(ii)  a voluntary incomes policy or 'social contract' relying on union cooperation and offering in return such benefits as tax cuts and extensive consultation in the drafting of legislation affecting the unions and employees.

In addition, more sophisticated methods of financing budget deficits were introduced. These included the limited issue of indexed government savings bonds and — important because it avoided monetary growth — the practice of maximising gilt sales just after long-term rates had peaked and when, in consequence, expectations of rising market values were widespread (Gowland, 1982, pp. 148−52).

## EARLY 'MONETARIST' POLICIES AND INCOMES POLICIES

The arrival of the 'monetarist' era took place, ostensibly, in the course of 1976. The first monetary targets were published in July, before recourse had to be had to the IMF to stem the collapse of sterling which culminated in October. It is possible that the government foresaw events clearly enough to adopt policies of a kind which would be likely to satisfy the IMF if its help were later to be required. On the whole, however, the likelihood is that no such foresight existed and that the government adopted the new targets under the influence of current thinking on the subject, combined with doubts about the efficacy of other controls if used on their own. Whatever the government's initial degree of commitment to its targets, its record in achieving them was imperfect, with the money supply overshooting its target in 1977/8.

The effects of Labour's monetary policy, which has been described as one of 'monetarily constrained Keynesianism', though hard to disentangle, were probably undramatic. What was less debatable was the short-run efficacy of the second main instrument of policy, incomes policy. Introduced in July 1975 soon after the referendum, the new policy was destined to run through three one-year stages. In 1975–6 Stage I laid down a £6 per week limit to pay rises, with a zero rise for high incomes; Stage II the following year set a norm of 6 per cent for the rise in average earnings with differing norms for different income-groups; while Stage III set a 10 per cent norm, with a minimum 12-month gap between settlements.

A widely-held opinion maintains that the policy, while it lasted, was more successful than its predecessors under the Heath and first Wilson governments. In general, studies of British incomes policies have tended to report some immediate success in restraining wages and prices below the level they would otherwise have reached, followed by a bout of 'catching up' after the policy's removal. Thus Henry and Ormerod (NIESR, August 1978, pp. 31–9), using different dummies to capture the effects both of different phases of incomes policies and of post-controls catch-up, found that 'over the period 1961–75 such policies reduced the rate of wage inflation below what it would otherwise have been but that there were offsetting wage increases in the period immediately following the end of the policies'. Henry (1981), updating the work using two separate models, embodying respectively an augmented Phillips Curve and a target real wage hypothesis (see Glossary), found the 1973–4 policy effective to a significant extent on the basis of one of the models but the 1975–7 phase effective on the basis of both. Even so, average earnings rose by 14.0, 8.9 and 15.0 per cent respectively in the three years of the policy's operation, an outcome not only far above what the government must have hoped for, but one which did not even move consistently downward.

By the late summer of 1978 the intense resistance of trade unions to the policy had resulted in its rejection by a TUC conference. In this the conference was probably influenced by the general expectation of a autumn election. Never since the early 1960s had either main party been willing to fight an election on a pledge to introduce or maintain an incomes policy, whatever they might do once in office. The time therefore seemed ripe for a union attack on the suggested Stage IV and its 5 per cent norm.

In fact, the worst possible outcome ensued. The election was delayed (apparently on a whim of the Prime Minister, Mr Callaghan) and by the time it was held early in May 1979 the incomes policy had broken down, probably beyond repair, amidst severe industrial disruption. Worse still, the newly elected Conservative government came to power committed to accepting proposals for public sector pay increases soon to be put forward by a Committee under the chairmanship of Professor H. Clegg. These in the event involved increases ranging from 5 to 21 per cent in addition to the 9 per cent already agreed, a figure which in the absence if any post-election incomes policy the private sector rapidly attempted to equal, gaining an average 1979–80 increase in wage rates of over 18 per cent. How far the wage explosion of 1979–80 represented unavoidable 'catching up' and how far it arose from the election promises remains a question incapable of a definitive answer.

## INFLATION UNDER LABOUR

Three features of Labour's anti-inflationary record deserve note. First, the 1975–8 incomes policy was in one respect unique in British experience. On one earlier occasion, in July 1972, the Chancellor had attempted to 'buy down' inflation by offering the unions cuts in indirect taxes and restraints on nationalised industry prices in return for moderation in wage settlements, a policy which on that occasion contributed to a dramatic growth in demand without yielding any perceptible wage restraint. In 1976, and again in 1977, the offer presented to the union was more blunt. In his 1976 Budget Mr Healey undertook to cut payments of income tax if, but only if, Stage II of the incomes policy was satisfactorily negotiated. In 1976 the deal was duly transacted and the policy widely hailed as a success, with average weekly earnings in the year to 1977:2 rising by only 10.4 per cent. In 1977, on the other hand, a repeat offer was followed by less satisfactory results, with the rate of increase if earnings rising sharply.

The deal broadly resembled one variant of the anti-inflationary proposal put forward by Wallich and Weintraub (1971), the central intention being to secure wage restraint by offering the unions tax cuts (or in the more general case wage subsidies) which would guarantee real wages at a time of rising prices — an indirect form of wage indexation. To the extent that the subsidy was financed by monetary growth the policy could thus be of an extreme anti-monetarist nature, offering to reduce inflation by *increasing* the money supply.

The weakness of the plan lay, however, in its underlying assumptions. One was that unions' pay ambitions would be predominantly defensive; only thus would they be willing to settle for tax cuts (wage subsidies) which did little or no more than compensate them for inflation. Another was that firms used mark-up pricing, so that wage restraint would lead to slower price inflation. To the extent that pricing was aggressive rather than defensive, this would not follow. Again, if the tax cuts (wage subsidies) were to prove unsustainable and had eventually to be phased out, a resurgence of prices could have followed and the only effect would have been to delay inflation (though even this might have reduced any self-aggravating 'snowball' effect). Perhaps most important of all, the policy would have been unlikely to succeed, and could have proved disastrous, if it had come into effect just before some exogenous shock imparted a new momentum to inflation. If, for example, the United States had adopted a subsidy-based incomes policy in 1979, as at one time seemed possible, the second oil shock might well have necessitated such large government deficits as to have engendered demand-led inflation on a much larger scale than in fact took place. The Healey policy therefore involved considerable risks and, perhaps unsurprisingly, proved only temporarily successful.

A second interesting feature of Labour's period of office lay in the extent to which control of the money supply was found to be inconsistent with control of the exchange rate. Thus, in October 1977, with the external balance benefiting from, *inter alia,* growing output of North Sea oil and related capital inflows, the government found that its attempts to keep the exchange rate down by selling sterling were leading to unacceptable monetary growth; it therefore felt obliged to concede defeat and allowed the exchange rate to rise by ten cents against the dollar, well above the level previously hoped for.

A third and still more dramatic episode during Labour's period of office was the slide of sterling in the spring and, more heavily, the autumn of 1976, with its inevitable inflationary effects. The causes were complex. On one view, the collapse was a delayed consequence of the ending of the guarantee of sterling balances under the 1968 Basle Arrangements, which, after extension, finally expired at the end of 1974 (Tew, 1982, p. 124). If this view is taken, however, some explanation of the lag between the end of the guarantee and the collapse has to be found; and the current account of the balance of payments does not seem to afford it, since in 1976 the deficit was far lower than in the preceding two years. Gowland (1982, p. 176) argues that, in the wake of cumulative growth of the broad money supply by £11,500 million during 1974–6, the authorities tried to restore British competitiveness by allowing sterling to fall in years like 1976 when the effect of wages in raising costs was limited. On this view, 1976 witnessed the voluntary release of some inflationary pressures previously suppressed via the support of the exchange rate. That any such 'release' far exceeded what was intended is, however, evident from the need to call in the aid of the IMF late in the year and to bind the country to a restrictive monetary policy set out in the Letter of Intent of 15 December.

## INFLATION UNDER THE CONSERVATIVES

The sources of the bout of inflation which peaked, in Britain, in

1980 went back well into the 1970s. By late 1978 the international business cycle had turned up again and inflation in other industrial countries, notably France and the United States, was accelerating. At home, the 1978 Budget had turned towards expansion with a cut of over £2 billion in direct taxes in a full year. True, by the year's end, despite the reflationary Budget, the growth both of M1 and £M3 slowed, as if in further warning of the perverse (or perhaps random) behaviour of the money supply; but with a modest pre-election boom now set in motion, the acceleration of wage and price increases was already visible by the spring. This was, moreover, a year before the consequences of the election campaign began to be felt, with its endorsement (by both main parties) of forthcoming Clegg proposals on public sector pay. With the resurgence of inflation, still more ominously, went a deterioration of the balance of trade in manufactured goods, which, after recovering during the dramatic business downturn of 1979–81, was by 1983 to swell into a huge deficit on manufactures, the first of any consequence in British industrial history. The ensuing debate centred on how far the collapse represented merely the inevitable delayed result of longstanding competitive weaknesses and how far, though otherwise avoidable, it stemmed from soaring interest rates and their effects in raising the exchange rate and accelerating deindustrialisation.

The economic aims of the Conservative government which came to power in May 1979 were varied. One was to strengthen incentives to work, and in pursuit of this goal the new Chancellor, Sir Geoffrey Howe, made an immediate cut of 3 per cent in the basic rate of income tax, restoring the revenue by raising value added tax. Measures were also taken to cut public expenditure as a proportion of GDP, but partly because these were quickly followed by a rise in unemployment and its associated welfare expenditures, it was not until 1983 that a cut in the target ratio was in fact achieved. The foremost aim, however, was the defeat of inflation and the renewed economic growth which was expected to result. As means to this end the government adopted strategies, embodied in the Medium Term Financial Strategy (MFTS) announced the following spring, which fell under five main headings.

First, monetary policy was allotted the prime role in curbing inflation. Fiscal policy was, indeed, to be used, but chiefly as a means of cutting the PSBR and so, it was believed, curbing the growth of the money supply.

Second, government ministers set themselves the task of eliminating inflationary expectations. By emphasising continually that they would not 'print money' and so ratify inflation, they sought to convince trade unions and employers alike that excessive price and wage increases would lead to unemployment and bankruptcies. The indicators to which public attention was drawn in the hope that they would influence expectations were the intermediate targets, £M3 and the PSBR. These were now to be announced for several years ahead. It was also immediately clear that they were to be pursued with much more vigour than had been the case under Labour.

Third, inheriting already high nominal interest rates, the government showed itself willing to raise them still further, abruptly and by action in the market. In June minimum lending rate (MLR), the successor to the former Bank rate, was raised from 12 to 14 per cent and thence in November to a postwar peak of 17 per cent. The ceiling on banks' interest-bearing liabilities was also renewed, though evasion was reported to be widespread (Gowland, 1982, p. 191).

Fourth, the exchange rate was declared free to find its own level; and when this led to sterling's appreciation the latter was welcomed, at least for a time in some governmental quarters, as a means of checking inflation.

Fifth, there was, initially, to be no incomes policy. In the event strictly enforced norms for public sector pay were in fact soon introduced, but in the private sector no such policy reversal took place. Instead, a series of Acts of Parliament sought to curb the powers of trade unions and so to reduce inflationary wage pressures.

At a detailed level at least, few of these policies yielded much success. In announcing its monetary targets emphatically and well in advance, the government hoped to induce firms and unions sharply and suddenly to lower expectations of inflation and to adjust their own behaviour accordingly. In this respect the policy was based on a so-called 'rational expectations' effect and resembled what, it was often recalled, had happened in the European stabilisations of the 1920s. The results were, however, far different. The money supply target, £M3, both in 1980 and into the mid-1980s, was seldom achieved. Artis and Bladen-Hovell (1987, p. 27) note, indeed, for the period 1979–85, only two successes against five failures, a record a good deal worse than that of the Labour government, whose commitment to its chosen targets was clearly weaker. The PSBR did respond to restraints; but the fact that this could happen concurrently with runaway monetary growth cast doubt upon the theory that the PSBR, or that part of it which involved borrowing from the banking system, largely determined the money supply. One of the many ironies of the period is the fact recorded by Gowland (1982, p. 203), that the government's first success in achieving its targets occurred in the first year when those targets were not given priority. A yet more striking irony was the fact that monetary conditions throughout 1980 were generally agreed to be tight even though both £M3 and the PSBR continued to rise fast – in the case of the former, at an annual rate which at one point was to approach 20 per cent.

In other respects, policy was equally unsuccessful. A widespread view holds that the threat of bankruptcy which high interest rates posed in and after 1980 itself drove firms to borrow and actually stimulated the growth of credit and the money supply. Similarly, the growth of unemployment-related expenditures tended strongly to counteract measures taken to curb public spending. Third, as Kaldor (1980) points out, there seems to be little evidence that public sector borrowing from the banking system had any firm relationship with the money supply. High nominal interest rates, moreover, even though they became low (indeed, negative) in real terms as inflation rose to 22 per cent in the course of 1980, brought with them a reported unwillingness on the part of financial institutions to satisfy borrowers' demands even when finance was available, and so powerfully contributed to the ensuing high rate of company failures. Nor, finally, did monetary stringency lead to a drop in consumption and the desired tightening of belts. On the contrary, consumers' real expenditure remained roughly constant right through the trough of the recession, which was primarily, for several years up to and including 1982, a destocking recession damaging to output rather than to consumption.

The extent to which high interest rates damaged the balance of trade by attracting an inflow of foreign funds and so raising the exchange rate has been the subject of further debate. That there must have been such an effect, with sterling rising against the yen, for example, by over a third in the course of 1979 alone, is hard to doubt; and since the higher exchange rate was, not surprisingly, to prove unsustainable, its effects in curbing inflation were similarly transient. Sterling appreciation in part coincided, moreover, with the second oil shock which raised the dollar price of oil by some 130 per cent in the course of 1979–80. Since Britain adjusted its own oil prices to those existing in international markets the inflationary effect of the shock was not eliminated by the fact of British net selfsufficiency in oil. In addition to these factors, the new government's commitment to the Clegg public sector wage awards ensured an initial period of exploding wages; and there were sharp rises in import prices generally, totalling 10, 15 and 9 per cent respectively in the years 1979–81.

The costs of other government measures were also high. 'Monetarist' policy, designed to remove from the public mind, for the first time since World War II, the assurance that any shortfall in demand would quickly be reversed, contributed a good deal, both directly and indirectly, to the downturn of 1979–81. Artis and Bladen-Hovell (1987), indeed, are willing to attribute about one third of the recession to fiscal and monetary policy. The former of these is important, since it was 'Keynesian' policy, as exemplified by the Budget of 1981 and its intended cut of 1.6 per cent in the planning total for public expenditure in 1982/3 (albeit combined with a 2 per cent cut in MLR), which was generally interpreted as the severest deflationary blow. Whether this was the case is debatable in view of the fact that output began to recover, however feebly, only two or three months later. If it was, however, and if government anti-inflationary policy is to be criticised on the ground that raising taxes in 1979 would have been less damaging to industry than was the raising of interest rates, the argument must be that a rise in taxes then, when interest rates were still 'low', would, in the generally less crisis-ridden atmosphere of that year, have restrained activity in a more gradual and controlled way than it did in 1981. Unless such an argument holds, as it may, it is not clear that fiscal deflation would have avoided economic collapse to a greater extent than did monetary.

Yet, despite all the defects in the mechanisms postulated and despite the high costs incurred, inflation did fall sharply. Reaching a figure of only 6.2 per cent at the end of 1982, it then stood at less than a third of its peak little more than two years earlier. This happened, moreover, despite a rise in unit import values (measured in sterling) which totalled 16 per cent in the two years to 1982 and which continued, though at a slowing rate, until 1985. Why?

One obvious and major reason was the non-repetition of the Clegg wage upsurge. Just as, in view of pre-election promises by both parties, the upsurge seems certain to have taken place whichever party won, so it would almost certainly not have been repeated in subsequent years under a government of either party. To this extent a marked fall in wage-induced inflation after 1980 was virtually inevitable, and one which, though it could perhaps be attributed to 'policy', had little to do with unemployment. Nor should the extent of the fall which did take place be overestimated. Despite all the unemployment, even when the 'Clegg peak' had passed, average earnings still rose at a rate which subsided no lower than a roughly constant 6–8½ per cent between 1983 and 1986. There was, in fact, every sign that, as some had foreseen, unemployment constituted a threat to everyone in general and to no one (or to rather few people) in particular.

The role of other factors in reducing inflation was also substantial. Artis and Bladen-Hovell (1987, p. 23) venture the view that comparatively little of the decline in British inflation between 1979 and 1984 was due to domestic policy. Beckerman and Jenkinson (1986, p. 39) further present econometric findings in support of the claim that the decline in British inflation 1980–2 was not due to the direct impact of higher unemployment but principally to the collapse of primary product prices. The latter, they argue, executed, for the average industrial country, a dramatic 'turn-round' (measured as the difference between the initial rate of increase and the final rate of decrease) of 50–60 per cent between 1980 and 1982. Even in countries with declining exchange rates, like Britain, the effect was to slow down the rise in import prices as a whole. To point this out is not, of course, to contradict the view that restrictive policies in the industrial countries *collectively* were powerful in bringing about the collapse of raw material prices. The claim being made is that in the course of those three years only a trivial influence on price trends was exerted by *British* policy in curbing wage inflation via domestic unemployment (as distinct from the non-repetition of Clegg). Other writers have, however, claimed to rediscover a a British Phillips Curve for the same period and it would be premature to say that consensus on Beckerman's claim has yet emerged.

Table 11.1: The British economy, 1967–82

| Year | % Unemployment s.a., UK, excl. school leavers 4th qtr. | Wages & salaries per unit of output 1980 = 100 | Retail prices 1975 = 100 | £M3 £m, s.a. 4th qtr. |
|------|------|------|------|------|
| 1967 | 2.4 | 24.0 | 46.2 | 14,380 |
| 1968 | 2.4 | 24.5 | 48.4 | 15,490 |
| 1969 | 2.4 | 25.3 | 51.0 | 15,820 |
| 1970 | 2.6 | 27.7 | 54.2 | 17,300 |
| 1971 | 3.8 | 30.2 | 59.3 | 19,530 |
| 1972 | 3.4 | 32.5 | 63.6 | 24,740 |
| 1973 | 2.3 | 35.2 | 69.4 | 31,380 |
| 1974 | 2.8 | 42.8 | 80.5 | 34,660 |
| 1975 | 4.7 | 55.7 | 100.0 | 36,960 |
| 1976 | 5.4 | 61.3 | 116.5 | 40,440 |
| 1977 | 5.7 | 65.4 | 135.0 | 44,570 |
| 1978 | 5.3 | 72.5 | 146.2 | 51,290 |
| 1979 | 5.0 | 82.7 | 165.8 | 57,800 |
| 1980 | 7.9 | 100.0 | 195.6 | 68,850 |
| 1981 | 10.8 | 108.7 | 218.9 | 77.960 |
| 1982 | 12.2 | 114.0 | 237.7 | 93,850 |

Underlining indicates a break in the series.

*Source:* Economic Trends, Annual Supplement, 1984.

It had long been a government view not only that low inflation was necessary for growth but that it would itself stimulate growth. How far did the fall in inflation bear out this claim? By March 1981, alarmed by the effects of high interest rates on companies and also on the exchange rate through the attraction of capital inflows, the government had lowered MLR to 12 per cent. The following summer output started to rise. The claim that this constituted recovery proved, however, to have too sanguine a ring. Subsequent rises in interest rates abroad, spreading to Britain, disrupted the early stages of expansion, while the appearance of many new entrants to the labour market prevented such growth of output as there was from stopping the steady rise in unemployment. In manufacturing, moreover, even in 1987 not only employment but also output was still below its 1979 level. The growth of productivity, at rates which seemed for a time to exceed any sustained previous postwar experience, constituted, in a sense, one encouraging aspect of events. But the claim that falling inflation would itself stimulate growth received little immediate support; and it was government reflationary measures in 1986 and 1987 which were first followed by any important fall in the underlying level of unemployment.

## SUMMARY AND ASSESSMENT OF CAUSES

Between 1967 and 1982 not only did Britain experience its most severe and sustained inflation of the twentieth century. With it there came also an unaccustomed and high degree of volatility of interest rates, the trade balance, capital movements and the exchange rate. More pertinently for our purposes, modern economic theory was applied to practical policy-making to an extent unequalled even at the time of the 'dash for growth' and National Plan in the 1960s. The episode is therefore a good one for helping us to assess the truth and practical utility of the theories involved. Our first task is to allot relative importance to the various impulses affecting the inflationary spiral in its different phases.

In 1967 devaluation, probably resulting from earlier protracted excess demand, and the ensuing upsurge of wages led the way. Wages, however, overcompensated for the rise in the cost of living. From late 1969, perhaps because of real wage resistance and certainly because both government policy and union attitudes were affected by the approach of an election, wages again led. During the Barber boom the push of import prices, including that of oil, and the accelerated rise of wages were accompanied by some excess demand, most strikingly in the market for real property. Even so, unemployment was high enough for some further explanation of the inflation to be needed. Various 'structural' explanations were offered, positing changes in union behaviour, skilled labour shortages and the delayed effects of long-term assured full employment on union militancy. The growth of such rigidities in the labour market provided evidence for Godley's view (Krause and Salant, 1977, pp. 449–92) that inflation took effect initially in factor markets and raised product prices through the markup mechanism, even when there was little *general* excess demand.

The second inflationary bout of 1979–82 made a primarily demand-centred theory no longer credible. Not only were supply-side shocks in the form of food and oil price rises too evident to be ignored. Import prices as a whole were rising at an annual rate of 15 per cent, while wages, propelled by the Clegg award in the public sector and emulative behaviour in the private, were rising considerably faster, and more than was necessary to compensate for the real reduction previously sustained. Meanwhile, unemployment stood at 8.8 per cent and was rising fast. Demand deficiency seemed unquestionable and costs clearly the main immediate source of the revived inflation.

In the summer of 1980 inflation turned down and thereafter remained at much lower levels throughout 1982–7. This owed much to falls in raw material prices. The approximate simultaneity of the downturns in inflation and monetary growth seems hard to reconcile with the common claim made by 'monetarist' writers (e.g. Laidler, 1974) that such changes are marked by a time lag of about two years. Even harder for such writers to explain was the monetary explosion, at rates of up to 19 per cent, which marked the years 1984–7 without, in that period at least, producing the predicted hyperinflation. Instead, inflation edged downwards. If monetary growth does unfailingly produce inflation, it can certainly take longer to do so than monetarists have predicted. Even in periods when money and inflation did move together, moreover, the direction of causality seems sometimes to have differed from what monetarists had claimed. Much of the monetary growth of

1979–80 resulted directly from fresh credit extended to help firms badly hit by the fall in demand accompanying interest rate increases. In 1972–3 money caused inflation; in 1979–80 much of it was created as a result of measures taken to check inflation.

Our period therefore saw a varied and continually changing mix of causal factors at work. Exogenous factors clearly included the world commodity price booms of 1972–3 and 1979–80. Political shocks, including almost every general election of the period as well as the EEC referendum of 1975, were also of major importance, contributing to inflation through the medium of pre-election promises and booms, and through the abandonment or delaying of policies of restraint until forthcoming elections were over. The effect was in each case the same. With uncanny regularity the advent of elections was favourable to inflation.

One further shock to the inflationary process worked, at least in the short run, in the direction of stability. This was the early decision of the Thatcher government to leave the exchange rate to be determined entirely by the market, with the result that when, in 1979, interest rates were raised to record levels, the resulting revaluation brought about a marked abatement of the rise in sterling import prices. The high exchange rate, however, like the high interest rates, was, not surprisingly, to prove unsustainable and sterling relapsed gradually over the early 1980s. Moreover, the effects in destroying manufacturing firms were grievous.

Even the strongest exogenous shocks impinged, however, upon a domestic economy which itself contained marked inflationary characteristics, many of them established long before severe inflation began. Thus, in the early 1970s excess demand certainly played a major inflationary role both through the domestic market and via the newly-floated exchange rate. Towards the end of the decade the country's high and rising propensity to import also came to constitute a major threat to price stability via the exchange rate. Even the modest boom of 1979–80 showed signs of bringing to a critical level growing balance-of-trade weaknesses which in the long run could scarcely fail, via exchange devaluation, to add to inflation.

More fundamental, however, was the underlying behaviour of wages. In part, wages adjusted to past price increases, as in the late 1960s and again after the end of the Wilson–Callaghan incomes policy in 1979–80. In larger part, however, wages rose faster than inflation – a general rule to which exceptions occurred only briefly in the periods of extraordinarily fast inflation associated with the two oil shocks and for a time during the 1975–8 incomes policy. In general, as Professor Phelps Brown points out (1983, pp. 147–67), real wages, powered by considerations of fairness which were often mutually inconsistent and by comparability links which bore little relationship to productivity or to supply and demand, tended to press steadily upwards through boom and slump alike. The tendency became more pronounced in and after the late 1960s, when a new and more aggressive attitude on the part of workers led, not only in Britain but in many industrial countries, to an increase in shopfloor militancy and visibly stronger pressure for higher wage settlements. For this change perhaps the most persuasive explanation so far advanced is the one mentioned above: that the influence of younger workers with no recollection of pre-war unemployment had by now come to dominate workers' collective behaviour. It was the problem posed by some such change as this, producing both persistent wage–cost pressures and continual overshoot in wages' reaction to price shocks, which constituted the chief unanswered challenge to anti-inflation policy, both in the 1970s and after inflation subsided, however temporarily, in the early 1980s.

## SALIENT FEATURES

Some main features of the inflation deserve special mention. The first concerns the attempt at indexation, for which the general case is discussed in Chapter 13. Here we merely note that the British experience revealed one strong argument in favour, one against. The argument in favour rests on fairness. During most of the 1970s and for most of the population, real rates of interest on some of the most widespread forms of saving – most especially, government bonds and savings certificates – were negative. As a result vast numbers of small savers suffered cuts in their real wealth, which the indexation of savings instruments (introduced in stages towards the end of our period) could have and belatedly did help to prevent, albeit at a price in the form of higher interest payments by the Treasury.

The argument apparently pointing in the other direction concerns wage indexation: the Heath government's foray into this field late in 1973, accompanying the boost to inflation given by the oil shock of late 1973 as it did, almost certainly led, as we have noted, to a much higher rate of inflation than would otherwise have occurred. The British evidence by itself is, of course, too partial to settle any issue; but it is interesting in providing vivid illustrations of two of the main arguments about indexation, one for and one against, which theorists have advanced.

Linked to the question of indexation was that of the redistribution of income and wealth. Here the customary doctrine that inflation is a major redistributor proved only too true. The real value of the national debt fell as the nominal pounds in which it was expressed lost over three quarters of their purchasing power during 1970–82, expropriating bondholders on a grand scale. The large proportion of the population who held deposits in building societies also suffered, even after reinvesting income, a real loss of wealth. Thus, between 1974 and 1986 the owner of a share account deposit would have seen his wealth grow by about 150 per cent while the retail price index rose by 195 per cent. Indeed, the newsletters issued by unit trusts in the early to mid-1980s, choosing their dates carefully, claimed real losses as great as 45 per cent. A large number of citizens with outstanding mortgage debts meanwhile benefited not only from tax reliefs but also from the fact that house prices rose, on trend, faster than the general price level while their money-dominated mortgage debts depreciated in real terms. In so far as these classes were not coincident, a redistribution of wealth must have ensued.

To say so much is to admit that one traditional strand of standard theory proved a poor guide to events. The doctrine that interest rates adjust to inflation in such a way as to preserve the real rate of return to savers − 'Fisher's Law' − was refuted in the early 1970s; and for several years the range of real interest rates for small savings, whether calculated prospectively or retrospectively (using the expected or the actual rate of inflation) remained negative. This situation continued until declining inflation and the competition afforded by more widespread availability of indexed government savings instruments combined to make positive real rates more generally available. The belief that negative real rates would lead to a fall in personal savings was likewise undermined. On the contrary, perhaps because of widespread anxiety about the future, the ratio of personal savings to personal disposable income rose sharply after 1972 to a peak of 12.4 per cent two years later, and to a second peak of 15.4 per cent in 1980, the peaks almost coinciding with times of maximum inflation.

The role of elections in economic management also deserves additional elaboration. To any observer in the later 1960s, the way in which the Labour government effectively ceased to implement its incomes policy and dropped its proposals for curbs on union power, previously described as essential, was hard to dissociate from the fact that a general election was approaching. Whether the 'Barber boom' was initiated, during the summer of 1971, in anticipation of a general election is disputable. Its prolongation for sixteen months after February 1974 seems certain to have been influenced by the expectation both of a second election, subsequently held in October, and of the referendum of the following summer, as the sharp change of policy thereafter testifies. Similarly, the relatively modest boom of 1977–9 pretty certainly owed something to electoral ambition while the wage push of the following year arose substantially from the direct and indirect effects of the pre-election promise to accept the Clegg recommendations. The unfailing tendency of electoral considerations to strengthen inflation in our period lends considerable force to the arguments of those who see in inflation the economic effects of inter-group conflict.

## INFLATION AND UNEMPLOYMENT

The summarist of inflationary thought in the 1970s can scarcely hope to avoid mention of the 'Phillips Curve'. Since, however, the topic has been discussed extensively elsewhere our treatment here will be brief.

A.W. Phillips' (1958) original claim, based on data for the years 1861–1957, was that during those years there existed a fairly stable inverse relationship, which could be graphed as a curve (see Glossary), between the rate of increase of wages and the level of unemployment; as either one rose, the other fell. Though the data were consistent with more than one explanation, the one which Phillips seems to have preferred was that wage changes were largely determined by supply and demand in the labour market.

Phillips also made a second claim. Dividing his period into individual business cycles and plotting data for each of these, he further argued that for any given level of unemployment the rate of wage increase was higher if unemployment was falling than if it was rising – an apparent sign of the influence of expectations upon wage settlements.

The statistical basis for the relationship, especially as it related to the distant past, did not escape criticism. Routh (1959), for example, argued that the standard wage rates used departed substantially from rates actually paid and that different series for wages and unemployment produced different results. Furthermore, it is fair to add that the most obvious examples of the Curve arise for years before 1923. Once the dramatic and well-documented relationship for the years 1913–22 had vanished, data for the later interwar years revealed a Curve which approached horizontality, with wage changes varying little as unemployment rose and fell. For the war years little more than amorphous bunching is perceptible, while in the early postwar years, when unemployment seldom varied outside a range of 1–2 per cent, the Curve became more nearly vertical. Both complete horizontality and complete verticality would, of course, indicate the absence of any relationship between the variables. None the less, the evidence presented by Phillips was copious and the correlation it yielded seemed in general strong, so that a large majority of economists accepted the Curve's existence not only for the years before 1957 but also, as it emerged, for those up to 1966.

With the second half of the 1960s, however, belief in the Curve suffered a severe setback. Throughout the whole of our period 1967–82, unemployment, on trend, rose steadily; and the trend continued through both of the major inflationary bouts. The Phillips Curve, with its 'trade-off' between inflation and unemployment, seemed to have vanished. Instead, the two variables seemed at best unrelated; at worst they were growing together.

One widely accepted interpretation of this joint deterioration, put forward by Friedman (1968) and Phelps (1968), centred on expectations. When the government stimulated demand in order to reduce unemployment, additional workers accepted employment in the expectation that the higher-than-usual wages they were offered would represent increased *real* wages. Employers, however, taking advantage of buoyant demand, passed their growing labour costs on in higher prices, so that the higher nominal wages before long proved deceptive. Workers and their unions then demanded further pay rises, thus reducing back to its initial level the number of workers firms were willing to employ. In this way employment was only enabled to rise beyond its 'natural' level – the equilibrium level, equating supply with demand, to which a free market would tend to move – by means of a temporary error arising from unanticipated inflation. The argument concluded that in order to cut unemployment permanently by means of demand reflation, it would be necessary to have *permanent unexpectedly high* inflation – in short, ever-increasing inflation.

Subsequent theorists, following the argument further, developed the theme of governmental powerlessness under the label 'rational expectations'. This line of thought accepted the premise that only *unanticipated* government action would thwart the workings of the market. It claimed, however, that normally the public, taking account of all relevant information and applying neoclassical economic theory, would *expect* expansionary policies to produce inflation, so that those policies would fail to lower unemployment, an effect which could have arisen only because of workers' erroneous expectations. In short, government reflationary policies could work only by inducing mistaken beliefs; and economic agents were too 'rational' to succumb to these.

These later theoretical developments are insufficiently relevant to our subject to warrant comment here. The virtue of the new expectations-augmented Phillips Curve was that it seemed to account for the failure of inflation to fall as unemployment rose. Further, it drew attention to the rigidity of the labour market and the need for institutional reform rather than unaided reflationary policy — a contention endorsing the widespread suspicion that policy should aim primarily to improve supply-side efficiency rather than merely control demand.

In retrospect, however, a number of writers came to feel that the aggregates plotted in drawing the Phillips Curve concealed more than they revealed. As Phelps Brown (1983, p. 153) points out, the manifold imperfections of the labour market had even before 1966 been evident to those involved in pay negotiations. Unions obtained pay increases from loss-making firms; pay rose in contracting, as well as in expanding industries; and 'key' wage settlements in a few leading industries were replicated in others where labour market conditions were far different. There was also some evidence that both low pay rises and high unemployment were twin effects of economic depression, with the level of profits exerting a direct influence, independent of the demand for labour, on wage settlements. Indeed, growing doubts about the Phillips Curve even gave some economists pause as to the habits of mind which their subject tended to instil in its students. Phelps Brown (1983, p. 152) wrote:

[The Curve] was seized on by economists who, perplexed by the persistent and seemingly self-propelled rise in wages, increasingly felt the need for an explanation of this movement that would be consistent with the general assumptions of economic theory. They were not historians, content to accept each year's wage level as emerging . . . as the outcome of a vast number of factors making for or resisting change. Nor had they been moving close to the daily affairs of labour management. The minds they brought to the study of inflation had been trained to arrange their observations within a framework of equilibrating forces. A study of the general level of wage-rates that, on a survey of the data, ascribed its movements to the impersonal forces of supply and demand in the labour market, carried conviction with them instantly.

Kaldor (1972, p. 1240) likewise viewed economists' enthusiasm for the Phillips Curve as a sure sign of the pre-scientific state of the subject. The two warnings are salutary. In fact, however, it is highly arguable that anyone wishing to defend the original Phillips Curve against its critics need only study Phillips' paper in detail. Phillips himself omitted from consideration any data for years in which cost of living adjustments arising from exogenous price shocks seemed large enough to upset his relationship. In particular, such years were those when import prices rose fast enough to make resulting cost of living adjustments to wages both unabsorbable by productivity increases and unconcealable beneath the usual rise in wages due to competitive bidding between employers. The years concerned he judged to be those in which import prices rose at a rate exceeding a stated critical level of 13 per cent. The formula by which he arrived at this figure was based on the assumption that the value of imports was equal to one fifth of total national expenditure. A 10 per cent increase in import prices would thus be necessary to raise the overall price level by 2 per cent, or, put otherwise, to counteract the price-lowering potential of a 2 per cent rise in productivity. By the 1970s, however, the import ratio had risen closer to three tenths, and if, using Phillips' formula, we take account of this higher ratio, the critical percentage falls. The rise in import prices now needed to offset a 2 per cent rise in domestic productivity is 6.7 per cent and the new critical limit is not 13 but 10 per cent.

The importance of this is that in every year between 1973 and 1980 (inclusive) except 1978 the year-on-year rise in import prices exceeded 13 per cent and *a fortiori* any lower percentage. Moreover, between 1980 and 1982 it is highly arguable that the missing Curve briefly reappeared. The years of the 'missing curve' thus shrink to 1969–72 inclusive. If one is prepared to allow that a Phillips Curve ever existed, it is possible, with a little *ad hoc* explanation of 1969–72 in terms of the demise of the Wilson incomes policy and subsequent catch-up, to argue for the continued existence throughout our period of the Phillips relationship, as originally specified. Whether the effort of formalising that relationship in a Curve is worthwhile may be doubted. None the less annual data for 1980–2 seem *prima facie* consistent with the existence of some broad 'Phillips effect'. To this, moreover, may be added two further features of the labour market during our period, namely: the marked propensity of tax encroachment, devaluation and expansionary policies alike to stimulate wage inflation; and the apparent tendency, after a series of external shocks, for wage inflation to accelerate continuously with little regard for the level of unemployment.

## MONETARY TARGETING: AN ASSESSMENT

It remains to ask what broad conclusions, if any, may be drawn from the 'monetarist' policies of the late 1970s and early 1980s.

One finding which, though obvious, deserves emphasis, is the scarcity of reliable relationships between macroeconomic variables not only in the Thatcher years but throughout 1967–82. The stable demand for money function which some researchers had claimed to identify in the 1960s later proved elusive (Artis and Lewis, 1974), even if it was not, indeed, misspecified in the first place. The velocity of circulation proved far from constant, varying by almost 50 per cent, for example, between 1974:1 and 1979:4. There was little success in relating that part of the PSBR which was funded by borrowing from the banking system with the growth of the money supply (Kaldor, 1980). On occasion, a lagged correlation between monetary growth and inflation did, by general admission, seem to emerge, as generally in the period 1968–73; but the rise in inflation late in 1969 despite slackening demand, casts grave doubt on any simple causal explanation of the link. On the other hand, the rise in interest rates in November 1979 clearly *was* a cause of the promptly following rise in the exchange rate, with its unhappy effects on output and exports. The most certain causal relationship of the period thus operated to damage the economy, not to help it. Not surprisingly, reliance on £M3 as a monetary target and on its previously popular correlations with other variables was later abandoned. By 1986 economic policy bore far more clearly the signs of step-by-step choice between the conflicting aims of lower unemployment, lower inflation and greater external surplus – what the Chancellor termed a policy of 'common sense' – than of any of the monetary doctrines with which the Conservatives had come to power.

A second lesson of the 1979–82 experiment concerns the government's initial hope of altering expectations of inflation, and so inflation itself, though the announcement of money supply targets for several years ahead. There seems no doubt that this experiment failed. The announcements had little or no perceptible effect on wage bargainers or price setters. Still worse, financial markets did pay attention and when, as continually happened, the targets set were exceeded, rates of interest rose, with apparent perversity, in anticipation of tougher government action. Even without this unforeseen effect, however, a policy designed to control the supply of money in the presence of persistent shifts in demand could in any case hardly have failed to produce interest rate instability and an ensuing instability of exchange rates. In two separate ways, therefore – through shifts in the demand for money and through different effects on expectations in different markets – monetary policy led to increased instability.

A further conclusion hard to dispute is that attempts to control the money supply were unsuccessful. Of the three possible methods – direct controls, control of a monetary base precisely linked with the money supply, and high interest rates – only the last was used with any persistence.

What may broadly be accounted a version of the first was already in use when the Conservatives assumed power. This was embodied in the supplementary special deposits scheme, which penalised banks for any unduly fast growth of interest-bearing liabilities. It was, however, soon abandoned, partly because it was widely avoided, partly because it was believed to limit and distort competition. Abandonment was itself accompanied by a sharp growth in the money supply as, through a process known as 'reintermediation', large amounts of private lending were rechanneled through the banks.

The second possible monetary curb, via control of a monetary base, was never used. The government therefore fell back on the third, higher interest rates. These, too, generally failed to curb monetary growth. In the short run they stimulated monetary growth through distress borrowing, while any effect in the longer run seems to have operated more through reduced demand than through supply. Their side effects, moreover, were gravely damaging. Not only did they contribute to the rise of the exchange rate, which is hard to dissociate from the dramatic worsening, as soon as recovery started, of Britain's trade balance in manufactures. They showed, too, the propensity, noted decades earlier by Alvin Hansen (1949, p. 166) to have little effect up to some critical psychological level, but above that level to 'put the economy into a nosedive'.' Once lodged at a high level, moreover, interest rates proved remarkably difficult to lower, partly because of external considerations, partly perhaps for fear of unleashing the private sector's vastly increased money balances in a fresh inflationary spending spree.

On the severe rebuff received by quantity theory during the inflationary upsurge of our period we have already commented. It would, however, be unwise to assume that even this negative conclusion has general validity. The mistake may lie not so much in the theory as in the assumption of its universality. The velocity of circulation, falling sharply, if irregularly, into the 1980s, played a part in enabling very modest inflation to be reconciled with a dramatic rise in £M3, at an annual average rate of 11.75 per cent, between 1980 and 1985. (H.M. Treasury, 1986, p. 2). Moreover, aggressive competition between banks succeeded in increasing the money holdings of private sector institutions. Unease persisted, however, about the likely permanence of these changes of behaviour, especially in the event of a marked fall in real interest rates. Economists had, on a grand scale, taken to quantity theory in the early 1970s. Now that their expectations had been dashed, some foresaw a danger that quantity theory and its attendant unpopular 'monetarist' policies might be forgotten too completely in any future recovery.

## MONETARISM: AN OBITUARY?

The Mansion House speech of 1985 may be taken as marking the end of the era of monetarist policies in Britain. In his speech not only did the Chancellor declare the broad money supply £M3 no longer a target. In addition he acknowledged the importance of influencing the exchange rate in line with government objectives, a policy rejected through the period of soaring exchanges a few years before. Although a new monetary aggregate, MO − the value of notes and coins in circulation and in bankers' balances at the central bank − was duly announced as a target, the speech in effect was an admission that intermediate targets were too distantly related to ultimate targets to be of much use; a corresponding shift was therefore made towards far broader assessments of policy and towards attempts to influence the more conventional 'Keynesian' instruments: the exchange rate, interest rates and fiscal revenue and expenditure. The speech was to be followed by the announcement of public spending increases and tax cuts the following month, and by steps towards fiscal reflation in 1986 and 1987, an election year. Indeed, but for the continuing PSBR target and the refusal to introduce an incomes policy in the private sector (which would probably have been unacceptable to the unions in any case), all of the macro economic policies of 1979 had by then been abandoned.

The end of the monetarist era in Britain, three years after its end in the United States, should provide a good point for drawing some general conclusions. Expressed in the broadest terms, the object of the policies of 1979–85 was to make people responsible for the consequences of their own actions. With the money supply strictly restrained, wage increases would visit unemployment upon those who had insisted upon them. If this fact could be impressed on trade unions they would curb their wage claims and unemployment would be avoided. Hence the importance attached to 'announcement effects'. As we have seen, a fresh access of responsibility was not so easily evoked. The effect of the policy thus proved to be harsh, probably far harsher than the government had ever envisaged, raising unemployment to the extent of perhaps an additional half million by July 1981, in Pratten's (1982) view, and again very substantially thereafter. In the view of Artis and Bladen-Hovell (1987, pp. 23–47), economic policies accounted for about a third of the 1979–84 recession. The only defence for those policies could be the claim that they worked, curbing inflation in the short run and thus promoting long run growth. But as we have seen, though inflation certainly fell, the fall owed much initially to the non-repetition of Clegg, an *administrative* decision, and to the fall in world commodity prices.

As far as the Medium-Term Financial Strategy (MFTS) is concerned, the short-term lesson seems to be that intermediate monetary targets are neither easy to hit, nor, if hit, of reliable usefulness. Fforde (1983, p. 207) argues that the targets served a purpose in enabling the government 'to stand back from output and employment as such and stress the vital part played' by industrial costs. That is, the strategy allowed the government to shift responsibility for the growing unemployment from itself to those unions which refused to accommodate their demands to the (theoretically) restricted money supply. Up to a point,

Fforde's argument rings true. The change in public opinion on inflation and unemployment during the early Thatcher years was indeed striking. But two strands in it must be distinguished. While, according to successive opinion polls, many people accepted that the government *could* do nothing to reduce unemployment, many fewer people seemed happy that it *should* take no action if it could. In short, acceptance of union blame for unemployment commonly depended on the belief in governmental powerlessness. This link between two quite different beliefs greatly weakens the case which Fforde presents for the effectiveness of government policies. Furthermore, whatever the effect of the government's arguments on public opinion generally, they seemed to have little influence on the unions; real wages and unemployment still rose together and it remained always doubtful how long the belief would persist that the government had no power to reduce unemployment in the long run.

A third line of defence seems to carry more weight. The Conservatives had from before 1979, always acknowledged that monetarism alone was 'not enough'; other structural reforms were also needed. The high unemployment towards which their policies substantially contributed afforded an opportunity that might not otherwise have arisen for introducing, and gaining general aquiescence in, gradually intensifying legislation to curb unions' powers and to democratise their procedures. No doubt the legislation did less to achieve this acquiescence than did government victory in the miners' strike of 1984–5. That too, however, owed something to the low demand for, and high stocks of, coal arising from the recession. A cautious judgement on the whole period would be that government economic doctrines, however untrue and costly they proved, combined with world recession to bring about a tilt in the perennial conflict between government and unions and in this unpredicted way may have done more to curb long-run inflation than they did directly through monetary policy.

As for the automatic stimulus to recovery and long-term growth expected to result from disinflation, the evidence is mixed. The economy as a whole, and particularly manufacturing, showed throughout 1980–87 widespread and convincing signs of benefiting not only from the microchip revolution but also from the increased authority of management which recession conferred and from the end of overmanning in a wide range of industries, both private and nationalised. Productivity as a result grew at sustained and high rates. On the other hand, above average productivity growth is normal in any recovery and it remained to be seen whether the growth of the 1980s would persist beyond the cyclical upswing and the once-for-all cuts in overmanning. The base for future growth was certainly low. Not until 1985 did industrial production again reach its 1979 level, while even in early 1987 manufacturing had still not made good the fall in output from its 1979 peak.

Given the circumstances of May 1979, with incomes policy in ruin probably beyond early repair, a domestic wage explosion already assured and soaring worldwide inflation, did there exist, contrary to Mrs Thatcher's repeated assertion, any alternative to the monetarist policies chosen?

The 364 economists who, in a celebrated letter to *The Times* in the spring of 1981, gave a negative answer to the question were most open to criticism for their failure to agree on any precise alternative policy. Limited space here confines us to considering only one of the possibilities, This is the policy of restraining inflation primarily by tax increases and only secondarily by interest rate increases designed to influence monetary growth. Such was, substantially, the 'Keynesian' policy used, admittedly in less extreme circumstances, after the devaluation of November 1967 to prevent excessive domestic demand curbing exports and to restrain wage increases designed to compensate for, and therefore largely cancel, the effects of devaluation.

Both in 1968–70 and in 1979–85 unemployment was rising while demand fell, partly as a result of government policy. In both cases sterling import prices were rising, while wage restraint and disinflation were primary objectives. In other respects, however, the situations differed. In 1967–8 current external payments were in deficit; in the early 1980s, because of North Sea oil, they were in surplus. In the 1960s an incomes policy, albeit by this time of dubious effectiveness, was ostensibly in operation. In the 1980s, such a policy was applied effectively, though only in the public sector. The late 19670s saw an initial sharp rise in import prices followed by a marked fall. In the

1980s the initial rise was far steeper and in terms of sterling, though not of dollars, continued, albeit at a much reduced pace, into the mid-1980s.

These different circumstances make comparison imperfect. Even so the contrast is sufficiently marked to deserve note. Under the policies of the earlier period there was no crash and no major recession despite tax increases of extreme severity. The PSBR fell rapidly to negative values, compared with only a slow fall in the 1980s. The current account improved sharply after an eighteen-month time-lag, compared with a sharp deterioration of the non-oil balance in the later period; not all of this contrast can be attributed to the very different levels of demand prevailing in export markets in the two periods, nor to growing real wage resistance over time, not to the unaided exchange rate effects of North Sea oil. In the 1960s the growth of broad money fell sharply in successive years, in contrast with persistent failure to respond adequately to the monetary targeting of the 1980s. Perhaps most strikingly, the inventory recession, not combined with any substantial fall in real consumption, which formed the backbone of the 1980–3 slump led to continuously soaring bankruptcies; tax policy in the earlier period produced nothing on this scale. Finally, the earlier period followed and reinforced a devaluation with the potential for favourable effects on trade; the early 1980s saw a sharp and sustained revaluation with opposite consequences. Making all due allowance for the different circumstances and the greater severity of the problems facing Mrs Thatcher's government in 1979, it is hard to believe that either the control of monetary aggregates, the avoidance of grave side-effects or the achievement of ultimate disinflationary objectives was as successful in the later period as would have been the case had tax-based policies been used from the beginning. True, the 1981 Budget belatedly invoked large tax increases; but this was after the harm was done, when many firms were already in trouble because of earlier monetary policy and when their demands for liquid funds had already given rise to sharp monetary growth. Tax increases would not, of course, have been a move towards the Conservatives' desired goal of reducing taxation and cutting the size of the public sector. But these were two objectives which in any case became more distant in the government's early years, as both public expenditure and taxation rose in proportion to GNP. It is not clear that temporary tax increases need have delayed the move towards smaller government any more than happened in the event; and if they would, the question remains whether, even from a Conservative point of view, the trade-off might not still have been worthwhile. Certainly we should be wise to note the suspicion left by the events of our period that the goal of cutting the size of the public sector may be inconsistent with the achievement of disinflation without a severe slump. Meanwhile, the experience of 1979–83 affords a warning that high interest rates, inducing a rundown of stocks of final goods, can curb investment and production and lead to the scrapping of productive capacity on a large scale without much affecting the level of consumption which a belt-tightening exercise is presumably designed to curb.

# 12   American Inflation from Johnson to Reagan

## THE FIRST PHASE

In the United States, as in Britain, inflation began to accelerate long before the boom in import prices began. Through the mid-1960s President Johnson's administration broadly continued to pursue 'Keynesian' policies previously introduced by President Kennedy. Generally expansionist in tone, these depended heavily on demand management by fiscal and monetary means while also employing a number of more directly interventionist devices such as wage and price guidelines and an interest equalisation tax to check capital outflows. For several years policies of these kinds seemed on the whole to prove successful. The growth of output throughout the first half of the 1960s was widely regarded as satisfactory and was unaccompanied by any serious degree of inflation or by any marked deterioration in the balance of payments.

The turning point is generally taken to have been mid-1965 (e.g. Blinder, 1979; OECD, 1965–6–7) and the augmentation of defence spending in connection with the Vietnam War. In 1966/7 the emerging excessive strain on resources, with the federal budget deficit on a seasonally adjusted national accounts basis sextupling in less than a year, was countered by higher interest rates and a 'credit crunch' at the cost of a mini-recession; but at the end of this, continuous inflation finally emerged. By the following year the acceleration of inflation observed simultaneously in many countries was also unmistakable in the United States.

The main impulse at this stage continued to come from

domestic demand led by defence spending and the stockbuilding to which it gave rise (Shapiro, 1977, p. 276). In the year ending 1968:1 final real sales grew sharply. Federal government expenditure, of which 60 per cent was on defence, and business investment led the way. A 13 per cent growth of imports between the second half of 1967 and the first half of 1968 contributed towards a sharp worsening of the trade balance. Measures were taken to curb demand, including a tightening of banks' reserve requirements, a renewed rise in the Federal Reserve's discount rate and pressure on commercial banks' reserves through open market operations; but this time they proved inadequate. Even the belated passing into law in August of a tax increase to pay for military expenditure which the administration had first requested in January 1967, and further substantial rises in interest rates, did not prevent inflation worsening, year on year, into 1969.

The role of other factors seems to have been limited. US import prices were at the time rising at less than 2 per cent a year so that they can be ruled out as an important cause of the upsurge. Other countries' expenditure on American goods cannot be blamed, for net exports during 1968–70 were at the lowest level of the postwar period to date. The only doubt may concern a possible auxiliary role for wages. Perry (1980) argues that in each of the years 1968–71 the index of average hourly earnings, led by union wage settlements, rose faster than consumer prices, though not by so much as to have been unabsorbable by productivity increases; while Brown (1985, p. 99), using annual rates of change, draws attention to the concomitance of wage-push and an acceleration of expenditure in 1966 and 1968. Overall, therefore, war-related demand, possibly augmented by some wage pressure, seems to have been the principal source of the acceleration, proving too strong for the monetary restraints imposed.

The general expectation of the time was that a reduced level of demand would produce price stability. That this did not happen during the mini-recession of late 1969 and 1970 seems to have been largely attributable to wage inertia. An important part of the American labour force negotiated its pay under long-term contracts often of three years' duration, which therefore tended to embody workers' and employers' expectations about price movements for some time ahead. In this way wage increases agreed during the boom years may have continued to exert inflationary pressures even during the substantial unemployment of the 1969–70 recession. Shapiro (1977, p. 293) further argues that a second type of inertia, taking the form of a widespread determination of different groups to maintain their *relative* wage positions, is also likely to have played a part in keeping up the level of wage settlements. Blinder (1979) argues that observers may have been too quick to conclude that inflation had becomer insensitive to changes in the level of unemployment. Whereas in 1970 the rate of inflation of the consumer price index remained above 5 per cent despite a rise in unemployment by the year's end to 6 per cent, by April 1971 inflation had fallen to only 4.4 per cent. Others, however, (e.g. Popkin, 1977, p. 3) point to the continuation of a steeply rising underlying trend, if changes in the mortgage interest rate are omitted, right up to August 1971 and the beginning of President Nixon's incomes policy.

*Table 12.1: US Economic Indicators, 1967–9*

|  | 1967 | 1968 | 1969 |
|---|---|---|---|
| Hourly earnings index (1963 = 100) | 115.0 | 122.4 | 129.7 |
| Unemployment (%) | 3.8 | 3.6 | 3.5 |
| Broad money M2 (December) $ bill., s.a. | 345.7 | 378.0 | 386.8 |
| Rise in consumer price index (percentage) | 2.8 | 4.2 | 5.4 |

From the recovery of 1971 until late 1973 the US economy continued to show many of the usual signs of worsening inflation, though because of controls this was in part suppressed rather than overt. Average hourly earnings rose substantially faster than retail prices, but whatever the role of wages in amplifying the inflation, the symptoms of pressure stemming immediately from other sources were widespread enough to make it doubtful whether wages were the main active initiator. The symptoms in question included a rising level of demand in relation to productive resources, falling unemployment, and a money supply which, broadly defined, was growing at double-digit rates. Furthermore, there occurred between 1970 and 1973 a huge growth of imports from $40 billion to $70 billion, and a consequent trend deterioration, which became dramatic in 1972, in the balance of payments on current account. Between the ultimately unsuccessful Smithsonian conference of December 1971, designed to stabilise world exchange rates, and May 1973, shortly after the final floating of the US rate, the trade-weighted value of the dollar on the foreign exchanges fell by about 9 per cent. Well before the first oil shock injected an exogenous inflationary shock into the American wage–price–exchange rate spiral, home-grown inflationary pressures, soon to be released by the ending of controls, were thus already mounting alarmingly.

## PRICE AND WAGE CONTROLS, 1971–4

Into this general picture the 'New Economic Policy' announced by President Nixon in August 1971 introduced price and wage controls of a kind previously unknown in the United States. The adoption of controls arose from the suspicion, which had grown since the experience of the late 1960s, that the ability of demand management policies to abate inflation had by now been seriously impaired. A further reason, in the view of many writers (e.g. Blinder, 1979; Tufte, 1975, pp. 6, 47–8; Stein, 1984, p. 187) was the President's desire to achieve popularity by combining at least temporarily low inflation with a high level of activity, in the hope of winning re-election in November 1972.

The details of the policy varied a good deal during its continuance up to April 1974. Phase One, a compulsory price and wage freeze, lasted for a ninety-day period ending in November. Phase Two, a more flexible but more complex regime, sought basically to limit the average price increases of firms with over 5000 employees to a maximum of 2½ per cent and to enforce a general pay 'standard' or norm of 5½ per cent, with a corresponding ceiling of 4 per cent for dividends. A Pay Board and Price Commission were set up to execute the new policies. When Phase Two ended in January 1973 compulsory price controls were continued in certain sectors (notably food, health care and construction), while elsewhere a policy of self-administered adherence to guidelines was instituted. The general standard for permissible wage increases was maintained but greater flexibility with more exceptions was tolerated and in general the Phase was seen as less severe than earlier policy. Inflation accelerated again and for two months in the summer of 1973 a second freeze was instituted in an attempt to check this. Finally, Phase Four beginning in August 1973 led, in a gradual and in some respects inconsistent manner, to final decontrol in April 1974.

The effectiveness of the controls has been the subject of intense econometric investigation. The method most favoured has been to use pre-controls data to estimate equations which can then be used to predict wages and prices as they would have been during 1971–4 in the absence of controls. The difference between these predictions and actual observed values is taken to measure the effect of the controls. Alternatively, data for the period of the controls have been used to estimate equations attempting to 'explain' the behaviour of prices or wages, and the coefficients of dummy variables in the equations have been taken to measure the effects of the controls.

Both methods are known to be open to serious criticism (see e.g. Blinder, 1979, p. 117), but the surprising degree of agreement in the results of the various studies may perhaps constitute some ground for accepting their general tenor. R.J. Gordon, in a series of papers (see esp. 1973) using both methods, arrives at estimates of the maximum restraining effect of controls on the price level which lie variously between 2 and 3½ per cent. In each case he finds that, when controls ended, prices caught up with the level they would have reached had there been no controls; indeed, in at least one case they actually overshot that level. Bosworth and Vroman (1977), using equations estimated for the precontrols period, found that the controls produced a reduction of about 0.5 per cent in the annual rate of price increase. Nadiri and Gupta (1977) similarly found small reductions in both wages and prices, while Al-Sammarie (1977) found a small effect upon prices but none on wages. Blinder, using a within-sample method, points to a possible maximum reduction in the consumer price index of 1.6 per cent, a result similar to Perry's (1980), but with post-controls catch-up. The results are, in short, remarkably similar to those commonly found for prices and incomes policies in Britain: the policy met with some small success while it was in operation; but it was very hard to maintain for long periods and when it ended catch-up was almost (or possibly even more than) complete.


## POLICY AFTER THE FIRST OIL SHOCK

The period of the controls was accompanied by a rising level of demand stimulated by expansionary fiscal policy involving large federal deficits. Between 1970 and 1973:1 expenditure on consumer durables and housebuilding rose at an annual rate of 17 per cent and business investment was buoyant.

Monetary policy is more difficult to interpret but the broad money supply expanded quickly and interest rates fell from about mid-1971 until early 1972, before beginning to rise again. Gordon (1980) finds that the close relationship between the broad money supply M2 and nominal GNP which he observes for a second postwar decade persisted in 1967–73, with a gap of two years between peak growth of M2 in mid-1971 and peak growth of nominal GNP. Furthermore, for 1960–77 he finds the velocity of M2 remarkably constant and suggests the conclusion that 'the boom of 1972–3 was primarily due to the influence of the acceleration in monetary growth in 1971, although some credit is due to consumer optimism engendered by the price control programme of 1971–2.' Certainly, in the first half of 1973 the level of demand was high enough for capacity shortages to be reported.

By that year, however, two further complicating factors had appeared. First, poor harvests and buoyant demand at home and abroad in 1972 had stimulated a rise in food prices which was to reach an annual rate of 15 per cent during the first three quarters of 1973 and which continued strongly upward thereafter. Second, in the fourth quarter OPEC quadrupled the price of crude oil, of which the United States was now a net importer, bringing about, for the three quarters to mid-1974, increases in retail energy prices at an annual rate of 44 per cent (Blinder, 1979, p. 76) and accounting for half the acceleration of inflation in that period. Nor were these the only commodity

*Table 12.2: US Economic Indicators, 1970–6 (per cent)*

|  | 1970 | 1971 | 1972 | 1973 | 1974 | 1975 | 1976 |
|---|---|---|---|---|---|---|---|
| Unemployment | 5.0 | 6.0 | 5.6 | 4.9 | 5.6 | 8.5 | 7.7 |
| Implicit consumption deflator | 4.6 | 3.8 | 3.7 | 7.4 | 11.0 | 6.1 | 4.8 |
| CPI | 5.6 | 3.5 | 3.4 | 8.3 | 12.1 | 7.4 | 5.1 |
| Broad money M2 | 5.9 | 13.5 | 12.8 | 7.2 | 5.9 | 12.1 | 13.3 |
| Weighted av. exchange rate | – 1.1 | – 5.7 | – 3.5 | – 10.6 | 2.0 | 2.7 | 2.7 |
| Hourly earnings index | 6.6 | 6.7 | 6.6 | 6.3 | 9.1 | 7.4 | 7.3 |

Unemployment figures are annual averages. All other variables are Q4/Q4 rates of change.

*Source:* Peter B. Clark (1985).

prices to soar. US import prices overall, expressed in foreign currencies, rose by 7 per cent in 1972 and 17 per cent in 1973, before rising to a startling post-OPEC rate of 44 per cent in 1974. The phasing out of controls in the months leading up to April 1974 and the subsequent catch-up of wages thus constituted only one more factor making for an acceleration of inflation, and one which at the peak period of inflation in 1974 helped to make non-food, non-energy prices rise almost as fast as prices generally. Blinder, indeed, points to a surprising degree of symmetry in the rise and fall of non-food, non-energy inflation, and notably in the prices of 'motor vehicles and parts' and of 'other non-durable goods'. That these items, which accounted for about half of the acceleration in inflation between the pre-peak period 1973:2–1974:1 and the peak period three quarters later, should subsequently have subsided substantially to their original level is, he argues, ground for supposing that some once-for-all shock must have been the predominant cause of the inflationary upsurge. His conclusion, accordingly, is that while the money supply may determine the rate of inflation in the longer run, its performance as a predictor of actual events in this period was poor.

Meanwhile, even though wages failed to keep pace with the cost of living in 1974, double-digit inflation appeared. By that time both fiscal and monetary policy were contractionary, with the oil price rise additionally lowering the level of activity, not only via higher prices and a drain of income abroad but also, it was plausibly argued, through its 'wealth effect' in lowering the real value of dollar-denominated assets and so producing a curtailment of expenditure. The level of economic activity fell sharply, reaching its nadir in the early months of 1975.

## THE MID-DECADE

As noted above, the persistence of inflation during the recession of 1970 had sown some doubt as to the efficacy of earlier anti-inflationary policies. By 1974 concern on this score had become acute as the country entered upon what Perry (1978, p. 2) was to describe as 'the first time in US history that a severe recession had failed to stop inflation'; for the growing suspicion that demand management could no longer curb the rate of price increases seemed to carry the implications that future expansionary policies might build up an ever-increasing level of continuing inflation.

To some commentators the inflation seemed less intractable than was widely supposed. As Arthur F. Burns (1975, pp. 625–6) noted, inflation fell from 11 to 5½ per cent as demand slackened between 1974:2 and 1975:2. In so far as residual inflation was indeed hard to eradicate, the explanation seems principally to have lain in wage inertia. It was not that US inflation drew much of its initiating momentum from wage push in the mid-1970s, as seems at times to have occurred in Britain. On the contrary, not only did real average hourly earnings fall for a time after the first oil shock but there was, according to Gordon (1981, p. 34; see also p. 24), 'no sign whatever of wage-push' in the period to 1973:1. Brown, too, finds wages rising as profits' share of value added fell (his specified symptoms of wage-push) only in 1974, a year in which other cost increases were also tending to reduce profitability. Perry (1978) finds that with many wages determined by long-term contracts, current wage increases, while showing some relation to earlier price increases, were more closely related to past wage increases than to any other relevant variable. More controversially, he argues that while the pressure of demand for labour, as measured by the level of unemployment, produced only weak effects on wages, it could none the less produce enough effect to slow inflation to an extent not much less than in the 1960s. The Phillips Curve, on this view, though perhaps in modified form, still perceptibly survived.

A related claim consistent with this general line of argument cites evidence due to Perloff and Wachter (1979) that among prime adult workers (whose wages were less responsive to recession than wages generally) the proportion out of work had fallen. This, it is argued, would explain the persistence of a given rate of wage increase in the presence of increased unemployment or, put otherwise, the acceleration of the rate of wage increase associated with any given level of unemployment. Proponents of the monetary theory of inflation, on the other hand, fortified by the surge in monetary growth which had preceded and in a widespread view caused the inflationary boom of 1972–3, explained the continued high inflation of the mid-1970s in terms of rooted expectations. What presented them with difficulties was the apparently shifting relationship between broad money and nominal GNP in the years 1973–9 (Gordon, 1980).

A broad summary of such conflicting opinions is perhaps impossible. Majority support could, however, be found for the propositions that the growth of demand, fuelled by monetary growth, played a major role in the inflation until it was submerged beneath external supply shocks; and that wages, though eluding close relationship with most other variables, seem at least to have displayed a good deal of inertia in relation to their own past rates of growth.

The worldwide recession which accompanied these developments arose primarily from a sudden large shift of export surpluses into the hands of a small group of oil-exporting countries not immediately able to restore to oil-consuming countries the demand they had thus withdrawn. The main interest of the US recession for the study of inflation lay in the failure of wages to respond in the expected way, or at least at the expected speed, to conditions of high unemployment. In the course of 1974 and 1975 some falls in real average hourly earnings, at times substantial, were observed. Thereafter, continuous real increases recommenced and for the rest of the decade as recovery proceeded, the rate of increase in nominal terms edged upwards once more. The consumer price index also accelerated, moving from a 5.1 per cent increase in 1976 to 12.8 in 1979; the corresponding rate for the personal consumption deflator, probably a more reliable indicator at this stage, rose from 4.8 per cent to 9.5 over the same period.

The economic policies of the middle of the decade were uncertain and varying; but with fiscal measures taken in January 1978 to boost the economy and with the money supply rising, at times ahead of the published targets, inflationary pressures, never far suppressed, were quick to return. From its year-on-year low point in 1976 the rate of increase in the consumer price index again topped 9 per cent in 1978:1. Food prices led at an annual growth rate of 16½ per cent and average hourly earnings gained 10 per cent. A downward trend in the dollar exchange rate aggravated the situation.

The anti-inflation programme announced in April of that year proposed a 5½ per cent ceiling to the salary rises of Federal employees and consultative procedures designed to decelerate inflation in the private sector. It was followed by a tightening of monetary policy and the announcement of voluntary price and wage guidelines in the autumn; but inflation continued to worsen throughout that and the following year. Supply bottlenecks had also begun to appear in some manufacturing industries. In October 1979 stiffer monetary measures designed to control bank reserves were implemented, accompanied by a sharp rise in the Federal Reserve's discount rate. A fall in the rate of monetary growth followed, but before this could be observed domestic influences, as in 1973, had been overwhelmed by international ones. The rise of over 130 per cent in crude oil prices in the course of 1979 and 1980 had set inflation, already stimulated by rising food prices, on the path to its postwar peak of about 12 per cent in the course of 1981. Meanwhile, the ensuing redistribution of world payments surpluses, combined with policies of retrenchment in the main industrial countries, were leading the world into its second major recession within a decade.

## POLICY UNDER REAGAN

The renewed inflationary upsurge at the end of the 1970s posed again all the problems of 1973–5 and in a form just as severe. The period is less researched than the earlier inflationary bout but even so a reasonable degree of consensus may perhaps be discerned. Few writers attribute much of the renewed acceleration in 1976 and 1977 to excess demand (G.W. Miller, 1979), though 1977 and 1978 did see the growth of the money supply gather momentum. With unemployment running at 7 per cent even in 1977 it is hard to see how this could have been a major active as distinct from accommodating cause, although Gordon allots it a role. It has to be remembered, too, that by the end of the decade estimates of the level of unemployment compatible with non-accelerating inflation (the 'NAIRU') had risen from the 3 or 4 per cent commonly cited in the 1960s to 5½ and even 6½ per cent – uncomfortably close to the level which by 1977 had been reached.

Nor do cash wages offer a strong or general explanation except in so far as the familiar inertia tended to make the new inflation start off from a higher base than had been usual in the past and sustained the price trend, after an initial fall in real wages, once it was established. *Total* labour costs to employers however, rose both in January 1978 and in 1979 because of increases in payroll taxes and the minimum wage, steps taken by administrative decision not market process but widely regarded as constituting almost as powerful an inflationary influence as were cash wage increases themselves. By 1979 spare capacity was becoming limited and production costs were rising at an annual rate of some 8 per cent. In other respects, too, circumstances bore a marked resemblance to those prevailing in the early 1970s. In 1978 and 1979 sharp rises took place in food, and notably meat, prices as well as in home ownership costs for new buyers, as mortgage interest rates rose. During 1979–80, moreover, the price of oil and oil-related products also rose sharply under the spur of supply restrictions and rising world demand. Along with the explosion of world food and energy prices went a renewal of worldwide inflation which communicated itself back to the United States in the form of sharply increased import prices. In Blinder's (1986) analysis supply shocks of this kind accounted for much the greater part of the acceleration, as distinct from the high underlying or 'baseline' level of inflation, in the late 1970s.

*Table 12.3: US Economic Indicators, 1977–82 (per cent)*

|  | 1977 | 1978 | 1979 | 1980 | 1981 | 1982 |
|---|---|---|---|---|---|---|
| Unemployment | 7.1 | 6.1 | 5.9 | 7.2 | 7.6 | 9.7 |
| Implicit consumption deflator | 5.8 | 7.9 | 9.5 | 10.2 | 7.5 | 4.9 |
| CPI | 6.6 | 9.0 | 12.8 | 12.5 | 9.6 | 4.5 |
| Broad money M2 | 11.2 | 8.0 | 8.1 | 9.0 | 9.4 | 9.3 |
| Weighted av. exchange rate | – 5.0 | – 12.6 | – 0.5 | 1.8 | 18.5 | 16.0 |
| Hourly earnings index | 7.5 | 8.4 | 8.0 | 9.6 | 8.3 | 6.0 |

See footnote to Table 12:2

*Source:* Peter B. Clark (1985).

In some ways the restrictive policies initially adopted to counter the stagflation of 1979–80, like some of the main causes at work, followed lines similar to those observed in 1974–5. At a deeper level, however, the two sets of policies differed substantially. Couched primarily in terms of monetary aggregates, the post-1979 policies seemed to embody a willingness to permit, and even to bring about, greater rises in interest rates than did the policies of five years before, and the Federal Reserve's discount rate at once edged up to 12 per cent. In the summer preceding the presidential election of 1980 the squeeze was replaced by vigorous monetary expansion but after the election of Ronald Reagan in November further restraint helped to raise discount rates to 14 per cent by May 1981.

The new President's fiscal proposals were also markedly different from any voiced by his predecessors in 1974–5. President Reagan planned large tax cuts, notably three successive annual 10 per cent cuts in income tax designed to restore supply side incentives and so favour expansion. On the expenditure side he favoured large cuts in non-defence, notably social security, combined with large rises in defence expenditure. The overall effects of these was to be the restoration of Federal budgetary balance by 1984/5.

The compatibility of slow monetary growth with the rapid rise in GNP which the administration seemed at the time to envisage, the realism of plans combining major tax cuts and higher defence spending with a return to budgetary balance, and the strength of the grounds for expecting faster growth to follow from lower taxation, or for that matter from lower inflation, are interesting questions which need not concern us here. Nor need the protracted process, marked by vacillation and inconsistency on the part of President and Congress alike, whereby substantial cuts in tax rates and increases in expenditure were at length approved. The central facts for our purposes are that by the end of 1981 the fiscal deficit was clearly set upon a high and rising path, while real and nominal interest rates were likewise high and variable, with consumer price inflation still running at 9 per cent and trend unemployment having still to reach its 11 per cent peak of the following year.

In the event, however, 1982 marked a turning-point. In June Mexico, which had borrowed heavily and at variable interest rates from US and British banks, threatened to default, a step which would have brought financial collapse to the US banking system. From then monetary policy was dramatically relaxed, in line with fiscal. The annual rate of growth of broad money – 7.9 per cent in the six months ending in June – rose to 16.4 per cent a year later; and the economy embarked upon a phase of fast growth powered, at the cost of growing weakness in the merchandise trade balance, by the federal deficit. Discount rates eased from 12 to 8.5 per cent over the next eighteen months.

Contrary to widespread expectations, the recovery of output did not bring with it a renewal of inflation. On the contrary, in the course of 1982 the rate of inflation halved to about 5 per cent. This was not due only to external factors, though energy prices fell and with them the dollar prices of many raw materials, including foodstuffs. The rise in wages also slowed, while the dollar, under the influence of high interest rates and an inflow of capital, appreciated by nearly 30 per cent 1979–82. Despite the United States' low exposure to foreign trade compared with other industrial countries, the appreciation must count as one fairly important, though all too reversible, source of the country's declining inflation.

For those who had argued that cost shocks of a once-for-all nature, rather than any major rise in 'baseline' inflation, accounted for the inflationary peak of 1979–80 the subsequent collapse of inflation gave ground for considerable satisfaction. On this view the removal of import price inflation, indeed the substitution for two years of positive disinflation, had removed the cause of the malady and the result had been renewed stability. As the expectation of continued low raw material prices spread and wages after a suitable lag adjusted to price deceleration, the Phillips Curve would reappear and with it the lower inflation rates of the 1960s.

From 1981 to 1983, if annual figures are used (Brown, 1985, pp. 373–4), the Phillips Curve, steep but none the less sloping, does indeed seem to have reappeared. The growth of hourly earnings slowed dramatically, halving between late 1980 and the end of 1982. In the years of recovery which immediately followed, however, the most striking thing to emerge was that the recovery of demand in most sectors of the economy did not halt the decline of inflation; and wage inertia, which had been a cause for widespread concern only a short time before, showed signs of having been curbed beyond all but the most optimistic predictions. Attention correspondingly turned from explaining the rigidities of the labour market towards explaining its superior flexibility when compared with those of many European economies. The attempt fully to account for the success, in the 1980s, of anti-inflation policies which seemed to many at best unplanned and at worst inconsistent promised to prove as difficult and controversial as had earlier attempts to explain the failures of the 1970s.

## SUMMARY OF EVENTS; AMERICA AND BRITAIN

The great importance of the United States economy for the study of inflation in recent years arises from its sheer size; the conceptual and policymaking problems which it poses are not different in kind from those posed in other industrial countries.

Our general comments on the years 1965–82 can therefore be brief.

Demand inflation led by defence expenditure broke the era of relative price stability that preceded 1965; wage inertia maintained and increased the inflation; wage–price controls delayed, but do not seem to have reduced the total extent of the inflation; and both in 1973–4 and again in 1979–80 the upsurge of world commodity prices, notably food and oil prices, added powerful momentum to the two main upsurges. In the later episode particularly, shocks from the world market seem to have predominated, although excess domestic demand and the 'self-inflicted wounds' of administered cost increases also played a part. In the downturn, accordingly, the non-repetition of the oil and food price shocks itself provided a major explanation of the disinflation; but with the dramatic shift from boom to slump, wage inertia subsided more rapidly than most observers had expected.

Even to recount the main influences thus briefly is to highlight a number of main differences between the US economy's behaviour during the period and Britain's. First, the role of oil shocks, especially during the second bout, seems to have been of greater proportional importance than in Britain, and their cessation correspondingly a stronger stabilising influence. Second, the reaction of American wages was nowhere near so violent as in Britain. Inertia existed, but it amplified the initial shocks far less than in Britain, and indeed less than in much of western Europe generally; and when in the early 1980s a slump became well established wage increases subsided faster and to lower levels.

On the other hand, there were also similarities of experience. Both countries seem to have owed a part of their respective inflations to governments' electoral ambitions, though the British debt seems incalculably greater. Suggested reasons for this difference in the degree of susceptibility have not been slow to appear. Among those suggested have been: the greater size of the United States, its less centralised federal structure, the greater scope for channelling rewards for electoral support through individual government contracts, the payment of rewards after rather than before elections, and the more staggered nature of elections. Explanations along these lines are persuasive yet to many seem only partly to explain why British governments seem to stimulate, so much more blatantly that their industrial neighbours, pre-election booms with their accompanying tax reductions, followed after the election by inflation and balance of payments crises.

A second similarity worth mentioning was the policy, followed in the early years of the Reagan and Thatcher administrations respectively, of allowing the exchange rate to rise in response, among other things, to interest rates movements, and thereby eliciting a new curb upon inflation. In the United States the anti-inflationary effect was widely held to be, relative to the prevailing levels of inflation, more powerful than in Britain. In both countries, however, the high exchange rate proved ultimately unsustainable and, in so far as it worsened the current balance of payments, a means merely of exporting inflation until a later date. In both countries, moreover, the period of high exchange levels was followed to different extents by a plunge in the balance of payments on current account. Other factors, of course, played vital parts here: the highly expansionary fiscal deficit of the Reagan administration, and Britain's long-run competitive weakness. Even so, the lessons drawn by the Reagan and Thatcher administrations respectively by the mid-1980s were of great significance: exchange rates could not be left completely free to adjust to market forces; some international coordination was highly desirable; and the use of higher exchange rates as weapons against inflation was circumscribed indeed.

One of the most instructive resemblances between the two countries' experiences was that on both sides of the Atlantic incomes policies seem to have achieved some temporary success but proved, politically and administratively, difficult to maintain; and little or none of their success long outlasted their abandonment. Furthermore, the timing both of the introduction and of the withdrawal of wage-restraining policies proved to be of unexpectedly great importance. Just as the introduction of the Heath governments policy of wage-indexation in Britain coincided with the first oil shock and amplified the shock's immediate effects, so the unfortunate timing of the end of President Nixon's controls, just after the same shock, added an extra momentum to inflation at the time when it was least welcome. It is fair to say that the catch-up effects following incomes policies were less well known then than now. In both cases, however, it may be concluded that it is an important disadvantage of such policies that their successful operation depends on timing decisions which may be very hard to make and carry out satisfactorily. It is not always possible for a government wishing to introduce wage indexation to foresee the occurrence of exogenous supply shocks; and it may not always be politically possible to persist in wage–price controls, at least of a kind enforced by adminstrative fiat, until a suitable time for their abolition arises.

# 13 Lessons from Modern Western Inflations

## ARE THERE LAWS OF INFLATION?

The foregoing chapters have reviewed the events and literature of a wide range of inflations and drawn conclusions for the particular episodes concerned. We now turn to broader questions. It has recently been claimed that there exist known laws of inflation which hold true over a wide range of circumstances. The claim is clearly important. Should it be true, the laws concerned would enable us to predict the course of economic events and would thus entitle to be regarded, in one widespread and reputable usage of the word, as a science. How far, then, have any such laws emerged?

If by 'laws' we mean regular and reasonably precise conjunctions of economic events or circumstances, then the overwhelming import of the evidence considered here is to undermine any such claim. In explaining events once they have taken place economics has had some success. But in finding laws and making predictions from them success has eluded us. Repeatedly, alleged laws formulated, not without reason, after study of one series of events has proved inapplicable, or only partly applicable, in the course of another.

Thus Professors Friedman and Laidler have proposed, as a general law of inflation, that when a country's money supply increases faster than output inflation will result within about two years. Often the claim has been borne out by events. Yet in Austria between August 1922 and December 1924, and again in Britain after 1984, the proposed law failed. Again, it has been suggested as a 'law' that a necessary condition for inflation is monetary growth. Yet the experience of France between December 1920 and December 1923 seems to show that inflation can long persist without that growth. The growth of money in relation to output is not, in general or in any reliable way, either a sufficient or a necessary condition for inflation.

The list can be extended. Large and persistent state deficits do not always produce inflation, as the American experience of the 1980s has shown. Despite theories to the contrary, the velocity of circulation can vary quickly and unpredictably. There is no rule for foretelling how an expected rise in national income will be divided between higher prices and higher output. The equation of exchange has provided no more than a framework which can be used to describe events but into which *any* event will fit. Purchasing power parity theory, except in post-rationalising versions produced after the events which the theory aims to predict, has similarly proved either a truism or unhelpful. The Phillips Curve, even if it existed before 1923, has since shown a sad propensity to shift between sloping, vertical and horizontal; and, as Phillips allowed, when import prices rise rapidly it seems to vanish altogether. There is no convincing evidence – in France during 1924–6, for example – that the purchasing power of money is stably related to the value of expected budget surpluses. Nor is there any rule to help us judge how far government investment intended to increase the level of economic activity will be thwarted by a worsening of the trade balance or by higher interest rates which curb private investment – versions of what has been called the 'crowding out' doctrine. Equally badly, we may note in passing, have fared the theory of Open Economy Monetarism (see Glossary), its associated Law of One Price and the doctrine of the futility of devaluation (more generally, of altering nominal magnitudes) (Isard, 1977; Williamson, 1983(II)).

Yet, though we have discovered no laws, we have discovered a number of marked tendencies. To recall the disappointments economic theory has encountered is not, therefore, to conclude that formal theories of inflation are valueless. On the contrary, as reminders of general tendencies in various situations they can assist policymaking. They may also help us to distinguish between different causal mechanisms and draw attention to the logical implications of views held or policies pursued. The unhappy, even tragic, effects of policies based on economic theories in recent years have arisen largely because the theories were taken, by governments and academics alike, to be scientific and exact – guides to actual events rather than to general tendencies. As the 1979–82 bout of inflation recedes, we still face the central problem: how to find out and tell in advance which of the various principles proposed will apply in any given situation. Some broad guidelines are already visible, But if economics aims to become a science, the matter will have to be taken much further; laws or principles are empty unless we know when they will apply. Meanwhile, until laws can be reformulated in terms precise enough to be useful for prediction, questions about how far, in any given situation, any particular one of them is relevant remain very much a matter of historical judgement.[1]

## CAUSES OF INFLATION

As to causality, our case studies have revealed a wide variety of mechanisms tending to produce inflation. The most widespread single active cause has been domestic demand, often springing from persistent state deficits, sometimes from the excessive extension of credit to the private sector, and occasionally from exogenously caused accelerations in the velocity of circulation of money. Wages, rising faster than productivity, have, as in Britain, often worsened inflation. So have the movements of exchange rates, provoked by a wide variety of circumstances, including reparation payments, overseas military expenditure and, occasionally, panic flights of capital of a dubiously rational kind. Profit inflations, on the other hand, in MDCs if not in Latin America, have been few in our period.

Because of the profusion of causal factors, general theories of inflation have been hard to sustain. Monocausal theories, in particular, gain little support from our evidence – a point which might seem too banal to be worth making but for the great upsurge of contrary opinion in high places, both academic and governmental and on both sides of the Atlantic, in the late 1960s and 1970s. Certainly, to return to the best-known example, a greater increase in the stock of money than in output, issued to finance a budget deficit, may propel a country into inflation, as happened widely in the Europe of the 1920s and 1940s; interestingly, both there and in Latin America railway deficits played a major role, an important instruments of nineteenth century growth thus leaving a lasting legacy of increased inflation-proneness behind it in many countries. But the full explanation of an inflation is often far more complex than can be explained by a simple relationship between money and output. The volume of money may grow as an effect rather than a cause, responding wholly or partly to the demand for it, as in Britain in 1980; monetary growth may, in fact, merely ratify an inflation which has other active causes – an important strand even of the German hyperinflation. A rising velocity of circulation may also enable a constant money stock to finance rising prices. Nor are money-induced inflations always caused by contemporary budget deficits. By the time the French inflation of the 1920s became acute such deficits had been almost eliminated, and even the effects of past monetary growth had largely worked their way into the price level. It is arguable that the expectation of future budget deficits played an important role. But insofar as the French inflation of 1924–6 owed anything to *concurrent* monetary growth, the latter occurred not chiefly to finance budget deficits but through the discounting of large volumes of commercial bills. The Real Bills Doctrine (see Glossary and Chapter 6) appears, indeed, both before and after the stabilisations of the 1920s as a persistent source of price increases.

In demand inflations, what induced governments to run public deficits which created or fuelled the malady? In discussing the Germany of the 1920s monetarist writers have often cited ignorance as the reason, by which they mean ignorance of the quantity theory of money and belief in reparations as the chief inflationary pressure. Ignorance there may have been, but as we have seen, the role or reparations was in reality large and, as the International Committee of Experts clearly saw, a firm prospect of at least a temporary settlement of the issue was a necessary part of any stabilisation. In another inflation, that of modern Britain, not ignorance but political misjudgement – the Prime Minister's postponement of a general election from October 1978 to May 1979 – also seems likely to have swelled the inevitable resurgence of inflation in 1979–80 by guaranteeing the breakdown beyond early repair of an incomes policy which might otherwise have been refurbished to exercise some restraint after an earlier election.

Misjudgements and ignorance apart, we have found in our studies from recent history cases of governments which felt themselves *obliged* by extreme circumstances to continue, at least temporarily, with inflationary methods of finance, as in Hungary 1945–6 and the Soviet Union 1922–4. French governments of the 1920s were also compelled so to behave largely by public distrust of their financial competence and by their parliamentary weakness; while German governments in 1921–3 may consciously or unconsciously have preferred inflation to the payment of the reparations.

More recently, governments have doubtless risked and incurred inflation in the pursuit of electoral popularity. Excess demand has been financed in order to reduce unemployment, partly as a goal in itself and partly to win elections. The practice has seemed, on the whole, less sinister than the picture monetarists have sometimes painted of governments secretly plotted to impose, via inflation, unlegislated taxation upon the public; the ill consequences of inflation may often have been underestimated but at least there were also public benefits. Even so, the regular recurrence of electoral spending sprees, regardless of the longer term economic consequences, has been an unappealing sight. Whether governments' proneness to the failing can be cured through growing public education and the inoculative effect of experience remains one of the central questions of economic policy for the future.

The inflationary role of monopolies, whether of firms in product markets or of trade unions in the labour market, emerges from our review as ambiguous – possibly important and yet imperfectly explained. In Poland (as well as in such diverse countries as Hungary, Chile and Argentina) a high degree of concentration in many industrial sectors is often cited as a cause of inflation. The problem is that the usual textbook model depicts a monopoly as choosing and maintaining the price which maximises its profits. On this model, the existence of a high degree of monopoly, thought it would explain *high* prices, would not explain persistently *rising* prices. Only a continuous *increase* in the degree of monopoly in an economy would explain that. Even an inflation due to a persistent rise in variable costs would not, moreover, necessarily be worsened by the existence of monopolies. On the contrary, in the basic textbook model with linear demand curves, monopoly would tend to damp down, more than would the working of a competitive market, the extent to which rising costs were passed on in rising prices. Clearly, monopoly is not by itself sufficient to explain inflation.

In the case of labour monopolies the need for a fuller explanation is even more evident, since trade unions do not maximise profits but rather some other objective, possibly their membership or the average earnings of their members. The usual supposition is that militant behaviour on the part of the unions persistently pushes up wages and so causes inflation. Much observation supports this view; what is less clear is the source of the initial militancy. On one well-evidence view, unions in industries where productivity is rising fast demand wage increases and comparability requires workers elsewhere to be treated similarly. To this Rowthorn (1980) adds that when firms cannot pass on the cost increase in higher prices because of constraints on the money supply, the government slackens the constraints to restore the rate of profit and so finances inflation. The story rings true for many countries recently.

There can be little doubt, too, that in the half-century beginning in 1918 the market economies changed in such a way as to strengthen inflation and make its control more difficult. Money wages became more rigid downwards. The huge fall in earnings associated with sliding scale arrangements which accompanied the slump of 1920–2 – itself something of a freak even for that time – was never repeated, however high the level of unemployment; even in the CPEs money wage cuts came to be widely regarded as unacceptable. The expectation that governments would maintain full employment as a top priority became deep-rooted, weakening the effectiveness of attempts to stabilise prices by means of announcements that no more money would be 'printed'.

A further aggravating factor was the persistent abandonment or failure of such anti-inflationary measures as incomes policies, which weakened the credibility of those policies in the future, immunising wage bargainers against their influence. Again, the growth in the size and complexity of the world's financial markets, where financial instruments increased vastly in volume and variety, made the definition, interpretation and still more the control of monetary magnitudes enormously harder. Nor can we overlook the huge growth of international trade and payments in relation to world output after World War II, which magnified the importance of internationally transmitted inflation when it took place. Against these factors, the continuing volatility, downwards as well as upwards, of primary commodity prices and the willingness, after 1980, of governments in the MDCs as a whole to permit a slump to develop had by the mid-1980s provided a temporary counteracting force. It was not, however, one with any great likelihood of remaining effective in the long term. Inflation remained endemic in the world economy and no general or reliable cure for it was yet in sight.

## GENERAL FEATURES AND EFFECTS OF INFLATION

Two well-known claims concerning regular concomitants of inflation deserve further mention. The best known, often springing from an overselective reading of Irving Fisher, is the claim that the velocity of circulation of money, somehow defined, remains broadly constant. Opposed to it, we have the assertion of the Radcliffe Committee (1959, p. 133) to the effect that:

. . . we cannot find any reason for supposing, or any experience in monetary history indicating, that there is any limit to the velocity of circulation . . .

No reliable statistics exist to test either view in respect of 'transactions velocity' − the average value of transactions carried out per unit of money. Records of trade in secondhand goods are simply not kept. Even for the calculation of 'income velocity', money supply figures for our case studies are inadequate. In the hyperinflation of the 1920s and 1940s, and in the inflation of the 1970s and 1980 in Poland, foreign or privately-created monies came into widespread use, depriving the ratio of income to official money supply of much meaning. It is clear that in Britain and the United States recent inflations, though moderate, witnessed substantial changes in income velocity. Two reservations must, however, be noted. First, in modern and only mildly inflationary market economies the changes that have taken place in velocity have involved such inconvenience as to have been undertaken only tardily and gradually. Second, in hyperinflation velocity has not changed anything like proportionally with the growth of pretty well all other economic variables. In the German hyperinflation with its soaring billions, for example, Bresciani (1931, p. 168) suggests change by a factor of ten where values are measured in retail prices, and by forty for wholesale. Falush (1976, p. 52), writing on Hungary in 1945–6, for his part records change by 'about 300-fold'. Changes in prices, wages, money supply and exchange rates far exceeded such figures. Velocity is certainly variable; but, perhaps partly because it enters into income and the value of transactions as a multiplicative factor, it is not nearly as variable as most other economic magnitudes.

A second alleged regularity, known as 'Fisher's Law', claims that rising inflation produces, via an increased insistence on high money gains on the part of lenders, corresponding rises in nominal interest rates. Lipsey and Cagan (1978, Chapter 2) find support for this view in the United States after 1965; but elsewhere it gains little support. Certainly, neither recent British evidence nor that of Central Europe in the 1920s, seems to fit it. In Britain the low-risk form of portfolio investment most widely adopted by small savers offered for much of the 1970s a negative real rate of return: a building society share account investor reinvesting all his interest between 1974 and 1985 would have lost at least a quarter of his original real investment. In Germany in 1923 the highest rate that seems to appear in the literature – 20 per cent per day – still failed to keep pace with concurrent inflation.

As to the effects of inflation upon different classes of the community, the main perceived harm, and the main undesired effects for the community as a whole, have traditionally been expressed in terms of the following broad contentions:

(a) Inflation in effect imposes an unlegislated and unplanned tax on holdings of cash by reducing their purchasing power, as well as on assets and incomes denominated in money terms. By falling more heavily on some people than on others, it thus redistributes income and wealth arbitrarily and unfairly.

(b) By inducing people to reduce their cash holdings it imposes upon them the inconvenience of more frequent financial transactions.

(c) Because, when the rate of inflation rises, its volatility also usually rises, it imposes additional risks upon decision-makers, together with the financial costs of hedging or other insurance. It thus reduces the volume and impairs the quality of investment. (Against this, however, it is sometimes claimed (see e.g. in the case of Brazil, Baer, 1965, pp. 364–9) that when prices rise ahead of costs in a demand inflation, the redistribution of income towards entrepreneurs increases (forced) savings and facilitates faster growth.)

(d) By attracting labour and other resources into speculative and financial-administrative activities it distorts the pattern of employment and output, and ensures at least temporary unemployment after the inflation ends.

(e) It tends to accelerate as, increasingly quickly, workers incorporate higher expected prices in their wage claims and firms pass on expected costs in higher prices.

In the Central Europe of the 1920s all four effects were generally and clearly visible. More recently, the outcome has been more obscure. Inconvenience costs to the general public existed in all our case-studies and were large in hyperinflations, though, in the view of some writers, trivial in cases such as the American and British. Costs taking the form of lost growth are more debatable. Countries undergoing hyperinflation in the immediate wake of wartime devastation, such as Hungary in 1946 or the Soviet Union in 1922, were clearly far less susceptible to the distortion and reduction of investment than were countries in which output and investment were initially high. In Britain and the United States, however, recession resulted to a substantial extent from shocks to external balance, not simply from inflation as such. Moreover, the structure of Britain's economy was also being distorted by other factors. How far monopoly, inappropriate taxes and ill-judged public spending had this effect is a contentious issue but it would be hard to argue that generally agreed distortions such as the excessive growth of local government administration or overmanning in nationalised industries resulted from inflation rather than from separate government policies. Equally, the claim that low investment in the 1970s was due to inflationary uncertainties rather than to cyclical recession must remain, to say the least, debatable.

The redistribution of real income and wealth, a marked feature of interwar hyperinflations, though less researched in more recent times, has none the less still been visible. In the market economies fairly widespread formal indexation, in combination with real wage resistance by trade unions, did much to limit or prevent obvious losses on the part of conspicuous groups in the 1970s, but the negative real interest rates paid to huge numbers of small savers in Britain, for example, inflicted grave losses upon the less financially astute classes of society. True, many housebuyers made correspondingly large gains but these resulted not from inflation but from tax advantages deliberately and independently legislated; nor, except by chance, did the class of gainers coincide with that of losers.

Did inflation tend with any regularity to accelerate without limit? Between the wars, and after World War II in Hungary, clearly it did. More recently, in the CPEs, the build-up of inflationary 'overhang' seems to have worsened. In the United States discussions of inflation frequently centred on the rising rate of inflation to accompany any given level of unemployment, a trend which persisted almost to the end of our period; but the effects of external shocks were so marked and the acceleration, once faced with strongly disinflationary policies, so temporary that to draw the conclusion that there existed a self-aggravating 'snowball effect' more than mere inertia would be going beyond the evidence. On Phelps Brown's view, however, the widespread outburst of union militancy in the 1960s was a delayed effect of long-term full employment policies, a story remarkably similar to Rowthorn's (1980) account of cumulative inflationary pressures. Nor can one overlook the suggestion that the Latin American hyperinflations of the 1980s represented the peaks of long cumulative processes, however intermittent. On balance, the evidence seems to support claims for 'cumulation', though at widely varying rates.

## REMEDIES

A feature of the inflations of the 1970s and 1980s was the profusion of recommended cures which they evoked. Few of these were implemented but several deserve mention.

Any cure for inflation involves the curtailment of real income or expenditure on the part of some social group or groups. One way may be for the government to provide incentives which increase voluntary saving; in this case, those, usually taxpayers, who pay the additional interest costs forfeit income. If involuntary curbs are placed on expenditure (but not on income), forced savings and suppressed inflation result, along with their attendant queues and shortages, as has often happened in the CPEs. If only some categories of expenditure are curbed, for example by rationing, suppressed inflation results but only in those sectors, with worse inflation probably appearing elsewhere – a case discussed later. The alternative is to curb incomes, a policy which can halt inflation but only at a price, measured in terms either of statutory compulsion, compulsion through fear of unemployment or voluntary restraint. Policies involving the two types of compulsion are widely unacceptable and also of dubious efficacy in the medium term (because of enforcement difficulties in the first case and the unreality of the unemployment threat to most of the employed in the second). As a result the third policy, voluntary restraint, has usually been the initial favourite of most goverments; but its record in Britain and the United States has so far been one of little lasting success.

Each type of cure is likely to prosper most in a particular type of industrial relations environment. Demand deflation is likely to work at lowest cost when trade unions are weak and/or decentralised. Formal incomes policies should ideally have the cooperation of strong centralised unions able to discipline their members – a requirement not easily reconciled with wage determination that takes account of local market forces. A statutory price freeze unaided by demand deflation may, for its part, be regarded as leading to suppressed inflation, though one unlikely to be maintained for long unless accompanied by similar curbs on costs. Inflation can also be temporarily suppressed by 'exporting' excess demand via a trade deficit.

More recently proposed policies for curbing inflation aim to free the government's hands by instituting more automatic mechanisms. Some of the main ones may be presented schematically by likening them to proposals for dealing with two other problems which often result from the production of a desired level of output: (a) additional imports and (b) industrial pollution.

In each case, a variety of remedies is possible. First, the alleged 'evil' may simply be banned. For pollution, suppressive devices may be made compulsory. Imports may be forbidden. In the case of inflation, prices may be legally frozen. The weapon used – direct control – is a crude one. In each case the social cost may exceed the benefits gained. Thus, an unimportant amount of pollution may be avoided at a massive cost to the firm or industry. A small saving in imports may cripple a large export industry which is dependent upon the now-banned import. Or a small gain in price stability when prices are frozen may combine with rising costs to produce unemployment, or retard growth by preventing firms attracting necessary labour. The simple ban embodies no device for weighing, at the margin, the social costs of the polluting firm's activities against their benefits.

A second, less crude policy would therefore be the issue by government of a limited, 'optimal' number of licenses to pollute, to import or to raise prices. Here the assumption is one of governmental omniscience as to which level of the undesired effect is optimal. But in fact governments may not know which level of pollution, of imports or of inflation does least harm, or which firms, because they engage in the most socially beneficial activities, should be awarded the licences concerned. In that case the problem of blunt instruments arises again, as well as that of bureaucratic costs and delays.

A more sophisticated technique would be to auction the licences, one by one, to the highest bidder. Thus, that firm would buy the first licence which expected to gain the greatest profit from the activity causing the undesired effect; and since, in a competitive market, high profit can be taken to reflect the production of goods which have a high value to consumers, this, it is argued, would mean that the licence to pollute (or import or inflate) would go where the polluting activity had the greatest social value. Similarly, the second licence would go to the firm expecting to make the second greatest profit; and so on. The method still involves governmental estimation: licences would be auctioned only so long as the price paid for each licence exceeded the estimated cost inflicted on society at large by the licensed activity. But if the government is in a position to make reasonably accurate estimates of the social costs of the activity, the method might, it is argued, tailor marginal costs to benefits more closely than would the bureaucratic issue of licences; and the government would gain revenue − at some administrative cost. The whole argument depends crucially, however, on the realism of assuming that competitive markets will reliably establish a link between the amount a firm can and will pay for its licence and the benefits which its activities confer on consumers.

In a further attempt to curb bureaucracy, some have advocated a *market* in licences to import, pollute or inflate. Unofficially, some such market existed, in the form of 'compensation deals', for the restricted volume of foreign exchange available to finance imports into Germany in the 1930s; this therefore tended to go to the firms which could pay most. In the case of inflation, one can argue, along the lines of a proposal due to Lerner and Colander (c. 1980), for the issue to firms of Special Credit in limited quantities, which would be necessary to permit the growth of any firm's value added (wages plus profits). Those firms which sought to raise their value added more quickly than the normal allocation allowed would have to buy extra Credit from other firms willing to sell. In inflationary times demand for the Credit, and therefore its cost, would be high so that, through a market process, a kind of tax would be imposed on the fast-inflating firm.

A further variant much discussed would be to levy an outright tax on each or all of the undesired effects in question. A tax on pollution would mean that the polluter paid the costs he inflicted on society generally and so, in the course of maximising his profits, would equate his marginal gain to the marginal cost which his output inflicted not only on himself but on the whole of society. He would therefore cut his output to the 'efficient' level, at which no additional cost to society was incurred unless it was exceeded by the additional benefit or profit gained.

A tax on imports would be the familiar tariff. A tax on inflation, originally proposed by Wallich and Weintraub (1971) would in one version use wage increases as a proxy for inflation and penalise any firm which allowed its workers' average wage increase to exceed a stated annual norm; the penalty might, if desired, grow with the excess. Here the aim would be to encourage wage resistance by employers and wage restraint by employees for fear of harming the firm's prospects. Objections which have been raised arise from fears about enforcement, cosmetic compliance and evasion, as well as about possible non-response or perverse response by unions.

A further possibility – with pollution, imports and inflation alike – would be to subsidise an alternative. Thus the government could subsidise: (a) the fitting of devices to suppress pollution, or the relocation of firms in industrial zones where the social costs of their activities would be low; (b) the domestic production of import-substitutes; or (c) the payment of wages by firms granting lower-than-norm increases. In the first two cases the subsidy would aim to reflect the benefits to be gained by the community at large from avoidance of the 'undesired' activity. It would follow that any firm gaining benefits in excess of the subsidy from the undesired activity would be free to continue with it, and society as a whole would, it is argued, still gain. In the case of the wage subsidy, objections arise partly because of the problem of raising finance for the subsidy without unfairness or the distortion of the economy, and partly from doubts about the ease, once inflation had been abated, of phasing out a subsidy on which the existing level of prices, profits and wages might by then depend. If inflation were cumulative and accelerating, even a temporary curb might check its growth. Even so, the cumulative cost of the subsidy paid before that happened might be substantial.

## PARALLEL CURRENCIES

Of the types of remedy classified above rather few were actually used in the inflations we have discussed. The most obvious cases of implementation were: the temporary wage and price freezes in Britain and the United States; the penalties for 'excessive' price increases instituted in the same two countries; and, for Britain, the budget deal of 1976 which traded cuts in income tax for wage restraint.

A type of remedy more often implemented in our case studies, and one variously designed to cure or alleviate the effects of inflation, proceeded by putting into domestic circulation two or more currencies simultaneously, their values being linked by a floating exchange rate: i.e. 'parallel' currencies.

Proposals of this general kind are by no means all archaic. One put forward only recently by Professor Hayek (1978) argues that multiple currencies should be legalised by permitting any firm or individual to establish a bank which would issue its own notes, the stability of the monetary system being ensured by market competition between note-issuers. Controversially and with little concern for the growth of inter-bank dependency over the last century, Lawrence H. White (1984) cites Scottish experience between 1716 and 1844 in support of such a proposal, even referring with approval to the system of unlimited shareholder liability as a useful stabilising factor. Since these proposals had no particular relevance to the inflations discussed above, we do no more than mention them here.

The evidence of our case studies throws more light on a second proposal, known in its most popular form as the All Saints' Day Manifesto (ASDM) (*The Economist,* 1975, pp. 33–8; Vaubel, 1978; Fratianni and Peeters, 1978). The Manifesto, briefly summarised, aims to achieve monetary union in the European Community (EMU), and at the same time to halt inflation. These results are expected to follow from measures of five kinds:

(a) Limited issue, in exchange for national currencies, of a new, European currency, the Europa, which would have constant purchasing power. Its value would be calculated as being equal to the value of a weighted average of the goods contained in the RPI (retail price index) 'baskets' of the member countries, the weights being, it is suggested, each country's share in intra-Community trade (or else Community GNP)[2].

(b) To prevent excessive fluctuations in exchange rates, Europas would be valued in terms of national currencies by means of a crawling peg system, whereby changes in relative purchasing power would be reflected only after a time-lag.

(c) Initially Europas would be issued only in exchange for national monies. In time, central banks would introduce them also through open market operations, EC expenditure and the rediscounting of bills to the commercial banks.

(d) Citizens of all member countries would be legally free to use the money of their choice but it is expected that eventually the more stable Europa would replace national monies completely.

(e) The final currency would be managed by an independent monetary authority whose members would be appointed or elected for long periods.

The advantages claimed for the ASDM proposal must be compared with those springing (a) from a continuance of national monies, and (b) from the following of alternative paths towards monetary union. In the first respect, ASDM is said to afford a gain in convenience for international traders similar to the gain from the abolition of barter within a country; conversion costs and exchange rate uncertainty would both vanish. The countries within the Union would also gain by being able to economise on their (pooled) reserves since reserve losses would tend not to occur for all of them at once (Christie and Fratianni, 1978, p. 5). The proposers of the ASDM do not allow that EMU would weaken national governments' power to curb unemployment, believing national policy to be powerless in that respect in any case, except possibly in the short run – the doctrine of the vertical Phillips Curve. The need for a Community regional policy to offset the low productivity of peripheral regions is, however, accepted.

The ASDM is also compared favourably with the alternative policy of working gradually towards a union of exchange rates and thereby currencies. The latter policy, it is argued, has made little progress over many years and seems unlikely to fare better in the future, involving as it does coordinated fiscal and monetary policies, huge loans between central banks and a willingness on the part of surplus countries to diminish their surpluses for the good of less disciplined neighbours. Any policy leaving currencies in national hands entails continuing exchange risk and makes wage-fixers unwilling to adjust their behaviour to the needs of the wider market. The continuing use of low-interest loans between central banks, Vaubel adds (1979, p. 158), by shielding countries from the external effects of their policies, creates an incentive to inflationary behaviour. Convergence of exchange rates is, moreover, at least in some versions, likely to confer on one country's currency, probably Germany's, a hegemonic status whereby that country could in effect control the Community's money supply. Thygesen (1979, pp. 156–83) argues that such a status, quite apart from being unwelcome to all EC members, might well be inconsistent with an expanding international role for the Community. In short, the EC might encounter the familiar dilemma which requires a currency widely held in reserves to be both plentifully available and at the same time scarce enough to command general confidence.

The chief virtues claimed for the ASDM in its own right are:

(i)  that the Europa would be introduced gradually, avoiding sudden recession in inflation-prone countries, and by the free choice of citizens rather than by government fiat.

(ii)  that the Europa's stable value would oblige member states to curb inflation in order to induce their citizens to go on holding national currencies throughout the period of transition to complete EMU. The greater ease of control over the new currency and the psychological effect of its being new would both make stabilisation easier via the ASDM than by any other method.

(iii) that, while a common currency would be provided early in the transition, national governments would remain free to control their internal policies until much later, giving citizens and firms time to adjust.

Objections to the ASDM have been numerous. Many deny that governments are powerless to influence the level of employment. Some argue that the proffered price stability seems all too likely to give rise to huge destabilising and dubiously desirable capital movements within the Community. Thus, the Europa–pound exchange rate and the Europe–DM rate would both, according to the original version of the proposal, be determined in proportion to relative purchasing powers; yet the pound–DM exchange rate would inevitably also be influenced by capital movements and by expectations. As a result, the possibility of large gains from arbitrage could scarcely fail to arise. If, on the other hand, the Europa's real value was allowed to vary in order to preserve consistency between exchange rates (say, by issuing a fixed quantity of Europas and floating all the rates), then the claim to have stabilised Europa-demoninated prices would no longer hold; and if the Europa appreciated, a rush into Europas might well occur. Similar objections would arise because the time-lag inherent in the crawling peg system might well prevent exchange rates adjusting promptly to reflect purchasing powers.

A further problem concerns the speed at which Europas would replace national currencies. On this issue, the likelihood is that governments would continue to use national monies for taxation and public expenditure, a policy which could greatly slow down the spread of Europas. Further, it is argued, the fact of a floating exchange rate might prevent Gresham's Law operating and tend to keep the 'bad' (depreciating) national currency in circulation. In either circumstance, progress to EMU could slow to a halt. If, on the other hand, expected future depreciation of the national money led the public to rush into Europas, the resulting stabilisation might be almost as sudden, and have as damaging effects, as the stabilisations of the 1920s.

Our chapters on Hungary in 1945–6 and the Soviet Union in 1922–4 seem to provide strong evidence that the instabilities feared could arise. In both countries the introduction of parallel currencies, one of them indexed, was accompanied by a rush into the indexed one, with correspondingly worsened depreciation of the other. In the Soviet Union, changing expectations of inflation in the two currencies led to highly disruptive surges of money between them. In neither case did the changeover win much time for the nation to adapt to price stability. In neither case, indeed, did the new stable-value currency in fact preserve its value; and in Hungary it depreciated to worthlessness. Certainly, neither of the old currencies had the protection of a separate national government, as they would under the ASDM proposal. Even so, fiscal policy, which in both earlier cases proved to be the decisive factor in stabilisation, would not be harmonised under ASDM until after EMU was achieved (Laidler, 1978, p. 60), and in the meantime the possibility of sudden rushes of money between the two currencies would present participant governments with a highly unstable situation. There is no general presumption that a parallel and indexed currency will curb inflation or reduce instability; it could well do the reverse.

## IMPLICATIONS FOR 'GRESHAM'S LAW'

The period of parallelism in Hungary deserves note not only for the experience of financial instability which it affords but also because of its apparent rebuttal of Gresham's Law. For as we have narrated, the tax pengo – the more stable of the two currencies – drove the old pengo out of use, first as a medium for hoarding and saving, and then as a means of exchange. How are we to account for this? A consideration of the question reveals that the behaviour of parellel currencies is a good deal more complex than the simple 'Law' suggests.

As predictors of which type of money will 'win', in the sense of driving out the opposing type, in an economy where alternative monies circulate, the following four criteria have been suggested:

1. Is the good money plentiful? If so, then even after hoarders' demands are satisfied there may still be some of it left in circulation. If not, then, as in Germany in the 1920s, it may all be withdrawn into hoards and in this sense 'driven out' by the bad.
2. Are the two monies readily distinguishable? Lack of distinguishability hinders the victory of either. But if the good money antedates the bad, people who held it before the bad was issued may keep it out of circulation. In practice, indistinguishability is likely to be only partial, and only partially thwart 'driving out'.

3. Is the exchange rate between the two monies fixed or floating? If fixed, the willingness to pay out good (stable-value) money may be less, so that it may be withdrawn into hoards.
4. Who usually decides which money is to be accepted in any transaction – the payer or the recipient? If the former, bad money will tend to be the main means of exchange; if the latter, good.

It is important to bear in mind the distinction between money driven out of use into dustbins and museums, as happens to bad money when good is freely available, and money withdrawn into hoards, as happens to good when it is scarce, or hard to distinguish, or when it may have to be exchanged for bad at a fixed rate. In general, when good money wins, the bad becomes useless; when bad wins, the good is merely hoarded.

Noting this distinction, we may answer as follows. If two monies are indistinguishable, neither 'wins'. If they are distinguishable and linked by an exchange rate *securely* fixed (i.e. confidently expected to stay fixed), then again neither wins. In any other case (i.e. insecure fixing or a flexible exchange rate), the outcome depends upon who decides which money shall be used. If payers decide, bad money will tend to drive out good; if recipients, the reverse. The prime condition for the truth of Gresham's Law is thus not that the inter-currency exchange rate should be fixed but that payers, not recipients, should determine in what currency transactions are financed. If, as is usual, the recipient decides, then bad money will not readily be accepted and will eventually tend to be driven out of circulation (and even out of hoards). If the payer decides, bad money may survive much longer.

## INDEXATION

One point noted above in connection with Hungary – that indexation, in safeguarding one sector of an economy or one flow of income, may worsen inflation elsewhere – is central not only to discussion of indexed currencies but also to the whole debate over the desirability of indexation. To this we now turn.

The chief candidates which have been proposed for indexation are: (a) the tax system; (b) government transfer payments; (c) the interest on government bonds and savings certificates; and (d) wages. A common additional recommendation is that the private sector should follow the public by indexing an increasing number of its contracts.

The case for indexation generally rests on fairness, honesty, the reduction of allocative inefficiency due to inflationary distortions and, in one view, its power to moderate inflation or make it more tolerable. A strong case on the ground of fairness may readily be granted in the light of the confiscations of income and wealth narrated in earlier chapters. As to honesty, many governments have found themselves pushed by inflation into the dubious position of urging citizens to save by offers of savings certificates and bonds which, even with accumulated interest, stand to make not a real gain but a loss. Similarly, there is, to many people, something morally repugnant about the way in which governments can gain tax revenue without overt legislation in times of inflation via 'fiscal drag' – the rise in revenue which occurs as taxpayers on constant real, but rising money incomes move into higher tax brackets under a progressive tax system. The indexation of the tax system would avoid this type of underhand-seeming practice.

The case on grounds of allocative efficiency is more debatable. Certainly, if all incomes are indexed and their relationship therefore unaffected by inflation it follows that inflation will not by itself reallocate resources away from their most efficient pattern. The trouble is that all incomes can never be indexed; in particular, investment incomes, incomes gained from overseas, and income which depend on import prices cannot. While, then, allocative efficiency may be preserved between indexed incomes, it will not be preserved between indexed and unindexed. The distortions of inflation are not eliminated by indexation; they are only shifted. The shift may be a net improvement; but there is no general presumption.

Similarly, indexation does not eliminate inequities, but only moves them. The small saver whose saving certificates are indexed is freed from loss; but the government has to meet the loss. This may well be an improvement. But as we shall see, not all the redistributions due to indexation are so harmless.

Moreover, it is fair to point out that many governments, past and present, are politically or administratively so weak that if they undertook to pay indexed interest even on a modest amount of the savings of each citizen, the resulting costs to the budget would drive them to money creation and so in all probability make inflation worse. Nor, if inflation arises as a mechanism for adjusting a country's standard of living downwards after a worsening in its external terms of trade, is it obvious that bondholders should be exempt from the common need to make economies. In a given situation − where, for example, bondholders are known to be a notably needy class − such a policy may be best. But again there is no watertight rule; the introduction of indexation may provoke a rush into bondholding on the part of the wealthy.

Perhaps the strongest case for full indexation arises in the case of social security payments to the needy. These people, if any, seem to deserve full protection against the depredations of rising prices. In all probability this will be true. Yet even here if the indexed incomes of those out of work were to be allowed to rise too high in relation to any unindexed earnings of other citizens, both fairness and the incentive to work could be impaired.

The point is relevant to the claim often made that indexation is 'an all-or-nothing affair'; indexation of one income flow has consequences for another. Thus, the indexation of earnings for tax purposes seems to require, in fairness, indexation of capital gains, which for some people may be a close substitute for earnings, and also of the yield from bank and building society deposits − another deferred return to saving. Again, if to avoid hardship to small savers the government were to offer for sale indexed savings certificates and bonds, competition for funds might compel building societies and banks to raise the interest rates they paid on deposits to the same extent. Yet if savings institutions were, *de facto* or formally, to have their liabilities indexed they would naturally insist on indexing their loans. The very high mortgage interest rates which could result during a severe inflation, though low in real terms, might still produce widespread family bankruptcies. Furthermore, borrowers for house purchase would be hard to find, and as housing costs rose the mobility of workers between different houses might be much impaired. Grievous consequences of this kind could be minimised if payments of interest and capital on mortgages were, in real terms, spread more evenly over the repayment period through the adoption of 'real value mortgages'. Even so, times of high inflation bring with them marked variations in mortgagees' real incomes. Unless wages were indexed, some bankruptcies would still occur. The example illustrates two main points: first, that indexation cannot itself abolish distortions or hardship, only shift them; and second, that once one flow of income is indexed, logic and fairness tend to demand the indexation of other flows; yet indexation of *all* flows is impossible.

Perhaps the most complex debate has concerned wage indexation. On this subject, at a theoretical level, a substantial measure of agreement now seems to have been reached. Summarising the literature, Carmichael, Fahrer and Hawkins (1985, pp. 78–102) write as follows:

The major theorem of the literature on this topic is that wage indexation tends to stabilize output in response to nominal or demand-side disturbances, to destabilize output in response to real or supply-side disturbances, and to amplify the reaction in prices to all disturbances. The first formal statements of this proposition are usually attributed to Gray (1976) and Fischer (1977) . . . Despite considerable extension and refinement by the subsequent literature, this key result appears to have survived largely intact.

The analysis underlying these results is as follows. During a demand inflation, wage indexation ensures that all wages rise in line with prices, thus greatly reducing any incentive for firms to increase supply; in a word, the aggregate supply curve becomes less elastic. As a result, when demand increases, variations in output are limited, but fluctuations in prices are amplified. During a supply-shock inflation, on the other hand, wage indexation ensures that wage rise with prices and so shifts the aggregate supply curve upwards more than would otherwise have happened. In a word, the cushion of reductions in real wages is removed. The result is that, with a supply curve shifting more dramatically along the demand curve, price and output fluctuations are both likely to be amplified; in Carmichael's words, 'the failure of real wages to adjust to supply shocks causes employment to bear the full brunt of adjustment.'

The foregoing argument assumes that without indexation real

wages would fall in an inflationary upswing, adjusting to prices less fully than would indexed wages. Other possibilities, however, deserve mention. The central issue is how far wage indexation alters the extent and timing of changes in real wages. If it merely brings about what trade union pressure would bring about in any case, and with the same time lag, it alters nothing. If it eliminates time lags and thus prevents temporary changes in real wages – for example, a fall in the inflationary upswing and a rise in the downswing, each due to the time trade unions take to adjust wages to recent price changes – then it accelerates both inflation in the upswing and disinflation in the downswing, without altering the price level ultimately reached, except in so far as such accelerations may trigger some cumulative 'snowball' effect (via, for example, a rising velocity of circulation). If, finally, indexation actually makes real wages lower than they would otherwise be, then it may reduce the overall rise in prices and perhaps curb unemployment. The general view related by Carmichael, with its prediction that wage indexation is usually likely to amplify inflation from whatever source, is based on the assumption of at least temporary real wage flexibility.

There is, however, one particular case where, on the mainstream view, a disinflationary effect can be claimed. Carmichael argues:

Since wage indexation amplifies the reaction in the price level to all disturbances, it will tend to be inflationary if most disturbances, including policy shocks, are expansionary. At the same time, the tendency for indexation to increase the price reaction and reduce the output reaction to demand-side shocks should minimize the cost of a programme designed to reduce inflation through monetary contraction.

Thus the argument of Friedman (1974; and in Shanahan, 1974) emerges. Once the peak of an inflation has passed, wage indexation will curb wage increases. Without indexation, these would be negotiated by unions and employers holding expectations of inflation which were formed during the peak period. With actual inflation falling, real wages would therefore rise and unemployment would result; workers would, in fact, price themselves out of jobs. With indexation, wages respond more promptly to the fall in inflation, real wages accordingly fail to rise and unemployment is minimised. Furthermore, inflation abates more rapidly that it otherwise would. The argument clearly hinges, however, on the assumptions made. Should indexation fail to reduce the time lag between price changes and wage changes, or should the prediction of rising real wages in the absence of indexation be false, the result need not follow.

One widespread view regards wage indexation as probably worsening inflation in the upswing but lessening it, in accordance with Friedman's argument, in the downswing. On this view, it might be thought best to introduce indexation at the peak, just before inflation begins to subside. One problem here is that trade unions may be reluctant to agree to a system which could limit wage gains in the downswing when no such indexation was offered to limit losses in the upswing. The recommendation assumes, too, that governments are able reliably to recognise the peak of an inflation when it is arriving; the evidence of the Heath indexation venture costs doubt on this. All too probably, a government contemplating wage indexation will find itself faced with the choice between having the system through worsening and abating inflation alike, and not having it at all.

Unfortunately, international experience in recent years casts only a little light on these theoretical reflections. Carmichael *et al.* find that in general the behaviour of governments suggests acceptance of the broad principles enunciated above. In particular, a number of countries have removed from the index which they use for fixing wages the effects of external and exchange rate shocks. The apparent implication is that they wish to avoid worsening the instability of output which, according to accepted theory, supply shocks bring, but are willing to index wages in the face of demand inflation, when accepted doctrine predicts stabilising effects on output rather than the reverse. Empirical surveys, however, show little clear evidence of the effects of wage indexation. Sheila Page and Sandra Trollope (1974), in an international survey for the years before the first oil shock, find little evidence that wage indexation either was, or was regarded as being, an anti-inflationary success in those countries which employed it; while the BIS (1977) and Williamson (in Milner, 1987, p. 255) report many other countries as diluting or abandoning their wage indexation arrangements in the light of experience.

Examining evidence from forty countries. Stanley Fischer (1981, p. 23) finds that 'no form of indexation, other than that of bonds, significantly affected comparative inflation performance after the oil shock' [of 1973]. Countries with bond indexation did, however, suffer worse inflation at that time than other countries. Two points made by Fischer elsewhere (1982, p. 186), moreover, may be thought to weaken the indexationist case. First, pure money-induced inflation — the kind under which wage indexation has no tendency to worsen fluctuations in output — is unlikely to occur. 'There is usually a real economic reason [why] the government has turned to inflationary policy. In these circumstances, contracts indexed to the consumer price index are likely to hamper adjustment rather than help.' Second, in practice we are almost certain to have to settle for a partially or imperfectly indexed economy, which Fischer regards as 'the worst of all worlds . . ..
Then inflation is likely to worsen the distortions of real prices that occur in the absence of indexation.' In a similarly rather pessimistic vein, Robert J. Gordon (1982) sees supply shock in an economy with monetary accommodation and a high degree of wage indexation, such as existed in Italy in 1973–4 for example, as leading to a *permanent* acceleration of inflation.

The conclusion seems to be that many measures of indexation may well be judged desirable on ground of honesty and equity or to prevent undesired income redistributions, and may reduce the recessionary effects of stabilisation at the same time as they speed up the disinflationary process. On the other hand, the price of these advantages may well be a tendency to increase the range of fluctuations in the inflation rate above what it would otherwise be; while in a supply-shock inflation, indexation may rigidify the economy in a way which increases the instability of real output. When, as in the case of wage idexation, the indexed 'sector' is very large, the worsening of inflation may be particularly severe. If, however, only the tax system, basic social security benefits and perhaps a limited issue of bonds to each purchaser are involved, the trade-off of slightly more inflation for a good deal more equity may well be judged worthwhile. Indeed, wage indexation for the lowest income groups in countries where low incomes barely cover subsistence could well excuse a more substantial addition to inflationary pressures.

The subject remains one of extreme complexity, to be settled very much in the light of national and conjunctural circumstances (Williamson, 1987). None the less, we venture below some broad and tentative guidelines for the reader's consideration. These would tend to support two objectives: first, to try to restrict indexation to a reasonable minimum, because of its limitations and inflationary potential; and second, to try to separate the fully indexed sector of the economy from the unindexed by a broad cordon of increasingly sub-indexed areas, in order to prevent any citizen finding himself at a clearcut juncture, with his liabilities indexed but his assets unindexed. In this way the inequities and distortions of inflation would be redistributed widely across that part of the population which was in a position to bear them.

In more detail, our proposal would tend to favour:

(i)   almost full indexation of the tax system (provided that the government is politically strong enough not to resort to inflationary finance when deprived of fiscal drag). An exception might arise in the case of tax on the interest from highly liquid assets such as bank and building society deposits. One reason for this would be administrative, arising from the volatile nature of such deposits. Another would be that the partial indexation of government bonds suggested below might via competition tend, to some extent, to raise the rate of return on these deposits and so lessen the need for indexation of the tax on them (see (iii) below). In so far as the resulting *de facto* 'indexation' of the return on the deposits was only partial, the object would be to spread the costs of inflation widely, not exempting the deposit holders. A further argument for excepting deposit interest from full indexation for tax arises from the already mentioned desire for a wide progressively sub-indexed sector of the economy separating the fully indexed sector from the unindexed.

(ii)  full indexation of basic social security benefits, where these represent a minimum acceptable standard of living.

(iii) Sub-indexation of interest on government debt (if, again, the government is strong enough to respond in a non-inflationary manner). The index used would omit the effects of exogenous supply shocks, including deteriorations in the external terms of trade, as well as of policy-induced price increases like those resulting from tax increases and cuts in subsidies. An argument for this would again be that if the whole nation has to sustain a cut in its standard of living there is no reason why bondholders should be altogether exempted. Possibly the amount of indexed debt available per citizen might be limited, If it was not, competition for funds might well drive up rates of interest on deposits in banks and building societies by the full extent of inflation, and with them the interest rates charged on mortgages and loans. The result, as mentioned above, might be to provoke, in times of fluctuating earnings, unacceptable numbers of bankruptcies.

(iv) for wages, non-indexation. At the most and *in extremis* semi-demi-indexation might be introduced. In the latter case, the index used should omit not only the factors named in (iii) but also any price increases due to rises of average earnings in excess of increased productivity. If this were not done, then large wage settlements gained by one group of workers could be transmitted rapidly, through prices, to all workers and the wage–price spiral powerfully reinforced. On the whole, however, any indexation of wages, however partial, might best be restricted to workers whose real wages threatened to fall below subsistence levels; and even here, because of the danger of creating unemployment by instituting such a minimum wage, alternative possible methods of succour should be considered first.

## STABILISATIONS

The Economic and Financial Committee of the League of Nations, in introducing its series of remarkably similar stabilisation plans in the 1920s, was at the same time at pains to emphasise that there existed no one guaranteed recipe for the treatment of inflation, no 'League of Nations method'. Yet, as experience in Britain and the United States half a century later showed, the League's success bequeathed to the future a deep belief in the efficacy of a package of policies including: sudden budget-balancing, a halt to monetary growth, the introduction of a new currency, the total or partial cancellation of 'old' money and the independence of central banks from government. These policies are even today widely seen as providing success in curing inflation in a market economy without government intervention. How far do our case studies support belief in the various strands of what has now become economic folklore?

One strand, the faith in sudden 'shock treatment', has taken a considerable beating since the 1920s. Alexandra Kafka (1967, p. 611) has, indeed, gone so far as to suggest that the circumstances conferring success upon the stabilisations of the 1920s were so rare as to make the successes of that decade unusual, even something of a freak. For Britain a House of Commons report (1981) was prepared to declare shock treatment an unacceptable policy. But more gradualist, Phillips-style attempts to exchange inflation for unemployment and vice versa produced varying and unpredictable results and one groups of writers (Sargent, 1986) continued to suggest that the degree of success of such policies in relation to their costs made sudden stabilisation preferable. Shock treatment only works well, however, if prices and wages adjust quickly to falling demand. Few modern accounts of product or labour markets in either MEs or LDCs hold out much hope of this occurring widely; and few MDCs have recently undergone inflations extreme enough to create conditions psychologically favourable to rapid adjustment. The hope that sudden deflation will *make* markets work efficiently gains little support from recent economic history. To note this is not to argue that demand management is unnecessary. It is merely to find it unsurprising that since the 1920s sudden stabilisations have been most successful and least costly when they were accompanied by price and wage controls or other extensive government intervention, no matter whether the controls preceded stabilisation, as in Germany in 1948, or accompanied it, as in Hungary in 1946.

As to the role of foreign credits in bringing about stabilisation, in 1946 Nurkse (p. 96) cast doubt on their general importance, pointing to the twelve European countries which achieved *de facto* stabilisation in the 1920s without them and to the doubtful need for loans in the case of several other countries. In one case at least, that of Poland, we saw reason to doubt this verdict. Foreign loans may be used either to bridge a budget deficit until corrective measures can be taken ( a case of a stable-value second currency being introduced as a transitional measure), or temporarily to bridge an external deficit. For the second purpose tariffs or quotas, by strengthening the external position, may sometimes serve as a substitute. For the first, it is harder to find substitutes other than tax-raising and the slow painful process of expenditure-cutting. In the 1920s a sudden access of confidence in the newly issued currencies of the day often increased governments' ability to borrow, while the ending of inflation sharply increased the real value of tax revenue; but results of this kind hinged crucially on the achievement of a dramatic change in public psychology. The general conclusion for more recent years, with most countries' foreign trade at a high level and little sign of announcement effects retaining their potency, seems to be that it is hard to dismiss the need for foreign credits as lightly as Nurkse suggested.

The necessity for central banks to be independent of government represents another traditional 'rule' − one which Friedman revived in the 1970s, with the added proposal that the central bank, once independent, should be instructed to forsake contracyclical policies and pursue a path of steady monetary growth. As on other occasions, citizens' 'rationality' is relied on to make them adjust their wage- and price-fixing behaviour to the expected monetary conditions.

Looking at our case studies, it is hard to glean any general support for the claim that central bank independence of government has prevented or lessened inflation. Indeed, some CPEs, such as the GDR, where banking has been under the closest government control, have suffered least from inflation. The observation prompts the question whether what is required is that the central bank should be independent of government or whether the need is to free it from popular influence of the kind which *democratic* governments commonly transmit. In part the absence of correlation between central bank independence and freedom from inflation may arise because many independent central banks within our survey were instructed to operate under insufficiently strict rules of monetary restraint. Thus central banks constituted in Austria and Poland in the 1920s seem likely to have failed to prevent the recurrence of inflation partly because their statutes permitted the unlimited discounting of sound commercial bills. Had tighter policies been pursued, inflation might not have reappeared.

In recent years, however, even the confident expectation, and indeed the reality, of tight money − which central bank independence is intended to bring about in inflationary times − has shown few signs of being able by itself to banish inflation. In Britain in the early 1980s repeated opinion polls claimed to show widespread disbelief both in the authorities' willingness, and in their ability, to reflate the economy and so remedy the high level of unemployment. We might therefore expect the British to have begun to expect price stability and consequently to behave in a markedly non-inflationary manner. Yet in fact wage claims and wage settlements continued to exceed by far the increase in prices or productivity. Since such claims cannot have stemmed from any confidence in job prospects *generally* it seems that they must have stemmed from the confidence which each individual wage-bargaining group felt in *its own* job prospects. Generalised conditions of monetary stringency allied with fiscal restraint were, in short, far from producing general wage restraint. For inflation of this type no degree of central bank independence or monetary restraint would by itself be a remedy.

None the less, the suspicion persists that even if such independence is not sufficient, it may be necessary for price stability. Certainly, a widespread opinion attributes a large part of postwar British inflation to the belief that at the first sign of remediable unemployment the authorities would relax fiscal restraint and boost demand, regardless of the implications for prices. Since any elected government is under great pressure to behave in this way, does not the necessity of an independent authority follow?

How far public opinion may be changed in such a way as to permit democratic parties to win elections without having to endorse inflation is so far an unanswered question. What can be said is that there exists, at least in Britain, a widespread feeling of repugnance against the transfer to a non-elected and unanswerable body, such as a central bank, of the power to create, or permit the emergence of, deep recession. Democratic control of monetary policy may lead to inflation; but it is doubtful if the nation would prefer undemocratic control of the state's power to influence unemployment.

One more doctrine to stem from the 1920s, minor and mainly folkloristic but none the less widely believed, asserts that democracy never for more than a few years survives a high rate of inflation. The recent experiences of, for example, Israel and Iceland disprove this view as a general rule. Yet our own case studies do attest that inflation brings with it pressure for a change of government. Usually the change is towards dictatorship, only rarely in the other direction. The stabilisations of the 1920s consistently involved governments in taking to themselves plenary powers. Similarly, the stabilisations attempted in many less developed countries, such as Chile in 1973, Brazil in 1964 and Argentina in 1966 and 1976, were the work of recently instituted military governments in whose accession to power fear of inflation had played an important role. Overall, the evidence is fairly impressive in favour of a general tendency for sustained severe inflation to lead towards autocracy. As for success in stabilisation, George Blazyca has written (1985, p. 433) that 'there is no evidence to suggest that military regimes have any advantage over other types when it comes to the control of inflation . . .' One stabilisation which casts grave doubt on this opinion is the German currency reform of 1948 which, in a widespread view, could not have been carried out under democratic rule.[3]

## IS COSTLESS STABILISATION POSSIBLE?

A final question which has occupied a large part of our investigations is how far stabilisation is possible without unemployment. The Phillips Curve, formally defined, we have discussed above and shall not consider further. The noteworthy fact here is that in every stabilisation after hyperinflation in the 1920s (with the sole and freak exception of that in the Soviet Union, where further collapse was almost impossible) stabilisation was followed by some degree of recession. One widely cited cause was the disruption caused by the elimination of inflationary distortions in the economy; a second was the post-stabilisation fall in the velocity of circulation of money. Third, Cagan and Fellner (1983) emphasise the effects of insolvencies arising from large debts at the time of stabilisation. Where such debts have been incurred only recently and in the expectation that repayment will be in depreciated currency, stabilisation − which falsifies such expectations − can easily produce widespread bankruptcy. In such a case, the slump provoked by ending a *hyper*inflation may tend to be less than that following a moderate inflation because in the former case lending is more likely to have dried up long before stabilisation day.

For the period since World War II, the evidence is more mixed. The Hungarian stabilisation of 1946 seems to have prompted immediate recovery of output, though from catastrophically low levels beforehand. The Soviet Union after 1947 and probably some other CPEs seem to have escaped recession because of tight controls over credit, velocity and the allocation of resources. In the longer run, however, the damage which controls wrought on supply must have worked against price stability. In Britain throughout the first half of the 1980s measures of domestic deflation and consequent falling velocity certainly contributed to recession; nor can the fall in velocity have been due wholly to financial innovations. On the other hand, shocks to the country's external balance and world depression certainly also exerted major recessionary influences. Even the high tide of bankruptcies during the period owed less to the ending of fast inflation than to the unsuccessful attempts at monetary targeting which preceded it. There seem, too, to be few signs that the correction of distortions due specifically to inflation were a major cause of recession.

If, however, recession is a regular result of stabilisation, in what circumstances, other than those of deep initial depression, can it be avoided? The first German stabilisation provides one answer. Between November 1923 and April 1924, *after* the stabilisation, the velocity of circulation fell in response to the belief that the inflation was over, but the money supply continued to soar. The stabilisation was, in short, a confidence trick; but the overall effect of two opposite tendencies, one (falling velocity) cutting demand for goods and services, the other (a soaring money supply) raising it, was to maintain a reasonably high level of activity.

Such a trick could not in its nature last long, and a recession, long delayed, was in due course to appear. Our evidence suggests, however, at least one alternative way of achieving stabilisation without recession: government controls, possibly including the direction of labour. The cost of such a policy in lost efficiency and lost freedom may be large and the freedom from unemployment purely formal, with many workers seriously underoccupied at their workplaces. None the less, the example of the CPEs, for example the Soviet Union in 1947, offers this as a solution relatively free from hardship for the workforce. In the longer run, however, the buildup of micro-inefficiencies under central planning (and also, in the Soviet case, the accumulation of unspent money balances) may itself create a grave threat of inflation. We are thus left with state-controlled stabilisation as an alternative to shock treatment, but one which can scarcely be held in place for long. On the other hand, such a method can be used under moderately normal conditions of civilisation. The orthodox 1920s solution, though brilliantly successful in anarchic conditions, or where – as in the Germany of 1948 – labour and other resources are highly mobile, seems unlikely to be acceptable in less extreme circumstances.

## THE INCOME SHARES APPROACH

What has been said so far gives little support to those who claim the existence of known general 'laws' of inflation, though considerably more to those who claim marked known tendencies. This is, perhaps, unsurprising in a subject long ago authoritatively described by J.N. Keynes (1891, p. 16) as 'a science of tendencies, not of matters of fact'. At a higher level of generality, however, it can be argued that all inflations everywhere do share a common basic nature. This is the income shares approach well expressed (in the context of Latin American inflation) by Rosemary Thorp (1971, p. 109):

Inflation is seen as an instrument for reconciling conflicting social groups: total product is expanding more slowly than is compatible with the aspirations of different sections of the community, and the solution of weak governments is to respond to all aspirations. The conflict is worked out through a continuous rise in prices . . .

On this view, all inflation, whatever its proximate cause, results fundamentally from inter-group conflict for mutually incompatible shares of available real income or wealth. Such a view of inflation finds strong support in almost all our case studies. The story of the German hyperinflation is substantially the story of a German government unable, or possibly unwilling, to exact from its taxpayers the full share of their income required by public spending, including reparations payments. German governmental weakness likewise reflects the governing parties' inability, until the evil of hyperinflation was far advanced, to secure the agreement of the business classes to halting the upward trend. The French inflation reflected deadlock in the legislature and in the country. In the Germany of 1945–8 the trouble lay primarily in the earlier issue, in the form of money, of excessive claims upon a much reduced volume of output. In Britain the struggle between government and trade unions, and between Britain and foreign oil exporters, lay at the heart of the inflation of the 1970s.

To the incomes shares approach, Rosemary Thorp raises two objections: first, that it cannot explain the *initiation* of inflation, only its continuance; second, that it assumes continuing and widespread 'money illusion' − the mistaking of money gains for real ones − since only if such an illusion exists can inflation succeed in reconciling conflicting claims to income where these exceed the total real income available.

The first objection, though formally correct, does little to weaken the income shares theory. In this century no country has lacked random shocks to initiate social conflict. From Poland we have reports of unrealistically soaring expectations; from the Soviet Union news of disappointing harvests; from the oil-importing countries, whether MEs, LDCs or CPEs, evidence of setbacks to living standards arising from price shocks in international markets. Once normal expectations are disppointed the income shares theory can provide an explanation of the inflation which follows.

The second objection is that money illusion cannot be so persistent as to allow inflation to resolve conflict indefinitely. The illusion must fade; learning from experience, people will try to insist on real gains and inflation will correspondingly soar. There is a good deal of evidence that this actually happens. Some of the experience of our period certainly seems to point to the transiency of money illusion. Such a belief is, for example, consistent with evidence of changes in the slope of the Phillips Curve both in Britain and the United States. Yet the central point remains: the fact that inflation may fail permanently to resolve conflict affords no evidence that it did not arise out of conflict. And in the end, a solution may be imposed. When inflation subsided in the industrial countries in the 1980s it may have been the unemployed who, though subject to no illusion, had to accept defeat.

The incomes shares theory is, however, inadequately stated. In a better formulation it is the view that inflation arises from inter-group conflict for income or wealth where the groups concerned possess roughly equal strength and when governmental and other regulatory bodies either cannot or will not impose, or persuade the conflicting parties to accept, a solution. The equality of the antagonists is important. Few writers doubt the existence of fierce inter-group conflict in South America before World War II, but because power at that time lay securely in the hands of a traditional oligarchy inflation was, except in Chile, seldom severe. The concentration of power in the hands of most eastern European postwar governments may similarly go far to explain why strong propensities in the direction of inter-group conflict led to only mild inflation. The absence of governmental imposition is also important. The worldwide struggle for income shares in the 1970s, essentially between oil producers and the trade unions of the developed countries, helped to cause inflation because neither group of antagonists was strong enough to win outright and no other organisation could impose a solution upon both, or persuade them to accept one.

## THE TRANSFER PROBLEM AND THE NATURE OF INFLATION

Our proposal, then, is that inflation has roots which lie deep in socio-political conflict. If this is so, it is not surprising that two economic mirror-images of social conflict occur repeatedly in the literature. The first, the 'scissors' phenomenon (see Glossary), refers to changes in the terms of trade, within a country, between town and country. The term first achieved wide notoriety in the Soviet Union of the 1920s, where it was observed that when the prices of agricultural output fell too low in relation to those for industrial goods the peasants began to hoard, or to consume or refuse to produce their own output. Higher relative agricultural prices became, in short, a prerequisite for increases in agricultural supplies and through them for economic growth and overall price stability. The latter therefore crucially depended on the achievement of internal terms of trade which were acceptable to the peasants. A similar 'scissors' phenomenon was noted in the 1970s in Poland. Writing of modern Argentina, Brown (1985, pp. 11–12) and others have also claimed that urban workers, suffering from adverse internal terms of trade, tried in the postwar years to recoup the loss in real income which higher food prices had inflicted on them by pressing for higher wages, and so gave a new impulse to inflation. Here again conflict between town and countryside seems to have fostered inflation. In Brown's version it is the fact that the same product (beef, in the case of Argentina) is both a basic wage good and the main export that lies at the heart of the problem, export incentives and inflation being barely separable. In the East European cases, similarly, food is described both as the farmer's wage good and as his export to the towns; high food prices are thus both an incentive to the farmer and a source of inflation and urban unrest. In each case the conflict between rural and urban interests is underlined.

A second fact indicative of underlying socio-political conflict is the frequency with which the so-called 'transfer problem' accompanies inflation. The problem is, indeed, to the international economy very much what the 'scissors' problem is to an agrarian country's domestic economy. No longer as well known as it was in the interwar period, it may be expressed, using one definition out of a range of interrelated possibilities, as the problem of specifying the circumstances in which the transfer of a given volume of capital from country A to country B will produce a corresponding transfer of real resources without disequilibrating the flow of payments between the two countries (see e.g. Harberler 1936, pp. 65–83; Viner, 1937, pp. 307–11). When, for example, £100 is transferred unrequitedly, as a gift or in the form of reparations, in what circumstances will the corresponding value of goods and services actually be transferred without balance of payments disequilibrium?

Perhaps the most widely suggested answer (e.g. Williamson, 1983 (I), pp. 178–80), applicable to a country whose current trade is initially in balance at full employment, states that the conditions for effecting a full transfer of reparations are: in the paying country, expenditure-reducing policies such as cutting real wages or expenditure, and policies switching expenditure away from foreign goods, perhaps via tariff increases or devaluation; and in the recipient country, the reverse. The circumstances of interwar Germany clearly differed from those envisaged in the model in certain vital respects. Reparations actually paid fell far short of the sums demanded; even those which were paid were more than wholly financed by net foreign borrowing, and not long after the borrowing dried up, the reparations were effectively cancelled. Yet the failure of German governments to fulfil the basic conditions for transfer is obvious. The point most relevant to our discussion here is that, by failing to curb real incomes and expenditure or to divert the latter to domestic output, German governments were, in fact and perhaps in intention, engaging in an international struggle for real resources; and this lay at the heart of the inflation.

The same cannot be said of the Western world's next major planned international income transfer, that embodied in Marshall Aid from the United States to former combatant countries in the late 1940s. This aimed at, and helped to achieve, a substantially non-inflationary recovery of output in the recipient countries. Governments in these countries were supplied with dollars which they allocated to their importers in exchange for local currency, known as 'counterpart funds'. They were then permitted to spend the counterpart funds for approved purposes connected mainly with reconstruction. In the recipient countries, therefore, the addition to demand could not exceed the addition to supplies which Marshall Aid made available. Even so, it deserves note that fears of demand inflation were expressed in the *donor* country; and this occurred despite the fact that on this occasion the aid, being voluntary, reflected a perceived coincidence of interests between donor and recipients and so constituted a transfer free from obvious inter-group conflict.

The most recent major transfer of purchasing power presents a much more inflationary picture. The OPEC oil crises of the 1970s do not strictly meet Harberler's definition of a transfer as an unrequited payment. None the less, the huge additional oil costs which suddenly became payable by oil importing countries to oil exporters clearly created, in all substance, a transfer problem. This becomes even more evident when we take account not only of the oil price rises of the decade but also of the accompanying increases in other raw material prices. Here, as in most such cases, including that of France when it was obliged to pay heavy reparations after the Franco-Prussian War of 1870 (Moulton and McGuire, 1923, Chapter 7), the transfer *in goods and services* was far from fully effected. Partly because the export surpluses of the OPEC countries were deposited in, and rapidly on-lent by, western financial intermediaries, any transfer in the form of goods and services was much moderated. Furthermore, the response of western trade unions to rising inflation and fast monetary growth helped rapidly to reverse the erosion of real wages, so that OPEC was never, even from the beginning, an outright victor in the conflict for income shares. The existence of negative real rates of interest on OPEC's lending in western countries further helped to damp down the real economic gains made. What concerns us, however, is the striking example the decade affords of inflation actively resulting not only from domestic struggles for income within individual nations but also from similar international struggles. A world may be imaginable in which a transfer of income or wealth is fully and quickly effected from a country with downwardly flexible incomes to others which stand in no danger of stimulating excess demand. Such a world could combine a fully effected transfer with price stability. It bears, however, little resemblance to the world of the 1970s or 1980s.

Drawing on the experience of the 1970s, Kaldor (1976) has drawn attention back to the need for commodity price stabilisation schemes, arguing that these are a prerequisite of reasonable stability for world prices and that in their absence remedial monetary policies are likely to prove inadequate. Any such schemes would inevitably amount to an attempt to control not only price fluctuations but also, in consequence, the huge shifts in the world's income distribution to which they give rise. The argument clearly carries force. The proviso has to be added, however, that the scheme concerned should aim primarily to smooth out price fluctuations, not to keep prices at permanently inflated levels. If this latter were to happen the schemes might affect primary commodity markets in much the same way as the rise of trade unions has affected labour markets and a persistent inflationary trend might result. With this proviso, however, it is hard to doubt that the advent of stabilising mechanisms in commodity markets could serve greatly to diminish world price instability and so serve as a means of lessening possible problems of income transfer.

## CONCLUSION

Is it possible, at the end of a lengthy and complex survey, to conclude by proposing any convincing generalisation about the origins of inflation? Could one, for example, argue that inflation, always and everywhere, springs from a transfer of income or wealth, actual or attempted, intra-national or international? Even this claim, though strikingly consistent with most of our evidence, would be too widely formulated. A sudden economic setback due to the advent of some persistent natural adversity can spark off conflict over a diminished total real income where no actual transfer is involved. Conflict itself may not initially be involved: mere incompetence, as in Peron's Argentina or Gierek's Poland, may provoke various economic groups to try to maintain their living standards by pressing for higher wages, profits or prices. Any generalisation about the nature of inflation, however simple, is hard to sustain. None the less, an attempt may be made. The matter may be worded as follows. In the modern Western world a central and regular source of augmented inflationary pressure lies in conflict over income shares. The conflict may arise fortuitously and be waged almost inadvertently. None the less, if no conflict were present, inflation would not persist. Furthermore, in fomenting conflict the disappointment of expectations, for any reason, plays a central part. Mere restraints on growth arising from natural or man-made misfortunes may stimulate it just as surely as actual falls in real income. But it is transfers of income or wealth, either between groups within a country or between countries, which seem most obviously and powerfully to stimulate economic conflict and the inflationary results which follow. Correspondingly, the cure must lie either in the imposition of a distributive solution by some authority, governmental or private, or in voluntary agreement upon a solution. Sadly, the evidence suggests that such voluntary agreement is often achieved only after all concerned have suffered the effects of a long and costly economic conflict.

## NOTES

1. The point above excessive claims to generality has wide relevance. It is normal in economic writing for accounts of models drawing on the experience of one or two episodes to be written in the present tense, giving the impression that the mechanism described holds generally. 'This is what happens,' the statement runs; not simply, 'This is what happened in July 1987.'
2. Statisticians constructing an index of prices typically take a 'representative' sample of goods (or 'basket') and sum the prices of the goods at a number of different dates – once for each year, say. The percentage rise in the value of the basket over time is then taken to represent the rise in the general price level. The ASDM proposal would, in the version cited, use an index based upon a basket of goods which would be the average of all national baskets, with their relative importance determined by the relative size, say, of the different countries' GNPs.
3. The Latin American evidence is also less clear than Mr Blazyca suggests. It is arguable that the Chilean government of President Pinochet, once it abandoned relative gradualism in 1975 and adopted a policy of 'shock treatment' did reduce inflation rapidly (Edwards, 1985, p. 226), though at a high cost. It can also be argued that its policies for inflation-free growth succeeded until it adopted new policies based on 'open economy monetarism' in the period leading up to June 1979. The Brazilian armed forces also had considerable success in reducing inflation until 1973.

Atrocious governments are not necessarily less effective in economic policy than humane ones.

# Abbreviations and Acronyms

ASDM: All Saints' Day Manifesto. A proposal for parallel currencies in the European Community as a means to monetary union, proposed on All Saints' Day, 1975.

CMEA: Council for Mutual Economic Assistance. One of the main organisations for fostering economic cooperation in Eastern Europe.

CPE: Centrally planned economy.

CPI: Consumer price index.

EC: European Community, successor to the three former Communities: the EEC or European Economic Community, Euratom and the European Coal and Steel Community.

EMU: European Monetary Union.

ERP: European Recovery Program, popularly known as Marshall Aid.

GARIOA: Government and Relief in Occupied Areas. Early postwar American aid for occupied countries, administered by the military authorities.

GDP: Gross domestic product. The value of all goods and services produced by a country within one year, excluding net property income from abroad.

GNP: Gross national product. GDP plus net property income from abroad.

G10: The Group of Ten. A group of the ten main banking nations which meets from time to time to discuss international financial and economic problems.

IMF: International Monetary Fund.

LDC: Less developed country.

MO, M1, M3, £M3: measures of the British money supply. See Glossary.

MDC: More developed, or advanced industrial country.

ME: Market economy.

MLR: Minimum Lending Rate. See Glossary of Terms.

MTFS: Medium Term Financial Strategy. Economic policy adopted by the British government after 1980, designed to abate inflation by achieving pre-stated targets for the broad money supply and the public sector borrowing requirement.

NAIRU: Non-accelerating inflation rate of unemployment. The minimum level of unemployment believed to be consistent with a steady rate of inflation.

NBER: National Bureau of Economic Research.

NEP: New Economic Policy. Term used both by Lenin to describe the partial and temporary return to private enterprise permitted after 1921 in the Soviet Union, and, presumably unwittingly, by President Nixon to describe his new policies in 1971, including price and wage controls.

NIESR: National Institute of Economic and Social Research.

NOW: Negotiated order of withdrawal. Name given to interest-bearing checkable accounts intoduced in American banks in the 1970s.

OECD: Organisation for Economic Cooperation and Development.

OPEC: Organisation of Petroleum Exporting Countries.

PSBR: Public sector borrowing requirement. See Glossary of Terms.

RPI: Retail price index.

s.a.: Seasonally adjusted.

STE: Soviet-type economy. An STE may be not centrally planned but, as in Yugoslavia, may allow much devolution of power to enterprises and regions. Equally, it would be possible for a centrally planned economy to be of a non-soviet type – as, for example, in a fascist state.

TUC: Trades Union Congress.

# Glossary

*Bank rate:* the Bank of England's lending rate, precursor of MLR (qv).

*'Crowding out':* any process whereby increases in public expenditure cut private expenditure, e.g. when borrowing for public investment drives up interest rates and so discourages private.

*Demand for money function:* mathematical expression purporting to relate the quantity of money which people and organisations wish to hold to the factors determining it.

*Discounting:* the purchase of a bill at a price below the price it will realise at redemption; the purchaser thus effectively earns interest by lending money to the drawer (issuer) of the bill.

*Equation of exchange:* $MV = PT$, where $M$ = the money stock, $V$ = the velocity of circulation of money (the number of times the average pound changes hands in the course of transactions during some given time period), $P$ = the general price level, and $T$ = the number of transactions taking place in the given period. As it stands, the 'equation' is an identity, true by the definition of the terms. It can, however, be used in framing a theory or hypothesis, which asserts either that $V$ and $T$ are in the short run constant, or equivalently, that the price level varies proportionally with the money supply, the latter being the determining cause. Around this hypothesis, and the reservations and elaborations added to it, the greater part of controversy about inflation has historically revolved.

*Eurocurrency:* currency deposited in (usually European) banks outside the country of the currency's origin.

*Extrapolative expectations* point to a continuance of present trends, regressive to a reversal of those trends.

*Fiscal drag:* the process by which, under a progressive tax system, incomes and expenditures rising only in line with inflation incur increasing amounts of tax.

*Fisher's Law:* the doctrine, attributed to Irving Fisher, that rates of interest will tend to rise to the full extent of inflation, so that the real rate of interest will remain constant.

*Gross Domestic/National Product (GDP/GNP):* see Abbreviations and Acronyms.

*Law of One Price:* the doctrine that free trade under fixed exchange rates will tend to equalise the price of any traded good in different countries.

*Liquid Assets Ration:* see Reserve Ratio.

*MO:* M zero. Measure of that part of the British money supply which consists of notes and coins which are either in circulation with the public or held as bankers' deposits with the Bank of England.

*M1:* narrow measure of the British money supply: notes and coins in circulation plus sterling sight (current account) deposits held by the UK private sector.

*£M3:* sterling M3. Broad measure of the British money supply: notes and coins in circulation plus *all* sterling bank deposits (including certificates of deposit) held by UK residents in the private sector.

*M3:* £M3 plus all deposits in other currencies held by UK residents in the private sector.

*Minimum Lending Rate:* the rate of interest at which the Bank of England was willing, during the 1970s, to lend to private financial intermediaries.

*Monetary base control:* proposed method of control of the money supply through control of the volume of 'high-powered money', of which the total money supply was believed to be (or to be capable of being made) a multiple.

*Open Economy Monetarism:* body of doctrine concerning the behaviour of economies, especially small ones, under free trade. One popular doctrine is that if a small economy fixes its exchange rate with respect to that of a major trading partner, its rate of inflation will, as trade equalises prices, tend to become equal to that prevailing in international trade generally.

*Opportunity cost:* the value of what is foregone by any action. Thus, interest is foregone by holding cash.

*Phillips Curve:* a graphic curve put forward by A.W. Phillips (1958) purporting to show, for Britain 1861–1957, an inverse relationship between the rate of increase of wage rates and the level of unemployment; as one rose, the other fell. Thus, percentage unemployment was plotted along the horizontal axis at the bottom of the graph, rising from a zero origin at the lefthand end, while the percentage rate of increase of wage rates was plotted on the vertical axis, rising from a zero origin at the bottom lefthand corner of the graph. Annual observations, when plotted, fell broadly around a curve, convex towards the origin, which sloped downwards on the graph (but at a diminishing gradient) from northwest to southeast. In short, by moving along the curve a country could, it was implied, substitute wage inflation for unemployment, or *vice versa*. The *expectations-augmented Phillips* Curve, which shows little or no trade-off between wage inflation and unemployment, explains the disappearance of the relationship between the two variables in terms of workers' and employers' expectations. Thus, in this account, reflationary policy only leads to higher employment because workers now accepting employment believe that the higher-than-usual wages they are offered represent a real wage increase. With costs rising and demand buoyant, however, prices rise, so that workers are disappointed. They demand further wage increases to restore their expected real wages and so the quantity of labour demanded falls once more to its pre-reflation level. The government's policy, designed to reduce unemployment, has merely boosted inflation. In diagrammatic terms, the Phillips Curve has become vertical, or may even slope upwards towards the northeast.

*Price equalisation system (Preisausgleich):* system in CPEs whereby a country insulates itself from price changes abroad by means of subsidies/taxes to imports and exports.

*Present value:* the value today of an expected flow of income in the future.

*Public sector borrowing requirement:* borrowing requirement of central and local government and nationalised industries. It was distinguished from the budget deficit, during our period, chiefly by its taking account of the cuts in borrowing made possible by the sale of publicly owned assets and industries.

*Purchasing power parity theory:* theory which, in its simplest form, claims that a freely floating exchange rate between two currencies will tend to approach equilibrium at a level which permits the equivalent amounts of the two currencies to purchase the same volume of goods and services in each of the two countries.

*Quantity theory of money:* the hypothesised equiproportional movement of the money stock and the general price level mentioned under 'Equation of exchange' above. The theory that the quantity of money determines the price level.

*Rational expectations:* expectations taking full account of all relevant information as well as of the predictions of economic theory. The particular theory usually meant is neoclassical, involving notably the quantity theory of money or one of its variants and relying on a belief in the efficiency of markets. The rational expectations hypothesis is commonly advanced to support the claim that governments are powerless to raise the level of output or employment, since such policies only work if citizens ignore the inflationary consequences of fiscal reflation, which, being rational, they will not do.

*Real Bills Doctrine:* the historical doctrine that money issued by the monetary authorities in the course of discounting sound commercial trade bills cannot be inflationary, since it only increases monetary demand in line with increases in real supply. Also called the Doctrine of Reflux, on the ground that such bills are redeemed, with consequent reduction of the money supply, when the real trade is complete and the bills mature.

*Real wage resistance:* the resistance of workers and trade unions to the erosion of real wages by tax increases, by inflation or by fiscal drag (qv).

*Reserve ratio:* the ratio which a bank maintains between certain reserve assets (e.g. cash, or liquid assets) and its total assets.

*'Scissors' phenomenon:* the inverse movement of agricultural and industrial prices, so that when the two price indices are plotted against time the lines representing them cross like the blades of scissors.

*Special deposits:* deposits which the British commercial banks were, during the 1960s and 1970s, required to make with the central bank. Since the deposits could not be counted in the banks' cash or liquid assets ratio they were often interpreted as being designed to result in a multiple contraction of bank lending along the lines of monetary base control (qv). The authorities, however, denied any such intention, claiming that the object was to raise interest rates and so restrict credit and the growth of the money supply.

*Supplementary special deposits:* in effect, a progressive tax imposed on British banks during the 1970s to the extent that their interest-bearing eligible liabilities grew beyond specified limits.

*Target wage hypothesis:* the hypothesis that workers or trade unions demand money wages designed to achieve a desired real wage.

*Velocity of circulation:* speed at which money circulates. Thus, income velocity is the number of times an average pound changes hands per year in the form of income; transactions velocity includes all transactions.

*Wage good:* basic consumer good on which an important part of wages is spent.

*Wealth effect:* any effect of a change in wealth, often upon the wealthholder's level of expenditure.

# Bibliographic Abbreviations

AEI:      *American Enterprise Institute for Public Policy Research*
AER:      *American Economic Review*
BEQB:     *Bank of England Quarterly Bulletin*
BPEA:     *Brookings Papers on Economic Activity*
CEH:      *Central European History*
EJ:       *Economic Journal*
Eca:      *Economica*
IEA:      Institute of Economic Affairs
JEL:      *Journal of Economic Literature*
JME:      *Journal of Monetary Economics*
JPE:      *Journal of Political Economy*
LBR:      *Lloyds Bank Review*
NBER:     National Bureau of Economic Research
NIESR:    National Institute of Economic and Social Research
QJE:      *Quarterly Journal of Economics*
RES:      *Review of Economic Studies*
REStat:   *Review of Economics and Statistics*
SS:       *Soviet Studies*

# Bibliography

(Double brackets indicate the date of the first edition. In the case of translations this may be the date of publication in the original language.)

Adirim, Isaak (1983), *Stagflation in the USSR,* Delphic Associates, Inc., Falls Church, Va.

Al Sammarie, A. (1977) and Roberts, B., 'The Effects of Phases I, II and III on Wages, Prices and Profit Margins in the Manufacturing Sector of the United States', in Popkin, J. (ed.), *Analysis of Inflation, 1965–74,* pp. 241–90.

American Enterprise institute for Public Policy Research (1974), *Indexing and Inflation,* Washington DC, 1974.

Angell, James W. (1926), *The Theory of International Prices: History, Criticism and Restatement,* Harvard U.P., Cambridge, Mass.

Argy V.E. and Nevile J.W. (1985), *Inflation and Unemployment,* Allen and Unwin, London.

Artis, M. and Lewis, M. (1974), 'The Demand for Money: Stable or Unstable?', *The Banker,* March, pp. 239–42.

Artis, M. and Lewis, M. (1976), 'The Demand for Money in the UK, 1963–73', *Manchester School,* no. 44, pp. 147–81.

Artis, M. and Bladen-Hovell, R. (1987), 'The UK's monetarist experiment, 1979–84', *International Review of Applied Economics,* vol. 1, pp. 23–47.

Ausch, S. (1958), 'The 1945–1946 Inflation Stabilization', Kossuth.

Baer, W. and Beckerman, P. (1980), 'The Trouble with Index-Linking: Reflections on the Recent Brazilian Experience', *World Development,* vol. 8, no.9, pp. 677–703.

Bank for International Settlements, *Annual Reports,* various years, Basle.

Beckerman, W., 'How the Battle against Inflation was Really Won',

*LBR,* January 1985.

Beckerman, W. and Jenkinson, T. (1986), 'What Stopped the Inflation? Unemployment or Commodity Prices?', *EJ,* vol. 96, pp. 39–54.

Bergson, A. (1964), *The Economics of Soviet Planning,* Yale U.P., New Haven.

Bernholz, P. (1982), *Flexible Exchange Rates in Historical Perspective,* Princeton Studies in International Finance, no. 49, Princeton U.P., New Jersey.

Birman, I. (1980), 'The Financial Crisis in the USSR', *SS,* vol. 32, pp. 84–105.

Birman, I. and Clarke, R. (1985), 'Inflation and the Money Supply in the Soviet Economy', *SS,* vol. 37, pp. 494–504.

Blazyca, G. (1982), 'The Degeneration of Central Planning in Poland', in Jean Woodall (ed.), *Policy and Politics in Contemporary Poland,* Frances Pinter, London.

Blazyca G. (1985), 'The Polish Economy under Martial Law', *SS,* vol. 37, no. 3, pp. 428–36.

Blinder, A.S. (1979), *Economic Policy and the Great Stagflation,* Academic Press, London and New York.

Blinder, A.S. (1982), 'The Anatomy of Double-Digit Inflation in the 1970s', in Robert E. Hall (ed.), *Inflation: Causes and Effects,* pp. 261–82.

Boltho, A. (1984), 'Is Western Europe Caught in an "Expectations Trap"?', *LBR,* pp. 1–13.

Bomberger, W.A. and Makinen, G.E. (1980), 'Indexation, Inflationary Finance, and Hyperinflation: The 1945–1946 Hungarian Experience', *JPE,* pp. 550–60.

Born, Karl Erich (1977), *Geld und Banken im 19. und 20.* Jahrundert, Kroner, Stuttgart.

Bornstein, M. (1962), 'The Soviet Price System', *AER,* vol. 52, p. 64.

Bornstein, M. (1978), 'The Administration of the Soviet Price System', *SS,* vol. 30, pp. 466–90.

Bornstein, M. (1985), 'Improving the Soviet Economic Mechanism', *SS,* vol. 37, no. 1, pp. 1–30.

Bosworth, B.P. and Lawrence, R.Z. (1982), *Commodity Prices and the New Inflation,* Brookings, Washington DC.

Bosworth, B. and Vroman, W. (1977), 'An Appraisal of the Wage-Price Control Program', in Popkin, J. (ed.), *Analysis of Inflation, 1965–74,* pp. 67–112.

Bresciani-Turroni, Constantino (1937 (1931)), *The Economics of Inflation,* reprinted 1968, Augustus M. Kelley, New York.

Brown, A.J., assisted by Jane Darby (1985), *World Inflation Since*

*1950: An International Comparative Study,* Cambridge U.P. for NIESR.

Brus, W. (1973), *The Economics and Politics of Socialism,* Routledge and Kegan Paul, London and Boston.

Brus, W. (1979), 'The East European Reforms: What Happened to Them?'. *SS,* vol. 31, pp. 257–67.

Buiter, W. and Miller, M. (1981), 'The Thatcher Experiment: The First Two Years', *BPEA,* no. 2, pp. 315–67.

Buiter, W. and Miller, M. (1983), 'Changing the Rules: Economic Consequences of the Thatcher Regime', *BPEA,* no. 2, pp. 305–79.

Buky, Jozsef (1946), *From the Pengo to the Florin,* Budapest.

Burns, Arthur (1975), *Federal Reserve Bulletin,* March, pp. 150–5.

Bush, Keith (1973), 'Soviet Inflation', in Yves Laulan (ed.), *Banking, Money and Credit in Eastern Europe,* pp. 97–105.

Cagan, Philip (1956), 'The Monetary Dynamics of Hyperinflation', in Friedman, M. (ed.), *Studies in the Quantity Theory of Money,* pp. 25–117.

Cagan, P. and Fellner, W., (1983), 'Tentative Lessons from the Recent Disinflationary Effort', *BPEA,* vol. 2, pp. 603–8.

Cagan, P. and Kincaid, G. (1977), 'Jacobs' estimates of the hyperinflation Model: a comment', *Economic Inquiry,* vol. 14, pp. 111–17.

Cagan, P. and Lipsey, Robert E. (1978), *The Financial Effects of Inflation,* NBER General Series, no. 103, Ballinger, Cambridge, Mass.

Cambridge (1981), *Encyclopaedia of Russia and the Soviet Union,* C.U.P.

Carmichael, J., Fahrer J. and Hawkins, J. (1985), 'Some Macroeconomic Implications of Wage Indexation: a Survey', in Argy V. and Nevile J. (eds), *Inflation and Unemployment,* pp. 78–102.

Central Statistical Office, *Economic Trends,* various issues.

Christie, H. and Fratianni, M. (1978), 'European Monetary Union: Rehabilitation of a case and Some Thoughts for Strategy', in Fratianni, M. and Peeters, T. (eds), *One Money for Europe,* pp. 3–34.

Clark, P.B. (1985), 'Inflation and Unemployment in the United States: Recent Experience and Policies', in Argy V. and Nevile J. (eds), *Inflation and Unemployment,* pp. 221–48.

Clarke, R.A. (1983), 'The Study of Soviet-Type Economies: Some Trends and Conclusions', *SS,* vol. 35, pp. 525–32.

Clarke, R.A. and Matko, D. (1972), *Soviet Economic Facts, 1917–1970,* John Wiley and Sons, New York.

Clough, S. (1939), *France: a History of National Economics, 1879–1939,* Scribner's, New York.

Coghlan, R. (1981), *Money Credit and the Economy,* Allen and Unwin, London.

Cohen, C.D. (1971), *Britain's Economic Policy, 1960–69,* Butterworth, London.

Committee on the Working of the Monetary System (1959), *Report,* (Radcliffe Report), Cmnd. 827, HMSO, London.

Corden, W.M. (1985 (1977)), 3rd edn, *Inflation, Exchange Rates and the World Economy,* Oxford U.P.

Courakis, A.S. (ed.) (1981), *Inflation, Depression and Economic Policy in the West,* Mansell, London and Alexandrine Press, Oxford.

Csikos Nagy, B. and Racz, L. (1983), 'The Rise of the Price Level and Its Factors in Hungary', *Acta Oeconomica,* no. 2, pp. 161–77.

Deane, P. and Mitchell, B.R. (1975), *European Historical Statistics,* Macmillan, London.

Debeir, Jean Claude (1982), 'Comment on Carl L. Holtfrerich, "Domestic and Foreign Expectations and the Demand for Money during the German Inflation, 1920–1923"', in C.P. Kindleberger and J-P. Lafargue (eds), *Financial Crises,* pp. 132–6.

de Bordes, J. van W. (1924), *The Austrian Crown,* P.S. King, London.

Dobb, M. (1948), *Soviet Economic Development Since 1917,* Routledge and Kegan Paul, London.

Dow, J.C.R. (1964), *The Management of the British Economy 1945–60,* Cambridge U.P.

Drewnowski, Jan (1982), *Crisis in the East European Economy,* Croom Helm, London, and St, Martin's Press, New York.

Dulles, Eleanor (1929), *The French Franc, 1914–1928: the Facts and Their Interpretation,* Macmillan, New York.

Edwards, S. (1985), 'Stabilization with Liberalization: An Evaluation of Ten Years of Chile's Experiment with Free-Market Policies, 1973–1983', *Economic Development and Cultural Change,* pp. 223–54.

Erhard, L. (1963), *The Economics of Success,* transl. J. Arengo-Jones and D. Thomson, Thames and Hudson, London.

Ehrlich, A. (1959), 'The Polish Economy After October, 1956', *AER,* vol. 49, no. 2, Papers and Proceedings pp. 94–112.

Estrin, S. (1982), 'The Effects of Self-Management on Yugoslav Industrial Growth', *SS,* vol. 34, pp. 69–85.

Fallenbuchl, Z. (1984), 'The Polish Economy Under Martial Law', *SS,* vol. 36, pp. 513–27.

Falush, P. (1976), 'The Hungarian Hyper-Inflation of 1945–46',

*National Westminster Bank Quarterly Review,* pp. 46–56.

Feldman, Gerald (ed.) (1982), *Die Deutsche Inflation: Eine Zwischenbilanz,* de Gruyter, Berlin and New York.

Feldman, Gerald (ed.) (1982), 'The Political Economy of Germany's Relative Stability During the 1920/21 World Depression', in Feldman G. (ed.) *Die Deutsche Inflation: Eine Zwischenbilanz,* pp. 180–206.

Feldstein, Martin (ed.) (1980), *The American Economy in Transition,* University of Chicago Press for NBER.

Felix, David (1971), 'Reparations Reconsidered with a Vengeance', *CEH,* vol. 4, pp. 171–9.

Fischer, S. (1977), 'Wage Indexation and Macroeconomic Stability', in K. Brunner and A. Meltzer (eds), *Stabilization of the Domestic and International Economy,* Carnegie-Rochester Conference Series on Public Policy, a supplementary series to the *JME,* North Holland, New York, pp. 107–48.

Fischer, S. (1981), *Indexing and Inflation,* NBER Working Paper Number no. 670, New York.

Fischer, S. (1982), 'Adapting to Inflation in the U.S. Economy', in Robert E. Hall, *Inflation: Causes and Cures,* pp. 169–86.

Fischer, I. (1966 [1911]), *The Purchasing Power of Money,* Macmillan, London, reissued by A.M. Kelley, New York.

Fforde, J.S. (1983), 'Setting Monetary Objectives', *BEQR,* vol. 23, *BEQR,* pp. 194–9.

Fratianni, M. and Peeters, T. (1978), *One Money for Europe,* Macmillan, London.

Frenkel, J. (1977), 'The Forward Exchange Rate, Expectations and the Demand for Money: the German Hyperinflation', *AER,* pp. 653–70.

Friedman, M., (1953), 'The Case for Flexible Exchange Rates', in *Essays in Positive Economics,* University of Chicago Press, pp. 157–203.

Friedman, M. (ed.) (1956), *Studies in the Quantity Theory of Money,* University of Chicago Press.

Friedman, M. (1968), 'The role of Monetary Policy', *AER,* pp. 1–17.

Friedman, M. (1974), *Monetary Correction,* IEA, Occasional Paper 41, London.

Friedman, M. and Friedman, R. (1980 (1979)), *Free to Choose,* Penguin, Harmondsworth, Middlesex.

Garvy, G. (1966), *Money, Banking and Credit in Eastern Europe,* Federal Reserve Bank of New York.

Garvy, G. (1977), *Money, Financial Flows and Credit in the Soviet Union,* publ. for NBER by Ballinger, Cambridge, Mass.

Gomulka, S. and Rostowski, J. (1984), 'The Reformed Polish Economic System, 1982–1983', *SS,* vol. 36, no. 3, pp. 386–405.

Gordon, R.J. (1971), 'Inflation in Recession and Recovery', *BPEA,* no. 1, pp. 105–58.

Gordon, R.J. (1972), 'Wage-Price Controls and the Shifting Phillips Curve', *BPEA,* no. 2, pp. 385–421.

Gordon, R.J. (1973), 'The Response of Wages and Prices to the First and Second Years of Control', *BPEA,* no. 3, pp. 765–78.

Gordon, R.J. (1975), 'The Impact of Aggregate Demand on Prices', *BPEA,* vol. 3, pp. 613–62.

Gordon, R.J. (1977), 'Can the Inflation of the 1970s be Explained?', *BPEA,* no. 1, pp. 253–77.

Gordon, R.J. (1980), 'Postwar Macroeconomics: The Evolution of Events and Ideas', in Feldstein, M. (ed.) *The American Economy in Transition,* pp. 101–62.

Gordon, R.J. (1981), 'International Monetarism, Wage Push and Monetary Accommodation', in A.S. Courakis (ed.), *Inflation, Depression and Economic Policy in the West,* pp. 1–63.

Gordon, R.J. (1982), 'Why Stopping Inflation May be Costly: Evidence from Fourteen Historical Episodes', in Robert E. Hall, *Inflation: Causes and Effects,* pp. 11–40.

Gordon, R.J. (1985), 'Understanding Inflation in the 1980s', *BPEA,* vol. 1, pp. 263–302.

Gowland, David (1982), *Controlling the Money Supply,* Croom Helm, London.

Graham, Frank D. (1967 (1930)), *Exchange, Prices and Production in Hyper-Inflation: Germany, 1920–23,* Princeton U.P., New Jersey, reissued by Russell and Russell, New York.

Gray, J.A. (1976), 'Wage indexation: a macroeconomic approach', *JME,* pp. 221–35.

Grubb, D. (1986), 'Topics in the OECD Phillips Curve', *EJ,* vol. 96, pp. 55–79.

Guillebaud, W.C. (1939), *The Economic Recovery of Germany, 1933–1939,* Macmillan, London.

Haberler, G. von (1936 (1933)), *The Theory of International Trade,* William Hodge, London.

Haddad, L. (1977), 'Inflation Under Socialism', *Australian Economic Papers,* no. 15/16, pp. 44–52.

Hall, Robert E. (1982), *Inflation: Causes and Effects,* University of Chicago Press, Chicago and London.

Hansen, A. (1949), *Monetary Theory and Fiscal Policy,* McGraw-Hill, New York.

Hare, P. and Wanless, P.T. (1981), 'Polish and Hungarian Economic

Reforms – A Comparison', *SS,* vol. 33, pp. 491–517.

Harrod, R.F. (1972), 'The Issues: Five Views', in Hinshaw, R. (ed.), *Inflation as a Global Problem,* Johns Hopkins Press, London.

Hartwig, Karl-Hans, (1983), 'Involuntary Liquid Assets in Eastern Europe: some Critical Remarks', *SS,* vol. 35, no. 1, pp. 103–5.

Hayek, F. (1976), *Choice in Currency, A Way to Stop Inflation,* IEA Occasional Paper 48, London.

Hayek, F.A. (1978), *Denationalisation of Money: the Argument Refined,* IEA, Hobart Special Paper 70, London.

Henry, S.G.B., Sawyer, M.C. and Smith, P. (1976), *NIESR Quarterly Review,* no. 77, pp. 60–71.

Henry, S.G.B. and Ormerod, P. (1978), 'Incomes Policy and Wage Inflation: Empirical Evidence for the UK, 1961–1977', *NIESR Quarterly Review,* no. 85, August, pp. 31–9.

Henry, S.G.B. (1981), 'Incomes Policy and Aggregate Pay', in Elliott, R.F. and Fallick, L. (eds), *Incomes Policies, Inflation and Relative Pay,* Allen and Unwin, London, pp. 23–44.

Hicks, J.R. and Rostas, L. (1942), *The Taxation of War Wealth,* Oxford U.P.

Hicks, Sir John (1975), 'The Permissive Economy', in *Crisis '75 . . .?,* IEA Occasional Paper Special, no. 43, London.

Hirsch, F. and Goldthorpe J. (eds) (1978), *The Political Economy of Inflation,* Martin Robertson,, London.

H.M. Treasury (1986), *Economic Progress Report,* no. 184, May-June.

Holtfrerich, C.L. (1983), 'Political Factors of the German Inflation 1914–23', in Schmukler N. and Marcus E. (eds), *Inflation Through the Ages,* Brooklyn College Press, dist. by Columbia U.P.

Holtfrerich, C.L. (1986), *The German Inflation, 1914–1923,* transl. T. Balderston, Walter de Gruyter, Berlin and New York.

Holtfrerich, C.L. (1982), 'Domestic and foreign expectations and the demand for money during the German inflation, 1920–23', in C.P. Kindleberger and J-P Larfargue (eds), *Financial Crises.*

Holzman, F.D. (1960), 'Soviet Inflationary Pressures, 1928–57: Causes and Cures', *QJE,* pp. 167–88.

Holzman, F.D. (1960), 'Soviet Inflationary Pressures, 1928–57: Causes and Cures', *QJE,* pp. 167–88.

House of Commons (1981), Treasury and Civil Service Committee, *Third Report,* Session 1980–81, 163–I, February, HMSO, London.

Hubbard, L.E. (1936), *Soviet Money and Finance,* Macmillan, London.

Huszti, E. (1977), 'The Social and Economic Impact of Inflation in

Hungary', *Acta Oeconomica,* no. 18, pp. 113–46.

Hutchison, T., (1986), *Economics and Economic Policy in Britain, 1946–66,* Allen and Unwin, London.

Hutchison, T. (1979), 'Notes on the Effects of Economic Ideas on Policy: the Example of the German Social Market Economy', in *Zeitschrift für die gesamte Staatswissenschaft,* vol. 135, part 3, September.

Isard, P. (1977), 'How Far Can We Push the "Law of One Price"?', *AER,* vol. 67, pp. 942–8.

Jacobs, R. (1975), 'A difficulty with monetarist models of hyperinflation', *Economic Inquiry,* vol. 13, pp. 337–60.

James, Harold (1986), *The German Slump: Politics and Economics 1924–36,* Oxford U.P.

Jèze, G. and Truchy, H. (1927), *The War Finance of France,* New Haven.

Kafka, A. (1967), 'The Brazilian Stabilisation Program, 1964–66', *JPE,* vol. 75, pp. 596–631.

Kaldor, N. (1946(I)), 'A Study in Inflation: Hungary's Classical Example', *Manchester Guardian Weekly,* 29 November, p. 299.

Kaldor, N. (1946(II)), 'The Hungarian Inflation: Stabilisation', *Manchester Guardian Weekly,* 13 December, p. 331.

Kaldor, N. (1970), 'The New Monetarism', *LBR,* pp. 1–18.

Kaldor, N. (1972), 'The Irrelevance of Equilibrium Economics', *EJ,* vol. 82, pp. 1237–55.

Kaldor, N. (1976), 'Inflation and Recession in the World Economy', *EJ,* vol. 86, pp. 703–14.

Kaldor, N. (1980), 'Monetarism and UK Monetary Policy', *Cambridge Journal of Economics,* vol. 4, pp. 293–318.

Kaser, M. (1982), 'Economic Policy' in Archie Brown and Michael Kaser, *Soviet Policy for the 1980s,* Macmillan, London.

Kaser, M. and Radice, E. (eds) (1986), *The Economic History of Eastern Europe 1919–1975,* Vol. II, Oxford U.P.

Katz, Samuel I. (ed.) (1979), *US-European Monetary Relations,* AEI, Washington DC.

Katzenellenbaum, S.S. (1925), *Russian Currency and Banking, 1914–24, P.S. King, London.*

*Keynes, J.N. (1955 (1891)), The Scope and Method of Political Economy,* reissued by A.M. Kelley, New York.

Kemp, Tom (1972), *The French Economy 1913–39,* Longman, London.

Kindleberger, C.P. and Laffargue, J-P. (eds) (1982), *Financial Crises: Theory, History and Policy,* Cambridge U.P.

Kindleberger, C.P. (1984), *A Financial History of Western Europe,*

Allen and Unwin, London.

Krause, L.B. and Salant, W.S., (1977), *Worldwide Inflation: Theory and Recent Experience,* Brookings, Washington DC.

Kushnirsky, F.I. (1984), 'Inflation Soviet Style', *Problems of Communism,* January-February, vol. 33, pp. 48–53.

Kushnirsky, F.I. (1985), 'Methodological Aspects in Building Soviet Prices Indices', *SS,* vol. 37, no. 4, October, pp. 505–19.

Laidler, D. (1978), 'Difficulties with European Monetary Union', in Fratianni and Peeters, *One Money for Europe,* pp. 52–63.

Laidler, D. (1974), 'A Policy for the New Government', *The Banker,* p. 216.

Laidler, D. and Parkin, M. (1975), 'Inflation: A Survey', *EJ,* vol. 85, pp. 741–809.

Laulan, Y. (1973), *Banking, Money and Credit in the USSR,* NATO, Brussels.

Laursen, K. and Pedersen, J. (1964), *The German Inflation 1918–1923,* North Holland, Amsterdam.

League of Nations (Layton, W.T. and Rist, C.) (1925), *The Economic Situation of Austria,* Geneva.

League of Nations (1925), *Twenty fifth Report by the Commissioner General of the League of Nations for Austria,* Geneva.

League of Nations (1926), *The Financial Reconstruction of Austria: General Survey and Principal Documents,* Geneva.

League of Nations (1926), (Sir Arthur Salter) *The Financial Reconstruction of Hungary: General Survey and Principal Documents,* Geneva.

Leontief, W. (1971), 'Theoretical Assumptions and Non-Observed Facts', *AER,* vol. 61, pp. 1–7.

Lerner, A.P. and Colander, D.C. (c.1980), *MAP: A Market Anti-Inflation Plan,* Harcourt Brace Jovanovich, New York.

Liesner, T. and King, M.A. (1975), *Indexing for Inflation,* Heinemann, London.

Lurié, Samuel (1947), *Private Investment in a Controlled Economy,* Columbia U.P., New York.

MacDougall, D. (1974), 'In Praise of Economics', *EJ,* vol. 84, pp. 773–86.

Maier, Charles S. (1975), *Recasting Bourgeois Europe: Stabilization in France, Germany and Italy in the Decade after World War I,* Princeton U.P., New Jersey.

Maier, Charles S. (1978), 'The Politics of Inflation in the Twentieth Century', in Hirsch F. and Goldthorpe J. (eds), *The Political Economy of Inflation.*

Marks, Sally (1969), 'Reparations Reconsidered: a Reminder', *CEH,* vol. 2, pp. 356–65.

Marks, Sally (1972), 'Reparations Reconsidered: a Rejoinder', *CEH,* vol. 5, pp. 358–61.

Mendershausen, H. (1955), *Two Postwar Recoveries of the German Economy,* North Holland, Amsterdam.

Mieczkowski, B. (1978), 'The Relationship Between Changes in Consumption and Politics in Poland', *SS,* vol. 30, pp. 262–9.

Millar, J.R. (1981), *The ABC of Soviet Socialism,* University of Illinois Press, Chicago.

Miller, William G. (1979), *Federal Reserve Bulletin,* pp. 113–30.

Milner, C. (ed.) (1987), *Political Economy and International Money,* Wheatsheaf, Brighton.

Mitzakis, Michel (1962), *Le Relèvement de la Hongrie et la Société des Nations,* Presses Universitaires de France, Paris.

Mlynarsky, F. (1926), *The International Significance of the Depreciation of the Zloty,* publ. by The Polish Economist, Warsaw.

Moorsteen, R. and Powell, R.P. (1966), *The Soviet Capital Stock, 1928–1962,* Yale U.P., Homewood, Illinois.

Moeller, Robert G. (1982), 'Winners as Losers in the German Inflation: Peasant Protest over the Controlled Economy, 1920–1923', in Feldman, G. (ed.), *Die Deutsche Inflation: Eine Zwischenbilanz,* pp. 155–88.

Montias, J. (1962), *Central Planning in Poland,* Yale U.P., New Haven and London.

Morgenstern, O. (1963) 2nd edn, *On the Accuracy of Economic Observations,* Princeton U.P.

Moulton, H.G. and McGuire, C. (1923), *Germany's Capacity to Pay,* McGraw Hill, New York.

Nadiri, M. and Gupta, V. (1977), 'Price and Wage Behaviour in the U.S. Aggregate Economy and in Manufacturing Industries', in Popkin, J. (ed.), *Analysis of Inflation, 1965–74,* pp. 195–234.

Nathan, Otto (1944), *The Nazi Economic System: Germany's Mobilization for War,* Duke U.P., Durham, N.C.

NIESR Quarterly Review, various years, London.

Nogaro, Bertrand (1948), 'Hungary's recent monetary crisis and its theoretical meaning', *AER,* vol. 38, pp. 526–42.

Nordhaus, W. (1975), 'The political business cycle', *RES,* vol. 42, pp. 169–90.

Nordhaus, W. and Shoven, J. (1977), 'A Technique for Analyzing and Decomposing Inflation', in Popkin, J. (ed.), *Analysis of Inflation, 1965–74,* pp. 333–55.

Nötel, R. (1986), 'International Credit and Finance', in Kaser and Radice (eds), *The Economic History of Eastern Europe 1919–1975*, pp. 170–295.

Nötel, R. (1986), 'International Finance and Monetary Reforms', in Kaser and Radice (eds), *The Economic History of Eastern Europe 1919–1975*, pp. 520–63.

Nove, A. (1969), *An Economic History of the U.S.S.R*, Penguin, Harmondsworth, Middlesex.

Nurske, Ragnar, (1946), *The Course and Control of Inflation after World War I*, League of Nations, Princeton, New Jersey.

Nuti, D.M. (1982), 'The Polish Crisis: Economic Factors and Constraints', in Drewnowski, J. *Crisis in the East European Economy*, pp. 18–64.

O'Brien, D. (1974), *Whither Economics? An inaugural lecture*, University of Durham.

O'Brien, D. (1975), *The Classical Economists*, Oxford U.P.

OECD, country reports, various, Paris.

OECD, *Economic Outlook,* various issues, Paris.

Okun, A. and Perry, G.L. (eds) (1978), *Curing Chronic Inflation,* Brookings, Washington DC.

Owen, Henry and Schultze, C.L. (eds) (1976), *Setting National Priorities: The Next Ten years,* Brookings, Washington DC.

Page, S.A.B. and Trollope, S. (1974), 'An International Survey of Indexing and Its Effects', *NIESR Quarterly Review,* no. 70, pp. 46–60.

Paish, F. (1966, (1962)), *Studies in an Inflationary Economy: the United Kingdom, 1948–61,* Cambridge U.P.

Parkin, M. (1978), 'Monetary Union and Stabilisation Policy in the European Community', *Review of the Banca Nazionale del Lavoro,* vol. 29, pp. 222–40.

Pasvolsky, Leo (1972 (1928)), *Economic Nationalism in the Danubian States,* Macmillan, London and New York.

Peel, George (1937), *The Economic Policy of France,* Macmillan, London.

Perloff, J. and Wachter, M. (1979), in Brunner K. and Meltzer, A., supplement to vol. 10 of *JME.*

Perry, George L. (1976), 'Stabilization Policy and Inflation', in Owen, H. and Schultze, C.L. (eds), *Setting National Priorities: The Next Ten Years,* pp. 271–321.

Perry, G.L. (1978), 'Slowing the Wage-Price Spiral', in Okun, A. and Perry, G.L. (eds), *Curing Chronic Inflation.*

Perry, G.L. (1980), 'Inflation in Theory and Practice', *BPEA,* pp. 207–48.

Perry, G.L. (1983), 'What Have We Learned about Disinflation?', *BPEA,* vol. 2, pp. 587–602.

Phelps, Edmund S. (1968), 'Money Wage Dynamics and Labour Market Equilibrium', *JPE,* vol. 76, part 2, pp. 678–711.

Phelps Brown, H. (1983), *The Origins of Trade Union Power,* Clarendon, Oxford.

Phillips, A.W. (1958), The Relation between Unemployment and the rate of Change of Money Wages in the United Kingdom, 1861–1957', *Eca,* pp. 283–99.

Pickersgill, Joyce, (1976), 'Soviet Household Savings Behaviour', *REStat,* vol. 58, pp. 139–47.

Pickersgill, Joyce, (1977), 'Soviet Inflation: Causes and Consequences', *Soviet Union,* vol. 4, part 2, pp. 297–313.

Pickersgill, Joyce (1980), 'The Financial Crisis in the USSR', *SS,* vol. 32, pp. 583–5.

Popkin, J. (1977) (ed.), *Analysis of Inflation, 1965–74,* Ballinger for NBER, Cambridge, Mass.

Portes, R.D. (1977), 'The Control of Inflation: Lessons from East European Experience', *Eca,* vol. 44, pp. 109–29.

Portes, R.D. (1978), 'Inflation under Central Planning', in Hirsch F. and Goldthorpe J. (eds), *The Political Economy of Inflation,* p. 72.

Portes, R.D. (1981), 'Prices', in *Cambridge Encyclopaedia of Russia and the Soviet Union,* pp. 362–4.

Portes, R.D. (1983), 'Central Planning and Monetarism: Fellow Travelers?', in P. Desai (ed.), *Marxism, Central Planning and the Soviet Economy,* pp. 149–65.

Portes R. and Winter D. (1977), 'The Supply of Consumption Goods in Centrally Planned Economies', *Journal of Comparative Economics,* vol. 1.

Portes R. and Winter D. (1978), 'The Demand for Money and for Consumption Goods in Centrally Planned Economies', *REStat,* vol. 60, pp. 8–18.

Portes R. and Winter D. (1980), 'Disequilibrium Estimates for Consumer Goods Markets in Centrally Planned Economies', *RES,* vol. 47, pp. 137–59.

Pratten, C. (1982), 'Mrs Thatcher's Economic Experiment', *LBR.*

Prest, A.R. and Barr, N. (1979), *Public Finance in Theory and Practice,* sixth edition, Weidenfeld and Nicolson, London.

Prittie, Terence (1979), *The Velvet Chancellors,* Frederick Muller, London.

Prout, Christopher (1985), *Market Socialism in Yugoslavia,* Oxford U.P.

Pryor, Frederic L. (1976), 'Some Costs and Benefits of Markets: an

Empirical Study', *QJE,* 41, pp. 81–102.

Radcliffe Committee, see Committee on the Working of the Monetary System.

Ringer, Fritz (1969), *The German Inflation of 1923,* Oxford U.P., London and New York.

Rist, Charles (1924), *La Déflation en Pratique – Angleterre, Etats-Unis, France, Tchéco-Slovakie,* Paris.

Robinson, Joan (1928), Review of Bresciani Turroni, *The Economics of Inflation, EJ,* vol. 48, pp. 507–13.

Rogers, J.H. (1929), *The Process of Inflation in France, 1924–27,* Columbia U.P., New York.

Routh, G. (1959), 'The relation between unemployment and the rate of change of money wage rates: a comment', *Eca,* NS 26, pp. 299–315.

Rowthorn B. (1980), *Capitalism, Conflict and Inflation,* Lawrence and Wishart, London.

Sargent, T.J. (1986), *Rational Expectations and Inflation,* Harper and Row, New York.

Sargent, T.J. and Wallace, Neil, 'Rational Expectations and the Dynamics of Hyperinflation', *International Economic Review* 14, pp. 326–50, 1973.

Schacht, H.G. (1927), *The Stabilisation of the Mark,* Allen and Unwin, London.

Shanahan, Eileen (moderator), *Indexing and Inflation,* American Enterprise Institute, 1974.

Shapiro, H.T. (1977), 'Inflation in the United States', in Krause, L. and Salant, W., *Worldwide Inflation,* pp. 270–94.

Schroeder, G.E. and Severin, B.S. (1976), 'Soviet Consumption and Income Policies in Perspective', in Joint Economic Committee of Congress, *Soviet Economy in a New Perspective,* USGPO, Washington DC, pp. 620–60.

Schuker, Stephen A. (1976), *The End of French Predominance in Europe: The Financial Crisis of 1924 and the Adoption of the Dawes Plan,* University of North Caroline Press, Chapel Hill, NC.

Shirer, William (1970), *The Collapse of the Third Reich,* Heinemann and Secker and Warburg, London.

Sirc, L. (1979), *The Yugoslav Economy under Self-Management,* Macmillan, London.

Smith, A.H. (1983), *The Planned Economies of Eastern Europe,* Croom Helm, Beckenham, Kent.

Spigler, I. (1986), 'Public Finance', in Kaser and Radice (eds), *The Economic History of Eastern Europe 1919–1975,* pp. 117–69.

Stein, Herbert (1984), *Presidential Economics: The Making of*

*Economic Policy from Roosevelt to Reagan and Beyond,* Simon and Schuster, New York.

Stolper, G., Hauser, K. and Borchardt, K. (1967 (1964)), *The German Economy, 1870 to the Present,* trans. Toni Stolper, Weidenfeld and Nicolson, London.

Tew, B. (1985, 3rd edn (1982, 1977), *The Evolution of the International Monetary System,* Hutchison, London.

Thorp, Rosemary (1971), 'Inflation and the Financing of Economic Development', in K. Griffin (ed.), *Financing Development in Latin America,* Macmillan, London, pp. 182–224.

Thygesen, N. (1979), 'Introduction and Summary of Optica Proposals', in Katz, S.I. (ed.), *US-European Monetary Relations,* pp. 135–55.

Tufte, Edward R. (1975), *Political Control of the Economy,* Princeton U.P. and Guildford.

Tulloch, G. and Campbell, C.D. (1954), 'Hyperinflation in China, 1937–1949', *JPE,* vol. 62, pp. 236–45.

Turcan, J.R. (1977), 'Some Observations in Retail Distribution in Poland', *SS,* vol. 29, pp. 128–36.

Vargas, Stefan (1947) I and II, 'Zerfall und Stabilisierung der ungarischen Währung', *Neue Zürcher Zeitung,* 7 and 8 January.

Vaubel, Roland (1979), 'A Europe-wide parallel currency', in S.I. Katz (ed.), *US-European Monetary Relations,* pp. 156–83.

Viner, Jacob (1937), *Studies in the Theory of International Trade,* Harper, New York.

Wallich, H.C. (1955), *Mainsprings of the German Revival,* Yale U.P., New Haven.

Wallich, H. and Weintraub, S. (1971), *Journal of Economic Issues.*

Wanless, P.T. (1985), 'Inflation in the Consumer Goods Market in Poland, 1971–82', *SS,* vol. 37, no. 3, pp. 403–16.

White, Lawrence H. (1984), *Free Banking in Britain: Theory, Experience and Debate, 1800–1845,* Cambridge U.P.

Wiles, P.J.D. (1977), *Economic Institutions Compared,* Blackwell, Oxford.

Williamson, J.G. (1983,I), *The Open Economy and the World Economy,* Harper and Row, Basic Books, New York.

Williamson, J.G. (1983,II), *IMF Conditionality,* Institute for International Economics, Washington DC.

Wilson, Duncan (1979), *Tito's Yugoslavia,* Cambridge U.P.

Wimberley, James (1981), 'The Soviet Financial Crisis? A Comment', *SS,* vol. 33, no. 3, pp. 444–5.

Wolfe, Martin (1951), *The French Franc Between the Wars, 1919–1939,* Columbia U.P., New York.

Wolff, R. (1943), *Economie et Finances de la France,* Brentano's, New York.

Yeager, Leland B. (1966), *International Monetary Relations: Theory, History and Policy,* Harper and Row, New York, Evanston and London.

Young, J. Parke (1925), *European Currency and Finance,* vol. 1, Government Printing Office, Washington DC.

Yurovsky, L.N. (1925), *Currency Problems and the Policy of the Soviet Union,* Leonard Parsons, London.

Zwass, Adam (1979), *Money, Banking and Credit in the Soviet Union and Eastern Europe,* M.E. Sharpe, White Plains, New York.

# Index

Because the book includes a detailed list of Contents and Bibliography, the Index is limited to the main themes, ideas, events and issues, together with the principal protagonists and those countries whose names do not occur in chapter headings or subheadings.